The Kaohsiung Incident in Taiwan and Memoirs of a Foreign Big Beard

The Kaohsiung Incident in Taiwan and Memoirs of a Foreign Big Beard

By

J. Bruce Jacobs

BRILL

LEIDEN | BOSTON

Cover illustration: Collage of images related to the Kaohsiung Incident and its aftermath, Taiwan 1979–1980.

Want or need Open Access? Brill Open offers you the choice to make your research freely accessible online in exchange for a publication charge. Review your various options on brill.com/brill-open.

Typeface for the Latin, Greek, and Cyrillic scripts: "Brill". See and download: brill.com/brill-typeface.

ISBN 978-90-04-31541-9 (hardback)
ISBN 978-90-04-31601-0 (paperback)
ISBN 978-90-04-31592-1 (e-book)

Copyright 2016 by Koninklijke Brill NV, Leiden, The Netherlands.
Koninklijke Brill NV incorporates the imprints Brill, Brill Hes & De Graaf, Brill Nijhoff, Brill Rodopi and Hotei Publishing.
All rights reserved. No part of this publication may be reproduced, translated, stored in a retrieval system, or transmitted in any form or by any means, electronic, mechanical, photocopying, recording or otherwise, without prior written permission from the publisher.
Authorization to photocopy items for internal or personal use is granted by Koninklijke Brill NV provided that the appropriate fees are paid directly to The Copyright Clearance Center, 222 Rosewood Drive, Suite 910, Danvers, MA 01923, USA. Fees are subject to change.

This book is printed on acid-free paper and produced in a sustainable manner.

In Memory of

Auntie Lim You A-mei 林游阿妹
Lin Liang-chun 林亮均 *and*
Lin Ting-chun 林亭均.

May Taiwan never forget your tragic sacrifices

∴

Contents

Preface IX
Note on Romanization XI

PART 1
The Kaohsiung Incident: A Tragedy of Errors?

1 **The Dangwai Setting** 3
  The Election of November 19, 1977 7
  The Aborted December 23, 1978 Election 12
  Dangwai Political Activities in 1979 14

2 **The Kaohsiung Incident, the Arrests, the Indictment and the Murder of Lin I-hsiung's Family** 23
  The Arrests 29
  The Indictment 33
  The Murder of Lin I-hsiung's Mother and Twin Daughters 40

3 **The Military Trial of the Eight Key Defendants** 43
  Day 1 of the Trial: Tuesday, March 18, 1980 44
  Day 2 of the Trial: Wednesday, March 19, 1980 46
  Day 3 of the Trial: Thursday, March 20, 1980 50
  Day 4 of the Trial: Friday, March 21, 1980 55
  Day 5 of the Trial: Monday, March 24, 1980 58
  Day 6 of the Trial: Tuesday, March 25, 1980 62
  Day 7 of the Trial: Wednesday, March 26, 1980 71
  Day 8 of the Trial: Thursday, March 27, 1980 78
  Day 9 of the Trial: Friday, March 28, 1980 81
  Question Time in the Taiwan Provincial Assembly and the Trial of Hung Chih-liang 84
  The Verdict in the Military Trial 85

4 **The Other Important Trials** 87
  The Civil Trial of the 33 Defendants 87
  The Military Trial of Reverend Kao Chun-ming and Nine Others for Concealing Shih Ming-teh 98

5 How the Kaohsiung Incident Contributed to Taiwan's Democratic Movement 103
    The First Group: The Defendants 104
    The Second Group: The Defense Lawyers 106
    The Third Group: Wives and Relatives of Defendants 108
    Conclusion 109

PART 2
Memoirs of a Foreign Big Beard 大鬍子外籍男子回憶錄

6 **Memoirs of a Foreign Big Beard** 113
    "Walking into the Tiger's Lair" 走進虎的巢穴 122
    A New Stage of "Protection" 126
    My Press Conference and Subpoena to Appear in the Prosecutor's Court 133
    My "Protection" Becomes More Relaxed 136
    Another Subpoena to See the Prosecutor 144
    Who Committed the Murders? 146

7 **Rip Van Winkle Returns to Taiwan** 148
    Rip Van Winkle Returns to Taiwan 149
    The Police Follow Me Constantly in 1993 156
    President Lee Teng-hui Helps Me in 1995 159
    The Report Commissioned by the Government of President Ma Ying-jeou 160
    Reconsidering the Lin Family Murder Case after 35 Years 163

Bibliography 165
Index 174

Preface

I started to write this book over three decades ago after I returned from Taiwan to Australia following three months of "police protection," resulting from official accusations that I was involved in the Lin Family Murders of February 28, 1980. I was not then—nor am I now—prone to nightmares, but as I started writing I began to have numerous nightmares. Rather than continue to write, I stopped and began other projects. After leaving La Trobe University at the end of 1990 and moving to Monash University at the beginning of 1991, I also came to have much heavier administrative loads at work.

In the meantime, commencing with the presidency of Lee Teng-hui (1988–2000), Taiwan began its process of democratization, a process that I have analyzed elsewhere.[1] The Kaohsiung Incident, as shown in this book, played an important role in Taiwan's democratization. Thus, I have long felt it important to give the Kaohsiung Incident a more detailed analysis. In addition, at the urging of many friends in Taiwan and elsewhere, I have completed the more personal memoir in Part 2.

For research and writing support, I especially wish to thank the Taiwan Foundation for Democracy (TFD), which gave me a small grant to help with the research and writing. I also wish to thank the Australian Research Council (ARC) for a Discovery Grant on "Democratizing Taiwan," which enabled some research on this project. An additional ARC Discovery Grant for "A History of Taiwan" has also facilitated the writing of this book.

By and large, especially from the 1970s onward, Taiwan's battle for democracy was relatively non-violent. As seen in this book, many people were beaten, tortured and imprisoned, but the number killed was relatively few. Two key exceptions were Professor Chen Wen-cheng 陳文成, a young Taiwanese professor at Carnegie Mellon University who died on July 3, 1981 from a fall from the fifth floor of the National Taiwan University Library after being in the hands of the Taiwan Garrison Command, and Henry Liu (Liu I-liang 劉宜良, Jiang Nan 江南), a Chinese Mainlander journalist who was murdered in California on October 14, 1984.[2]

---

1 J. Bruce Jacobs, *Democratizing Taiwan* (Leiden and Boston: Brill, 2012). For the perspective from the rural countryside, see J. Bruce Jacobs, *Local Politics in Rural Taiwan under Dictatorship and Democracy* (Norwalk, CT: EastBridge, 2008).

2 On the Liu murder see Richard C. Bush, *At Cross Purposes: U.S.-Taiwan Relations Since 1942* (Armonk, NY and London, England: M.E. Sharpe, 2004), pp. 206–209. For a useful book-length

To some extent, Chen Wen-cheng and Henry Liu were politically involved. The murder of Provincial Assemblyman Lin I-hsiung's 林義雄 mother, Lim You A-mei 林游阿妹, and his twin daughters, Lin Liang-chun 林亮均 and Lin Ting-chun 林亭均, is much more tragic as they were totally innocent victims. The Lin Family Murder Case was especially shocking in Taiwan because it was the first—and only—case where the family of a political prisoner was killed.

This book is dedicated to the lives and memories of Auntie Lim You A-mei, Liang-chun and Ting-chun. May Taiwan never forget your tragic sacrifices.

---

biography of Henry Liu and a study of his murder, see David E. Kaplan, *Fires of the Dragon: Politics, Murder, and the Kuomintang* (New York: Atheneum, 1992).

Note on Romanization

For scholars of Taiwan, romanization of Chinese words remains a difficult issue. Where known, for all personal names I have used the name preferred by the individual. Otherwise, I have used a simplified Wade-Giles romanization. As the final arbiter, I have used the Who's Who section in various annual editions of *Republic of China Yearbook/Taiwan Yearbook*. For all place names in Taiwan, I have used the common form used in Taiwan (prior to the introduction of tongyong romanization). For all Chinese-language publications and for the romanization of Chinese terms, I have used pinyin. I have also used pinyin for all Chinese place names and personal names.

PART 1

The Kaohsiung Incident: A Tragedy of Errors?

∴

CHAPTER 1

The Dangwai Setting

When the Chinese Nationalist Party or Kuomintang succeeded the Japanese colonial rulers (1895–1945), they in turn established a new colonial regime dominated by Chinese Mainlanders who systematically discriminated against the majority Taiwanese. Under the leadership of Chiang Kai-shek, this Chinese colonial regime massacred up to 28,000 Taiwanese following the February 28, 1947 Uprising. It then instituted "White Terror," under which many thousands were imprisoned and executed during the 1950s and 1960s.[1]

Chiang Kai-shek arranged for his son, Chiang Ching-kuo, to succeed him. This succession process began most clearly in 1969, when Chiang Kai-shek was already 81 years old. Partly as a result of such external pressures as the Diaoyutai Movement and Taiwan's leaving the United Nations, pressure for reform also built up within Taiwan. Chiang Ching-kuo, already somewhat of a reformer though not a democrat, used "reform" to increase his own political support, especially after his father nominated him to become Premier on May 20, 1972. Chiang Ching-kuo doubled the small numbers of Taiwanese in his cabinet where he also appointed younger and better educated ministers. As part of his reform, Premier Chiang Ching-kuo clamped down on corruption and even publicly arrested and sentenced important officers of the Taiwan Garrison Command, one of Taiwan's then most repressive security agencies, for corruption.

These reform efforts began a first phase of "liberalization" in Taiwan that lasted until the Kaohsiung Incident of December 10, 1979. Sometimes authoritarian regimes allow an increase in the scope of speech or the press. They may allow opposition politicians to win office in elections, but they do not relinquish ultimate control. It must be stated very clearly that such "liberalization" is not democratization.[2] Chiang Ching-kuo, right up to his death, never intended to relinquish control to any opposition.[3] He maintained his power

---

1 For details, see Jacobs, *Democratizing Taiwan*.
2 The present writer began to draw this distinction in 1981, see J. Bruce Jacobs, "Political Opposition and Taiwan's Political Future," *The Australian Journal of Chinese Affairs*, no. 6 (July 1981), p. 21.
3 J. Bruce Jacobs, "Chiang Ching-kuo Was No Democrat: The Difference between Liberalization and Democratization," in *Zhonghua minguo liuwang Taiwan 60 nian ji Zhanhou Taiwan guoji chujing* 中華民國流亡台灣 60 年暨戰後台灣國際處境 [*The Republic of China's Sixty Years of Exile in Taiwan and Taiwan's Difficult Postwar International Situation*], ed. Taiwan jiaoshou

through controlled elections as well as through his many security agencies and a controlled media.⁴

In order to maintain his colonial control in Taiwan following his forced retreat from the Mainland in 1949, Chiang Kai-shek arranged that the central parliamentarians in the Legislative Branch, the Control Branch and the National Assembly retained their power. With the Communist takeover, Chiang Kai-shek's regime could no longer hold elections on the Mainland, so it arranged for the Council of Grand Justices to give Constitutional Interpretation No. 31 on January 29, 1954, which extended the terms of the central parliamentarians initially elected on the Mainland during 1947 and 1948 until they could "be elected and convene according to law…"⁵

By 1969, the numbers of central parliamentarians had declined. The KMT used the excuse of Taiwan's growing population to have limited supplementary elections in 1969. Taiwan (including Taipei) elected fifteen additional National Assemblymen and eleven additional legislators on December 20, and on December 29 the Taipei Municipality Council elected two members of the Control Branch.⁶ These additional central parliamentarians, like the original central parliamentarians elected on the Chinese Mainland, all had indefinite terms.

By 1972, only half of the original National Assemblymen and Legislators and only one-third of the Control Branch members remained and their average ages had gone up to 63 in the National Assembly, 67 in the Legislature and 73 in the Control Branch. The twenty-eight new central parliamentarians elected in 1969 only accounted for one-seventieth of the membership. Thus, in 1972, after considerable debate, the KMT agreed to have further supplementary elections for the central parliamentary organs. Most importantly, these new central parliamentarians would have the three and six year terms fixed in the Constitution.⁷ However, this reform did not end Mainlander control. When the system was

---

xiehui 台灣教授協會 [Taiwan Association of University Professors] (Taibei: Qianwei 前衛, 2010), pp. 435–480. See also Jacobs, *Democratizing Taiwan*, pp. 47–68.

4   For Taiwan's press at this time, see J. Bruce Jacobs, "Taiwan's Press: Political Communications Link and Research Resource," *China Quarterly*, no. 68 (December 1976), pp. 778–788.

5   The text of Constitutional Interpretation No. 31 can be found in *Zhongyang ribao* 中央日報 (*Central Daily News*), January 30, 1954, p. 1 and *Lianhebao* 聯合報 (*United Daily News*), January 30, 1954, p. 1.

6   Taiwan Province was not given any new Control Branch members; see J. Bruce Jacobs, "Recent Leadership and Political Trends in Taiwan," *The China Quarterly*, no. 45 (January-March 1971), p. 133.

7   J. Bruce Jacobs, "Taiwan 1972: Political Season," *Asian Survey* XIII, no. 1 (January 1973), pp. 106–107.

finally abolished in mid-1990, during Lee Teng-hui's presidency, the "old thieves" (*laozei* 老賊) still occupied 76 per cent of the central parliamentary seats.[8]

The death of Chiang Kai-shek on April 5, 1975 provided some further opportunities for liberalization. On April 20, Premier Chiang ordered the Minister of Justice to prepare to shorten the sentences of criminals in accord with the "will" of the late President Chiang to "humanely and virtuously love the people." On May 30 the legislature passed a law "To shorten the sentences of criminals," to be implemented on July 14, the hundredth day after the passing of President Chiang,[9] and preliminary estimates suggested 9,000 criminals would benefit.[10] According to a modern source, 7,000 criminals were released as a result of their shortened sentences, but less than 200 political prisoners received shorter sentences and less than half of these were released.[11]

Later, in August 1975, Huang Hsin-chieh 黃信介 and Kang Ning-hsiang 康寧祥, two of the pioneers of the democracy movement, established a new magazine, *The Taiwan Political Review* (*Taiwan zhenglun* 台灣政論). Huang, born in 1917, had been elected a Taipei Municipality Councilman in 1961 and was re-elected in 1964. In 1969 he was elected as one of the new legislators with a permanent term. Kang, born in 1938, was elected a Taipei Municipality Councilman in 1969 after Taipei Municipality was raised to provincial status and in 1972 he won a three-year term to the legislature with the highest number of votes of any candidate in Taipei.[12]

Taiwan Political Review "was the first opposition magazine to raise the banner of 'Taiwan' since the Kuomintang had arrived in Taiwan."[13] As an opposition magazine it followed *Free China Fortnightly* (*Ziyou Zhongguo* 自由中國), *Apollo*

---

8   The "old thieves" held 88% of the National Assembly seats, 52% of the Legislative Branch seats and 38% of the Control Branch seats. Statistics from table in *Zhongyang ribao guoji ban* 中央日報國際版 [*Central Daily News International Edition*], June 23, 1990, p. 1.

9   *Zhongyang ribao* 中央日報, May 31, 1975, p. 1.

10 *Zhongyang ribao* 中央日報, May 31, 1975, p. 3. This page also has the text of the provisions for shortening prison sentences.

11 *Renquan zhi lu: Taiwan minzhu renquan huigu* 人權之路：臺灣民主人權回顧 [*The Road to Human Rights: Looking Back on Taiwan's Democracy and Human Rights*] (Taibei: Yushan, 2002), p. 29; *The Road to Freedom: Taiwan's Postwar Human Rights Movement* (Taipei: Dr Chen Wen-chen Memorial Foundation, 2004), p. 29.

12 Zhang Fuzhong 張富忠 and Qiu Wanxing 邱萬興, *Lüse niandai: Taiwan minzhu yundong 25 nian, 1975–1987* 綠色年代：台灣民主運動 25 年, 1975–1987 [*The Green Era: Twenty-Five Years of Taiwan's Democratic Movement, 1975–1987*], II vols., vol. I (Taibei: Caituan faren lüxing wenjiao jijinhui 財團法人綠色旅行文教基金會, 2005), p. 26.

13 Ibid.

(*Wenxing* 文星), and *The Intellectual* (*Daxue zazhi* 大學雜誌). With articles like "Can't We Criticize the Constitution and National Policy?" by Yao Chia-wen and "Let's Remove Martial Law As Soon as Possible" by Chen Ku-ying, the magazine clearly challenged the ruling party. The magazine published 50,000 copies for its fifth issue in December 1975. However, with the December 1975 legislative election looming, the authorities clearly felt the magazine had gone too far and they closed it.[14]

The excuse for closing the magazine was an article by Chiou Chui-liang, an academic at the University of Queensland in Australia.[15] Chiou wrote about his discussions with two people from the People's Republic of China. In fact, the content was mild. Probably the government used Chiou's article as an excuse to close down *Taiwan Political Review* because Chiou was overseas and did not need to be arrested.

The movement that led to the Kaohsiung Incident developed further as a result of the December 20, 1975 Legislative election. Although the key non-partisans who had won in 1972—Kang Ning-hsiang 康寧祥, Hsu Shih-hsien 許世賢 and Huang Shun-hsing 黃順興—all won re-election,[16] another prominent non-partisan, Kuo Yu-hsin 郭雨新, lost. Kuo officially obtained over 80,000 votes, but in his home Ilan County an additional 80,000 of his votes were declared invalid and he was defeated.[17]

In early 1976, Kuo launched a case against the election results led by two young lawyers, Lin I-hsiung 林義雄 also from Ilan County and Yao Chia-wen 姚嘉文, both of whom would lead the opposition movement.[18] In addition, several other key people became deeply involved in the opposition movement at this time including Chen Chu 陳菊 (who was Kuo's secretary) and Tien Chiu-chin 田秋堇, both also from Ilan, as well as Chiu I-jen 邱義仁, Fan Sun-lu 范巽綠, Wu Nai-jen 吳乃人, Wu Nai-te 吳乃德, Chou Hung-hsien 周弘憲 and Lin Cheng-chieh 林正杰 among many others.[19] Kuo himself left Taiwan for the United States in 1977, where he died in exile in 1985, but he left a burgeoning

---

14 Ibid., pp. 26, 29.
15 Qiu Chuiliang 邱垂亮, "Liangzhong xinxiang 兩種心向 [Two Ways of Thinking]," *Taiwan zhenglun* 台灣政論 [*Taiwan Political Review*], no. 5 (1975), pp. 31–34.
16 *Zhongyang ribao* 中央日報, December 21, 1975, p. 3.
17 Zhang Fuzhong 張富忠 and Qiu Wanxing 邱萬興, *Lüse niandai I*, 1, p. 29.
18 Their book provides many details of these battles, see Lin Yixiong 林義雄 and Yao Jiawen 姚嘉文, *Huluo pingyang? Xuanzhan guansi Guo Yuxin* 虎落平陽？選戰官司郭雨新 [*Has the Tiger Descended to Pingyang? Election Battles, Court Battles and Kuo Yu-hsin*] (Taibei: Gaoshan 高山, 1977).
19 Zhang Fuzhong 張富忠 and Qiu Wanxing 邱萬興, *Lüse niandai I*, 1, p. 30.

opposition movement that would come together in 1977. At this time, the Presbyterian Church re-entered politics declaring on August 16, 1977:

> We insist that the future of Taiwan be determined by the 17 million people who live there ... In order to achieve our goal of independence and freedom for the people of Taiwan in this critical international situation, we urge our government to face reality and to take effective measures whereby Taiwan may become a new and independent country.[20]

The Election of November 19, 1977

The term *dangwai* 黨外, literally "outside the [Nationalist] Party," gained new and ongoing currency as the name of the opposition during the campaign for the local elections of November 19, 1977.[21] In fact, the term was first used in the "Fifteen Demands" of March 18, 1960 during the movement that led to the aborted rise of the China Democratic Party headed by the Mainlander democrat, Lei Chen 雷震, and several Taiwanese politicians including Li Wan-chu 李萬居, Wu San-lien 吳三連, Kuo Yu-hsin 郭雨新, Hsu Shih-hsien 許世賢, Kao Yu-shu (Henry Kao) 高玉樹 and Yu Teng-fa 余登發.[22]

The elections of November 19, 1977 were "local" in that they chose sub-central level officials including provincial assemblymen and women, county executives and equivalent mayors, county assemblymen and women and township executives. In Taipei Municipality, city councilmen and women were elected.

These elections took place at the same time that the Kuomintang was making an important push for greater roles in local politics. Previously, under Chiang Kai-shek, the Kuomintang did not play a strong role in township-level

---

20 Presbyterian Church in Taiwan, "A Declaration on Human Rights," in *The Future of Taiwan: A Difference of Opinion*, ed. Victor H Li (White Plains, NY: M.E. Sharpe), pp. 186–187. This is also available on the web, see Presbyterian Church in Taiwan, "A Declaration of Human Rights," <http://www.taiwandocuments.org/pct04.htm>.

21 Zhang Fuzhong 張富忠 and Qiu Wanxing 邱萬興, *Lüse niandai I*, 1, p. 38. This source incorrectly states that this was the first use of the term *"dangwai."*

22 See Jacobs, *Democratizing Taiwan*, p. 39. For the text of the Fifteen Demands, see "Zaiyedang ji wudang wupai renshi duiyu ben jie difang xuanju xiang Guomintang ji zhengfu tichu de shiwudian yaoqiu 在野黨及無黨無派人士對於本屆地方選舉向國民黨及政府提出的十五點要求 [Fifteen Demands from Opposition Parties and from Non-partisans Addressed to the Kuomintang and the government concerning the Current Local Elections]", *Ziyou Zhongguo* 自由中國 22, no. 7 (April 1, 1960), p. 30.

elections. Higher levels controlled funds and, thus, the actual functioning of government, so the Kuomintang allowed local factions considerable electoral leeway in the township. However, about April 1975, the Kuomintang began to push for greater power at the local level and began to intervene in local elections and decision-making. Party membership also increased substantially during this period.[23]

This pressure created dissension within the KMT and contributed to the Kuomintang's unparalleled "loss" in the November 19, 1977 election.[24] In the county executive and equivalent mayoral elections, non-partisans defeated KMT nominees in four of twenty elections. Non-partisans also defeated fourteen of sixty-nine KMT nominees for provincial assembly. In addition, they won an additional seven provincial assembly seats that the KMT had allocated to non-partisans.

During the campaign for these elections, Huang Hsin-chieh and Kang Ning-hsiang, the two non-partisan legislators respectively elected in the supplementary elections of 1969 and 1972 (and again in 1975) and who also founded *Taiwan Political Review*, travelled up and down the island seeking support. The resulting *dangwai* movement proved to have considerable success. However, not all successful non-partisans belonged to the *dangwai*. Huang Hsin-chieh, who classified the non-partisans into "genuine" and "false" categories, claimed only thirteen of the twenty-one non-partisans elected to the provincial assembly were "genuine."[25] Interestingly, the right-wing opponents of the *dangwai* from *Gust (Jifeng) Magazine* claimed only eleven of the non-partisan provincial assemblymen belonged to the "Black Fist Gang."[26] In addition, interviews conducted in 1979 suggested that Huang Hsin-chieh's figures included a couple of non-political non-partisans.[27] So about half of the non-partisan provincial assemblymen and even fewer of the non-partisan county executives and Taipei Municipality Councilmen belonged to the *dangwai*.

---

23 Jacobs, *Local ... Democracy*, pp. 32–34, 37–39, 216–217, 222–246.
24 On the November 19, 1977 election, see Jacobs, "Political Opposition," esp. pp. 27–34. See also J. Bruce Jacobs, "Taiwan 1978: Economic Successes, International Uncertainties," *Asian Survey* XIX, no. 1 (January 1979), pp. 20–23.
25 Zhen Boya 甄伯牙, "Linshi wuju, bumou wucheng 臨事無懼，不謀無成 [If One Does Not Plan, One Cannot Successfully Approach a Crisis without Fear]," *Da Shidai* 大時代 [*Great Epoch*] April 5, 1980, pp. 13–14.
26 Ziliaoshi 資料室 [Reference Office], "Baifen zhi sa xuanpiao de shuzi moshu 百分之卅選票的數字魔術 [The Wizardry of the Thirty Per Cent Vote Figure]," *Jifeng* 疾風 [*Gust*] April 4, 1980, p. 49.
27 Jacobs, "Political Opposition," p. 34.

As noted above, Huang Hsin-chieh only included thirteen of the twenty-one non-partisan provincial assemblymen as "genuine." These were Chang Chun-hung 張俊宏 of Nantou County, Lin I-hsiung 林義雄 of Ilan County, Chiu Lien-hui 邱連輝 of Pingtung County, Tsai Chieh-hsiung 蔡介雄 of Tainan Municipality, Huang Yu-chiao 黃玉嬌 of Taoyuan County, Sung Hung Yueh-chiao 蘇洪月嬌 of Yunlin County, Chou Tsang-yuan 周滄淵 of Keelung Municipality, Chao Hsiu-wa 趙綉娃 of Kaohsiung Municipality, Fu Wen-cheng 傅文政 of Miaoli County, Lin Lo-shan 林樂善 of Chiayi County, Chen Chin-te 陳金德 of Taipei County, Ho Chun-mu 何春木 of Taichung Municipalilty and Yu Chen Yueh-ying 余陳月瑛 of Kaohsiung County.[28] Su Hung Yueh-chiao, the wife of long-term political prisoner Su Tung-chi, asked voters during her campaign, "Am I guilty?" (*wo you zui ma?* 我有罪嗎 ?)[29] Yu Chen Yueh-ying had married into the powerful Yu Teng-fa family. Many of these names will appear repeatedly throughout this book.

Among the four county executives, Huang Hsin-chieh only included Hsu Hsin-liang 許信良 of Taoyuan County. About Su Nan-cheng 蘇南成 of Tainan Municipality, Huang said, "He is very busy and we are also very busy, so we rarely see him." With regard to Tseng Wen-po 曾文坡 of Taichung Municipality, Huang simply said, "He is not with us." And with regard to Huang Yu-jen 黃友仁 of Kaohsiung County, Huang said, "We can communicate with him." Huang only included two of the eight non-partisan Taipei Municipality Councilmen as "genuine" non-partisans, Kang Shui-mu 康水木 and Wang Kun-ho 王昆和.[30]

The county executive election in Taoyuan County led to the famous Chungli Incident. Citizens feared that the government was stealing the election from Hsu Hsin-liang, leading to a series of demonstrations and the ultimate burning down of a major police station as well as six adjoining houses for police. According to an important book, "this was Taiwan's largest [incident of] violence since the February 28, 1947 Uprising."[31] However, it was not true to say that Taiwan's media did not cover the incident.[32] In fact, short stories appeared in the three privately-owned newspapers that the writer received at the time.[33] In the end, the authorities conceded the election to Hsu Hsin-liang. Fortunately,

---

28 Zhen Boya 甄伯牙, "Linshi wuju," p. 14. I have obtained locality from *Taiwan shibao* 臺灣時報 [*Taiwan Times*], November 20, 1977, p. 1.
29 Jacobs, "Taiwan 1978," pp. 21–22.
30 Zhen Boya 甄伯牙, "Linshi wuju," p. 14.
31 Zhang Fuzhong 張富忠 and Qiu Wanxing 邱萬興, *Lüse niandai I*, I, p. 46. For the whole incident, see ibid., pp. 44–47.
32 Ibid., p. 46.
33 See *Lianhebao* 聯合報 (*United Daily News*), November 20, 1977, p. 3; *Taiwan shibao* 臺灣時報 [*Taiwan Times*], November 20, 1977, p. 3; and *Taiwan ribao* 臺灣日報 [*Taiwan*

the Kuomintang under its then "liberal" leadership decided not to repress the violence at the time. However, on April 17 the next year, a court sentenced eight defendants to terms ranging from two years and four months to twelve years.[34]

The Provincial Assembly election also had consequences. On December 20, 1977, during the election for Speaker and Deputy Speaker of the Provincial Assembly, Lin I-hsiung demanded the withdrawal of administrative officials in order to facilitate a secret ballot.[35] On March 30, 1978, Lin I-hsiung proposed a motion "allowing the use of Chinese languages including Mandarin, Manchu, Mongolian, Hui, Tibetan, Miao and this province's aboriginal languages when the Provincial Assembly is in session." Seven provincial assemblymen and women supported the resolution, while forty-three opposed it and five abstained.[36] Then, on April 18, 1978, Chang Chun-hung, Lin I-hsiung and Lin Lo-shan all fiercely attacked the police during interpellation.[37] On September 11, 1978, twelve-non-partisan provincial assemblymen and women refused to participate in the six normal committees of the Provincial Assembly and instead established a "Seventh Committee" and elected Chen Chin-te as convenor and Chang Chun-hung as deputy convenor.[38] Clearly, the relatively large number of non-partisans in the Provincial Assembly was changing the dynamics of that institution.

The regime did not ignore these challenges. In the middle of the night on March 18, 1978, the authorities confiscated ten thousand copies of an important, but still unbound, book on the November 19, 1977 county executive election in Taoyuan County and the subsequent Chungli Incident.[39] On March

---

Daily], November 20, 1977, p. 3. A small additional item appeared in *Taiwan ribao* 臺灣日報 [*Taiwan Daily*], November 21, 1977, p. 3.

34 *Taiwan lishi nianbiao (1966–1978)* 台灣歷史年表 [*Chronology of Taiwan History*], vol. II (Taibei: Guojia zhengce yanjiusuo ziliao zhongxin, 1990), p. 342. Details can be found in the lead article,, *Lianhebao (Guowai hangkongban)* 聯合報 (國外航空版) [*United Daily News (Overseas Edition)*] April 18, 1978, p. 1.

35 *Taiwan lishi nianbiao (1966–1978)* 台灣歷史年表 [*Chronology of Taiwan History*], II, p. 336.

36 *Lianhebao (Guowai hangkongban)* 聯合報 (國外航空版) [*United Daily News (Overseas Edition)*], March 31, 1978, p. 2.

37 For two news articles and a commentary, see *Lianhebao (Guowai hangkongban)* 聯合報 (國外航空版) [*United Daily News (Overseas Edition)*], April 19, 1978, p. 2.

38 *Lianhebao (Guowai hangkongban)* 聯合報 (國外航空版) [*United Daily News (Overseas Edition)*], September 12, 1978, p. 3. The twelve included all of the thirteen mentioned by Huang Hsin-chieh as "genuine" non-partisans except for Chiu Lien-hui.

39 See Zhang Fuzhong 張富忠 and Qiu Wanxing 邱萬興, *Lüse niandai I*, 1, p. 53–54. This book was *Xuanju wansui* 選舉萬歲 [*Long Live Elections*] by Lin Zhengjie 林正杰 and Zhang Fuzhong 張富忠.

25, 1978 the Ministry of the Interior wrote to the Taiwan Presbyterian Church to "warn it to correct" the Taiwan Independence attitudes of a small minority of members following the Church's August 16, 1977 Declaration mentioned above.[40] The Ministry's letter came ten days after a *United Daily* editorial calling for clarification of the Presbyterian Church's political viewpoints.[41] In June, the Director of the Bureau of Investigation told the legislature that supporters of "Taiwan Independence" were "domesticated lackeys" (*huanyang yingquan* 豢養鷹犬) of the Chinese Communists.[42] In September, the government forced the owners of the *Taiwan Daily News* (*Taiwan ribao* 臺灣日報), an outspoken independent paper based in Taichung that had given excellent coverage of the Taiwan Provincial Government and the Taiwan Provincial Assembly, to sell to a new owner with close links to the Ministry of Defense.[43]

The security agencies took even stronger action against Chen Chu, who did not hold an elected public office. Chen had been Kuo Yu-hsin's secretary and still handled his affairs even after he left for the United States. She was also one of the key young *dangwai* leaders. In the early hours of June 16, 1978 police without a search warrant came to her residence, checked her identification card and confiscated some fifty items. That morning Chen left Taipei and stayed with an American Catholic priest in a Catholic Church in Changhua County. On June 23, the police surrounded this church and arrested Chen Chu. She was taken back to Taipei and subjected to four days of intensive interrogation and deprivation of sleep. Many people expressed concern as did the American embassy.

On July 5, 1978, the KMT Secretary-General Chang Pao-shu 張寶樹 called a meeting with the Director of the Security Bureau Wang Yung-shu 王永樹, the Commander of the Taiwan Garrison Command Wang Ching-hsi 汪敬煦, Minister of National Defense Kao Kuei-yuan 高魁元, and Minister of Foreign Affairs Shen Chang-huan 沈昌煥 to discuss how to deal with the situation. The meeting decided to release Chen Chu the next day.

On July 6 the Taiwan Garrison Command called a press conference and forced Chen Chu to "confess." In fact, Chen Chu was not released but taken on

---

40   *Lianhebao (Guowai hangkongban)* 聯合報 (國外航空版) [*United Daily News (Overseas Edition)*], March 26, 1978, p. 1.

41   *Lianhebao (Guowai hangkongban)* 聯合報 (國外航空版) [*United Daily News (Overseas Edition)*], March 16, 1978, p. 1.

42   *Lianhebao (Guowai hangkongban)* 聯合報 (國外航空版) [*United Daily News (Overseas Edition)*], June 27, 1978, p. 1.

43   Jacobs, "Taiwan 1978," p. 29.

a tour of the "Ten Great Projects" and Kinmen Island. Only on July 24 did the Garrison Command call her father to come and get her.

In late October, Chen Chu met Harvey Feldman, a senior State Department official then visiting Taiwan, at the Taipei Hilton Hotel. Feldman told Chen Chu that she had been released in exchange for the United States selling weapons to Taiwan.[44]

The Aborted December 23, 1978 Election

In preparation for the December 23, 1978 legislative election, on October 6 Huang Hsin-chieh established a "Taiwan *Dangwai* Personages Election Assistance Group. (*Taiwan dangwai renshi zhuxuantuan*), which released twelve common political viewpoints for *dangwai* candidates on October 31 including "respect the Constitution and re-elect all central parliamentarians, directly elect the provincial governor, nationalize the military [instead of having a military loyal to the party] ... end martial law ... oppose discrimination on the basis of provincial origin and language ... have a major amnesty for political prisoners."[45] Huang Hsin-chieh was the liaison person, Shih Ming-teh, released in June 1977 after serving fifteen years in prison for "Taiwan Independence," was the general manager, and Chen Chu was the secretary.[46]

On December 5, more than forty candidates and seven hundred people met in the Chungshan Auditorium in Taipei for a campaign rally and press conference, the first organized meeting in over thirty years of opposition on the

---

44 Zhang Fuzhong 張富忠 and Qiu Wanxing 邱萬興, *Lüse niandai I*, 1, pp. 55, 57. For a useful English summary of the case, see International Committee for the Defense of Human Rights in Taiwan (ICDHRT), "An Account of Chen Chü's June 23rd Arrest, Detention and Release," in *A Borrowed Voice: Taiwan Human Rights through International Networks, 1960–1980*, ed. Linda Gail Arrigo and Lynn Miles (Taipei: Social Empowerment Alliance, 2008), pp. 317, 319. For an account by a foreigner involved in the case, see Rosemary Haddon, "The Sky-blue Backpack: My Experience with Taiwan's Human Rights," in *A Borrowed Voice: Taiwan Human Rights through International Networks, 1960–1980*, ed. Linda Gail Arrigo and Lynn Miles (Taipei: Social Empowerment Alliance, 2008), p. 295. For another foreign account, see Linda Gail Arrigo, "Three Years and a Lifetime: Swept Up in Taiwan's Democratic Movement, 1977–79," in *A Borrowed Voice: Taiwan Human Rights through International Networks, 1960–1980*, ed. Linda Gail Arrigo and Lynn Miles (Taipei: Social Empowerment Alliance, 2008), pp. 314, 316.

45 Zhang Fuzhong 張富忠 and Qiu Wanxing 邱萬興, *Lüse niandai I*, 1, pp. 60–62.

46 Ibid., p. 62. For Shih Ming-teh's release, see ibid., p. 54.

island.⁴⁷ In preparation for this meeting, Huang Hsin-chieh told Shih Ming-teh that in singing the national anthem, the word "party" (*dang* 黨) should be changed to "people" (*min* 民). As a result, everyone was happy and no one protested singing the national anthem.⁴⁸ After two hours, when the meeting was about to close, some "anti-Communists" created a disturbance and protested the amended word of the national anthem. Chairman Huang Hsin-chieh said, "This meeting is a meeting protected by the Constitution. These are bad people sent by the Communist Party to disrupt the meeting. If someone beats these bad people to death, I will not be responsible!" The disrupters fled.⁴⁹

During the campaign, various candidates raised issues relevant to Taiwan and to democratization. Annette Lu 呂秀蓮 in Taoyuan discussed "the Taiwan Question," "The Community Concerned with Taiwan's Fate," and "Taiwan's Past and Future." In Changhua Yao Chia-wen talked about the constitution, martial law and the complete re-election of the legislature.⁵⁰

On November 1, 1978, two former members of the Kuomintang, Chen Ku-ying 陳鼓應, a Mainlander professor of philosophy at National Taiwan University running for National Assembly, and Chen Wan-chen 陳婉真, a former reporter for the *China Times* running for the legislature, issued a joint statement denouncing the Kuomintang's thirty years of rule in Taiwan.⁵¹ In addition, they established a "Democracy Wall" near the gate of National Taiwan University, where conservatives also launched a "Patriotism Wall."⁵² Their actions were colloquially summarized as "From within the Party, they hit their way out, joined with the *dangwai* and hit their way back in."⁵³

At least twenty-seven candidates actively ran for the legislature and National Assembly with the support of the *Dangwai* Election Assistance Group.⁵⁴ On December 16, 1978 in Taiwan, the American government announced it was establishing formal diplomatic with China as of January 1. This naturally raised concern in Taiwan and led to the government postponing the central parliamentary elections scheduled for December 23. In response, twenty-seven *dangwai* personages issued a statement calling on the government to quickly

---

47   Ibid., pp. 62, 64, 66.
48   Ibid., p. 64.
49   Ibid., pp. 64, 66.
50   Ibid., pp. 66, 68.
51   Ibid., p. 68. This source reprints their joint statement.
52   Ibid., pp. 66–71.
53   Ibid., p. 68.
54   Ibid., p. 71.

restore the elections and to "bravely oppose the lures and oppression of military rule."[55]

Dangwai Political Activities in 1979

With the indefinite postponement of the December 23, 1978 election, the *dangwai* continued its activities in an effort to stay in the limelight for the forthcoming election. Because of a conflict between Huang Hsin-chieh and Kang Ning-hsiang, several *dangwai* leaders went to Kaohsiung County to ask Yu Teng-fa, a founding member of the "China Democratic Self-Government Research Association" in 1960, who won election as Kaohsiung County Executive that year, to become the national "spiritual" *dangwai* leader. Yu Teng-fa agreed, though the leader of the Black Faction in Kaohsiung County had never participated in *dangwai* activities in the 1970s. Under his chairmanship, a *Dangwai* National Affairs Meeting (*Dangwai guoshi huiyi* 黨外國是會議) met on December 25 at the Ambassador Hotel in Taipei with 73 people despite attempts of the security agencies to inhibit the meeting.[56]

But divisions soon appeared in the *dangwai*. Some, like Yu Teng-fa, Huang Shun-hsing 黃順興 (who later went to China), Wang Tuoh 王拓, Chen Ku-ying and Su Ching-li 蘇慶黎,[57] the editor of *China Tide* (*Xia Chao* 夏朝), a leftist magazine that began publishing on February 28, 1976,[58] advocated unity with China. Others, including Shih Ming-teh, Lin I-hsiung, Hsu Hsin-liang, Yao Chia-wen, and Chang Chun-hung, favored a separate Taiwan.[59]

On January 21, 1979, the authorities arrested Yu Teng-fa and his son and charged them with "knowing a Communist and not reporting it." Yu Teng-fa was sentenced to eight years in prison on April 16. In a sense, the Yu Teng-fa case in itself is not important to Taiwan's democratization and I have analyzed it elsewhere.[60] More importantly, on January 22, the day after the arrest, Taoyuan County Executive Hsu Hsin-liang and other prominent *dangwai* leaders[61] went to Yu's home village and to Kaohsiung City to protest. In April, in

---

55 For this quote and full text, see ibid., p. 72.
56 Ibid., pp. 73–74.
57 Ibid., pp. 72–74.
58 Ibid., p. 55.
59 Ibid., p. 74.
60 J. Bruce Jacobs, "Taiwan 1979: 'Normalcy' After 'Normalization'," *Asian Survey* xx, no. 1 (January 1980), pp. 90–91.
61 A list of about twenty-five other leaders appears in Zhang Fuzhong 張富忠 and Qiu Wanxing 邱萬興, *Lüse niandai I*, 1, p. 79.

order to impeach Hsu, the Control Branch announced an investigation into Hsu's "taking leave without permission," participating in an illegal demonstration and signing leaflets that libeled the government.[62]

To support Hsu Hsin-liang as well as Yu Teng-fa, on May 26, 1979 the *dangwai* opposition organized a massive "birthday party" for Hsu Hsin-liang in his hometown of Chungli, the very location of the Chungli Incident eighteen months previously. Naturally, both the government and the opposition felt concern about the sensitive nature of the location. Between ten thousand and thirty thousand people attended to show support for the *dangwai* and to listen to the speeches, but the uniformed police and military stayed well away from the crowd. As the largest non-government sponsored, non-electoral peaceful political gathering in Taiwan's history, Hsu's birthday party was very important for the development of democracy in Taiwan. Unfortunately, the Committee on the Discipline of Public Functionaries suspended Hsu from office for two years. Hsu left for "study" overseas and promised to return to finish the final six months of his term in June 1981.[63]

On June 1, 1979, key members of the *dangwai* established *Formosa Magazine* (*Meilidao zazhi* 美麗島雜誌). As Shih Ming-teh told this writer in May, the opposition would establish a political party without using the term "political party." The magazine established county offices around the island, offices which they called "service centers" (*fuwu chu* 服務處). Ironically, this was exactly the same term used by the Kuomintang in its external nomenclature for its county party headquarters, though interviews several years later indicated the *dangwai* leaders did not realize this.[64] Naturally, this organization, as well as the language, scared the Kuomintang which had consistently prevented the establishment of any organization that could threaten Kuomintang rule.

In the meantime, as it could not gain publicity for the forthcoming elections in the Kuomintang-controlled media, the *dangwai* continued its public demonstrations throughout 1979. Two key demonstrations, the Taichung Incident of July 28 and the Chungtai Hotel Incident of September 8, deserve special analysis both for their importance in Taiwan's democratization movement and because they illustrate the difficulties that the *dangwai* faced in this struggle.

---

62   Jacobs, "Taiwan 1979," p. 91.
63   More details can be found in ibid., pp. 91–92.
64   At the township level, the Kuomintang used the external nomenclature of "Service Station" (*fuwu fenshe* 服務分社) rather than the internal nomenclature of "District Party Office" (*qudangbu* 區黨部). However, at the county level, the KMT generally used the internal nomenclature of County Party Headquarters (*xian dangbu* 縣黨部) rather than the external nomenclature of Service Center (*fuwuchu* 服務處).

In comparative terms, the Taichung Incident was relatively small. The twenty-odd *dangwai* demonstrators did not even have a microphone. They were met by "a group of super-patriots" who banged on their cars and shouted two sets of slogans, "Communist Party! Communist Party! Kill the Communist Party!" and "Taichung's citizens do not welcome you! Get out! Get out!"[65] The Fire Department also gave the demonstrators a "baptism" with fire hoses.[66] A picture of the event shows some twenty people in Taichung Park peacefully seated in a circle listening to Chiu Chui-chen 邱垂貞 play his guitar while singing Taiwan folksongs.[67]

On September 8, the newly formed *Formosa Magazine* held a cocktail party to celebrate the magazine's founding. The location was the Kowloon Room at the Chungtai Hotel (also known in English as the Mandarin Hotel) on Tunhua North Road in Taipei. In applying for permission to hold the cocktail party, the *Formosa Magazine* had met many obstructions. Originally, the *Formosa Magazine* had tried to book the Hilton Hotel, but had been rejected. They then were able to book the Chungtai Hotel and paid a deposit. The Chungtai Hotel also got cold feet and tried to return the deposit, but the *Formosa Magazine* refused. Finally, the *Formosa Magazine* told the authorities that if they did not receive permission to hold the cocktail party indoors, they would hold it outdoors either in a park near the presidential office or in front of the international airport in Taoyuan. The Deputy Secretary-General of the Kuomintang's Policy Committee, Kuan Chung 關中, then came forward and the cocktail party went ahead at the Chungtai Hotel as planned.[68]

When the five hundred guests for the cocktail party started to arrive in the afternoon, they were met by several hundred demonstrators organized by *Gust Magazine* (*Jifeng zazhi* 疾風雜誌) who had put up signs proclaiming such

---

65   Fan Zhengyou 范政祐, "Qi erba Taizhong naoju zhi wo guan: gei Taizhong shimin de gongkai xin 七二八台中鬧劇之我觀：給台中市民的公開信 [My Views on the Taizhong Farce of July 28: An Open Letter to Taizhong's Citizens]," *Meilidao* 美麗島 [*Formosa*], no. 1 (August 16, 1979), p. 74.

66   On the Taichung Incident, see ibid., pp. 74–76. See also He Wenzhen 何文振, "Qi erba Taizhong shijian zhenxiang 七二八台中事件真相 [The Truth about the Taichung Incident of July 28]," *Meilidao* 美麗島 [*Formosa*], no. 1 (August 16, 1979), p. 73. In their overseas editions, neither the *Lianhebao* nor the *Zhongyang ribao* reported on the Taichung Incident.

67   Zhang Fuzhong 張富忠 and Qiu Wanxing 邱萬興, *Lüse niandai I*, I, p. 88.

68   Wu Zhengshuo 吳正朔, "Zhongtai binguan shijian shimo 中泰賓館事件始末 [The Chungtai Hotel Incident from the Beginning to the End]," *Da shidai* 大時代 [*Great Epoch*], no. 4 (October 5, 1979), p. 9. This article is the classic account of the Chungtai Hotel Incident.

things as "Grand Meeting to Condemn the National Traitor Chen Wan-chen." In addition, when guests went into the function, the demonstrators shouted such things as "Various compatriots are prepared to destroy you at any time," "Kill him!" and "Destroy the Black Fist Gang!" Less violent shouted slogans included "Long Live the Republic of China!" and "Long Live President Chiang!"[69]

About 3.20 PM the formal part of the cocktail party began with Annette Lu as master of ceremonies. Led by the publisher of the *Formosa Magazine*, Huang Hsin-chieh, several people spoke. Kuan Chung, the KMT Deputy-Secretary of the Policy Committee, came and shook hands with several people before departing. Shih Ming-teh went outside to have a look and was called "Linda Arrigo's sex tool." There were also shouts of "Taiwan Independence!," "National Traitor!," and "Get Out!"[70]

The *Formosa Magazine* had booked the Kowloon Room until 5pm. At that time, Hsiao Yu-ching 蕭玉井, one of the *Gust* leaders, yelled: "Taiwan Independent elements, get out. It is already five o'clock. Please go out under police protection with your tail between your legs and get out!" Others in the crowd responded, "Get Out! Get Out! Get Out!"[71]

Clearly the *Gust* demonstrators posed a threat to the guests of the *Formosa Magazine*. The police sent three buses to the Chungtai Hotel and asked the *dangwai* guests to leave in the buses. The *dangwai* guests refused as they believed the demonstrators outside were those who were acting illegally. Around 7 PM it had already become dark and the police again sent buses and again the *dangwai* guests refused to board the police buses. The *Gust* demonstrators continued to hurl abuse. The riot police arrived and some used electric prods on some *Gust* demonstrators who fell down. Hsiao Yu-ching yelled, "Lie Down! Sit Down! Lie Down! Sit Down!" The demonstrators did as instructed. The riot police back off and surrounded the demonstrators.[72]

Around 7.40 PM, Lao Cheng-wu 勞政武, another *Gust* leader, spoke to the demonstrators, "We have already won. Now we must respect the requests of the police and go home and have a happy weekend." Finally, the crowd dispersed. About 8 PM, the *dangwai* organized about one hundred men into two lines who protected the elderly, women and children between the two lines. The *dangwai* participants proceeded to march out under police guard as well. Some yelled "Beautiful Island" and some yelled "One, two, one, two." A taxi drove into the crowd, but no one was hurt. By the time the *dangwai* marchers

---

69   Ibid., p. 8.
70   Ibid., p. 11.
71   Ibid., p. 12.
72   Ibid., p. 13.

reached Changchun Road, they were no longer in order. Other incidents took place like the sound of an explosion and people throwing rocks breaking windows.[73]

The Chungtai Hotel Incident was important for several reasons. First, it showed the *dangwai* could convene an orderly meeting. Second, it demonstrated that the threats to public order came from such right-wing "patriotic" groups as the *Gust Magazine*. According to the police, it was the *Gust* demonstrators, not the *dangwai*, who threatened public order.[74] The reports of the Chungtai Incident varied greatly among Taiwan's daily newspapers.[75] For example, some newspapers did not report the numbers attending the Formosa Magazine cocktail party, while other reported from several hundred to even a thousand people participating.[76]

The *Formosa Magazine* published four issues on August 16, September 25, October 25 and November 25, 1979. Many of those involved in the *dangwai* in 1979 were involved in the magazine according to the list published on the back cover of the first issue: Huang Hsin-chieh 黃信介, Lin I-hsiung 林義雄, Yao Chia-wen 姚嘉文, Chang Te-ming 張德銘, Huang Tien-fu 黃天福, Lu Hsiu-lien (Annette Lu) 呂秀蓮, Hsu Hsin-liang 許信良, Chang Chun-hung 張俊宏, Shih Ming-teh 施明德, Wei Ting-chao 魏廷朝, Wang Tuoh 王拓, Su Ching-li 蘇慶黎, Hsieh San-sheng 謝三升, Hsieh Hsiu-hsiung 謝秀雄, and Huang Huang-hsiung 黃皇雄. Many others were also involved as committee members including such people as Kang Ning-hsiang 康寧祥, Huang Shun-hsing 黃順興 and Hsu Shih-hsien 許世賢. The first issue had 100 pages including the two covers and each issue expanded until the fourth issue had 132 pages. Circulation increased until it reached about 100,000 for the fourth issue,[77] about one per cent of Taiwan's population.

The first issue of *Formosa Magazine* began with a statement launching the magazine by the publisher, Huang Hsin-chieh, entitled "All work together to push a political movement of the new generation!" Huang said that the break in relations with the United States "announced the bankruptcy of the KMT government's foreign policy for the past thirty years" and created the greatest political crisis for the KMT since it began to rule Taiwan. One political response

---

73 Ibid., p. 14.

74 Ibid., pp. 8, 13, 18.

75 Wen Chaogong 文抄公, "Ni kan de shi shenme bao? ge bao dui Zhongtai shijian de baodao 你看的是什麼報？各報對中泰事件的報導 [What Newspaper Do You read? The Reports of Different Newspapers on the Chungtai Incident]," *Meilidao* 美麗島 [*Formosa*], no. 2 (September 25, 1979), pp. 83–87.

76 Ibid., p. 83.

77 Katherine Lee, "Taiwan's dissidents," *Index on Censorship* 9, no. 6 (December 1980), p. 54.

has been to stop the elections. But "democracy will not die. Long live elections."[78] The statement also emphasized Taiwan: "This beautiful island (*meili zhi dao* 美麗之島) is our homeland where we have grown up. We deeply love this piece of land and its people, who have drunk its milk as they have grown. And we have concern about our future joint fate."[79]

In 1979 *Formosa* struck its readers as radical and new. Today, over thirty years later and after more than two decades of democracy, *Formosa* seems milder. The first issue had a six-page commentary entitled "Long Live Democracy,"[80] Two pages of legislative interpellation by Huang Shun-hsing[81] and five pages of Cabinet response.[82] With regard to the provincial level, the issue had a commentary on "What can the 'provincial chairman' do?"[83] and an article on the "ten best provincial assembly members" chosen by twenty-two relatively young observers of the provincial assembly. Of the fourteen finally chosen (five provincial assembly members tied for the tenth position), eight—including the first three place-getters—were non-partisans.[84] As previously discussed, the first issue also had two articles on the Taichung Incident of July 28.[85]

---

78 Huang Hsin-chieh 黃信介, "Fakan ci: gongtong lai tuidong xinshengdai zhengzhi yundong! 發刊詞：共同來推動新生代政治運動! [Words on Launching Magazine: All work together to push a political movement of the new generation!," *Meilidao* 美麗島 [*Formosa*], no. 1 (August 16, 1979), inside front cover.

79 Ibid., p. 1.

80 Ben she 本社 [Formosa Magazine], "Dangwai zhenglun: minzhu wansui 黨外政論：民主萬歲 [*Dangwai Commentary: Long Live Elections*]," *Meilidao* 美麗島 [*Formosa*], no. 1 (August 16, 1979), pp. 4–9.

81 Huang Shun-hsing 黃順興, "Xiang xingzhengyuan zhixun san ze 向行政院質詢三則 [Three Interpellations of the Cabinet]," *Meilidao* 美麗島 [*Formosa*], no. 1 (August 16, 1979), pp. 10–11.

82 Xingzhengyuan 行政院 [Cabinet], "Fulu: dui Huang weiyuan Shunxing zhixun zhi shumian dafu 附錄：對黃委員順興質詢書面答覆 [Appendix: Written Answers to the Interpellations of Legislator Huang Shun-hsing]," *Meilidao* 美麗島 [*Formosa*], no. 1 (August 16, 1979), pp. 12–16.

83 Huang Huang-hsiung 黃煌雄, "'Sheng zhuxi' neng zuo shenme? '省主席' 能做什麼？ [What can the 'Provincial Chairman' Do?]," *Meilidao* 美麗島 [*Formosa*], no. 1 (August 16, 1979), pp. 34–36.

84 Zhou Qingyuan 周清源, "Shi da shengyiyuan 十大省議員 [Ten Great Provincial Assembly Members]," *Meilidao* 美麗島 [*Formosa*], no. 1 (August 16, 1979), pp. 37–39.

85 Fan Zhengyou 范政祐, "Qi erba". He Wenzhen 何文振, "Qi erba."

The second issue of *Formosa* had two articles on the Chungtai Hotel Incident of September 8 discussed above.[86] In addition, the second issue had the text of three *dangwai* legislators interpellating Premier Sun Yuan-suan,[87] two responses to the article in the first issue on "Ten Great Provincial Assembly Members"[88] and the transcript of a long forum on the draft election and recall law[89] among other items.

The third issue contained an extensive interpellation of Premier Sun by Legislator Huang Shun-hsing on behalf of Taiwan's farmers.[90] Another extended article raised the very sensitive issue of Taiwanese/Mainlander relations.[91] The article began by pointing out that Taiwanese account for 87.8 per cent of Taiwan's population, while Mainlander account for 12.2 per cent. Of the Taiwanese, about two per cent are aborigines, Hokkien account for 83.1 per cent and Hakka account for 15.6 per cent. Among the Hokkien, those originating from Chuanchou account for 44.8 per cent while those from Changchou number 35.2 per cent.[92] Publishing these figures right at the front of the article broke many taboos.

---

86 Ben she 本社 [Formosa Magazine], "Dangwai zhenglun: Shaoshu pai yu baoli, ping Zhongtai binguan qian de naoju 黨外政論：少數派與暴力，評中泰賓館前的鬧劇 [Dangwai Commentary: The Minority Faction and Violence, A Critique of the Farce in Front of the Chungtai Hotel]," *Meilidao* 美麗島 [*Formosa*], no. 2 (September 25, 1979), pp. 4–5. Wen Chaogong 文抄公, "Ni kan."

87 Fei Xiping 費希平, Huang Hsin-chieh 黃信介, and Kang Ning-xiang 康寧祥, "Jiu women suo mianlin de san xiang zhengzhi wenti xiang xingzhengyuan Sun yuanzhang tichu zhixun 就我們所面臨的三項政治問題向行政院孫院長提出質詢 [Interpellating Premier Sun about Three Political Questions which We Face]," *Meilidao* 美麗島 [*Formosa*], no. 2 (September 25, 1979), pp. 7–8.

88 Chen Qiude 陳秋德, "Feichang jumianxia, shengyiyuan suowei heshi? 非常局面下，省議員所謂何事？ [Under Unusual Circumstances, What are Provincial Assembly Members to do?]," *Meilidao* 美麗島 [*Formosa*], no. 2 (September 25, 1979), pp. 20–23. Ye Fengsheng 葉逢生, "'Shida shengyiyuan' xuanba yup'. 十大省議員'選拔餘波 [Trouble After Selecting the Best 'Ten Great Provincial Assembly Members']," *Meilidao* 美麗島 [*Formosa*], no. 2 (September 25, 1979), pp. 24–25.

89 Ben she 本社 [Formosa Magazine], "Xuanju bamianfa cao'an zuotanhui jilu 選舉罷免法草案座談會紀錄 [Record of Forum on Draft Election and Recall Law]," *Meilidao* 美麗島 [*Formosa*], no. 2 (September 25, 1979), pp. 34–41.

90 Huang Shun-hsing 黃順興, "Wei nongmin quanyi xiang xingzhengyuan Sun yuanzhang zhixun 為農民權益向行政院孫院長質詢 [Interpellation of Premier Sun on the Rights and Interests of Farmers]," *Meilidao* 美麗島 [*Formosa*], no. 3 (October 25, 1979), pp. 35–42.

91 Liu Fengsong 劉峯松, "Yiqian babaiwan ren de Taiwan shi 一千八百萬人的台灣史 [The Taiwan History of Eighteen Million People]," *Meilidao* 美麗島 [*Formosa*], no. 3 (October 25, 1979), pp. 69–76.

92 Ibid., p. 69.

Next, the article asked who is Taiwan's *zhuren* 主人, a term meaning "master" or "lord" in this context. These are the aborigines who came many centuries before the Hokkien, but the Hokkien, Hakkas and Mainlanders do not discuss this.[93] After discussing the reasons Hokkien and Hakka came to Taiwan 200–300 years previously, the article gives statistics on Mainlander males and females arriving from 1947–1951.[94] In terms of modern scholarship, the article declines a bit. It divides Taiwan's history into period of unity with the mainland (216 years) and separation (139 years),[95] periods of rule by Chinese (56 years) and by others (299 years), and then subdivides the rule by Chinese into 4 years of unity (with China) and 52 years of separation.[96] In the last paragraph, the article concludes, "Lastly, this article raises democracy, because only with democracy can we change our unclear destiny. Only with democracy can the people here stand on this land and genuinely protect themselves."[97]

The fourth issue of *Formosa Magazine* covered a variety of areas including commentary of the 1979 coup against Park Chung-hee in Korea,[98] three discussions of matters relevant to provincial politics,[99] several articles on human rights and overseas human rights organizations such as Amnesty International,[100] and the transcript of a long forum on labor unions.[101] Shih Ming-teh had a detailed account of the demonstrations in support of Yu Teng-fa in January 1979.[102]

Formosa Magazine never published again. Three weeks later, on December 10, 1979, the *Formosa Magazine* sponsored a demonstration in Kaohsiung in celebration of Human Rights Day. Originally, this Kaohsiung demonstration was one of several planned until the legislative election. It was to be surpassed by a planned demonstration in Taipei on December 16, exactly one year after the United States broke diplomatic relations with Taiwan.

---

93   Ibid.
94   Ibid., p. 70.
95   Ibid., p. 73.
96   Ibid., p. 74.
97   Ibid., p. 76.
98   *Meilidao* 美麗島 [*Formosa*], no. 4 (November 25, 1979), pp. 4–5, 6, 70–77, 77–78.
99   Ibid., pp. 7–11, 13–16, 30–34.
100 Ibid., pp. 40–44, 51.
101 Ibid., pp. 52–69.
102 Shi Mingde 施明德, "Taiwan minzhu yundong huashidai de yitian: dangwai renshi wei Yu Dengfa an youxing kangyi jishi 台灣民主運動劃時代的一天：黨外人士為雨余登發案遊行抗議記實 [An Epoch-Making Day in the Taiwan Democratic Movement: A True Account of the *Dangwai* Personnages Marching to Resist the Yu Teng-fa Case]," *Meilidao* 美麗島 [*Formosa*], no. 4 (November 25, 1979), pp. 82–88.

Instead, what became known as the Kaohsiung Incident on December 10 ended in violence and, more than two days later, the arrests of the *dangwai* leaders. As Premier Sun Yun-suan had warned the legislature over two months before, "Now is not the time to establish an opposition political party."[103] The formation of an opposition political organization—even one that did not use the term "political party"—could not be tolerated.

The next chapter tells what actually happened in Kaohsiung on December 10, 1979.

---

103 "Sun Yunxuan yuanzhang da liwei zhixun ... 孫運璿院長答立委質詢 ... [Premier Sun Yun-suan answers the Interpellation of a Legislator ...]," *Lianhebao* (*Guowai hangkongban*) 聯合報 (國外航空版) [*United Daily News* (*Overseas Edition*)] October 3, 1979, p. 1. This response was to a joint interpellation of "Fei Hsi-ping, Huang Hsin-chieh and Kang Ning-hsiang, for text see Fei Xiping 費希平, Huang Hsin-chieh 黃信介, and Kang Ning-xiang 康寧祥, "Jiu women suo mianlin de san xiang zhengzhi wenti xiang xingzhengyuan Sun yuanzhang tichu zhixun 就我們所面臨的三項政治問題向行政院孫院長提出質詢 [Interpellating Premier Sun about Three Political Questions which We Face]," pp. 7–8.

CHAPTER 2

The Kaohsiung Incident, the Arrests, the Indictment and the Murder of Lin I-hsiung's Family

On December 10, 1948, the United Nations General Assembly adopted and proclaimed the Universal Declaration of Human Rights. Since then, December 10 has become Human Rights Day throughout the world. In order to commemorate Human Rights Day, the *Formosa Magazine* planned a demonstration in Kaohsiung on Monday, December 10, 1979.[1]

As we shall see, the Kaohsiung Incident had some violence, mostly from the government and security agencies. This violence was used as an excuse by the government to arrest, imprison and try the *dangwai* leaders. This process of arrest, imprisonment and trial made the Kaohsiung Incident important in Taiwan's human rights history.

Even before the actual events of December 10, 1979, tension had arisen in and around Kaohsiung. The *Formosa Magazine* office in Kaohsiung had been attacked with furniture destroyed and windows broken on November 6 and November 29. On November 29, the Taipei residence of Huang Hsin-chieh was

---

[1] In preparing this chapter, I have relied on many interviews conducted with participants in the Kaohsiung Incident during January-April 1980. In addition I have used an English translation of a tape made of the Kaohsiung Incident, *The Kaohsiung Tapes* (Seattle: International Committee for Human Rights in Taiwan, February 1981). This book can be obtained at <http://www.taiwandc.org/kao-tapes.pdf>. An important collection of oral histories around the Kaohsiung Incident is Chen Yishen 陳儀深, ed. *Koushu lishi, di 12 qi: Meilidao shijian zhuanji* 口述歷史，第 12 期: 美麗島事件專輯 [*Oral History, No. 12: Special Collection on the Formosa Incident*] (Taibei: Zhongyang yanjiuyuan jindaishi yanjiusuo 中央研究院近代史研究所 [Institute of Modern History, Academia Sinica], 2004). An important memoir by a key participant is Lu Xiulian 呂秀蓮, *Chongshen Meilidao* 重審美麗島 [*Re-Examining the Formosa Incident*] (Taibei 台北: Qianwei 前衛, 1997). A voluminous documentary source with the transcript of numerous phone calls from Taiwan to the United States is Zhang Yanxian 張炎憲 and Wen Qiufen 溫秋芬, eds., *Gaoxiong shijian: 'Taiwan zhi yin' luyin jilu xuanji* 高雄事件：'台灣之音 '錄音紀錄選輯 [*Witnessing Kaohsiung Incident: Selected Tape Recordings of 'Voice of Taiwan'*] (Taibei 台北: Wu San-lien Taiwan shiliao jijinhui 吳三連台灣史料基金會 [Wu San-lien Taiwan History Materials Foundation], 2006). Another important collection of materials is Zhang Yanxian 張炎憲 and Chen Chaohai 陳朝海, eds., *Meilidao shijian 30 zhounian yanjiu lunwenji* 美麗島事件 30 周年研究論文集 [*Compendium of Research Articles on the 30th Anniversary of the Formosa Incident*] (Taibei 臺北: Wu Sanlian Taiwan shiliao jijinhui 吳三連臺灣史料基金會, 2010).

also attacked.[2] On December 7, the night before the Pingtung Office of Formosa Magazine was to be opened, six youths attacked the office with axes, destroying furniture and wounding employees.[3]

The severe police beating of two *Formosa Magazine* volunteers during the night of December 9, the so-called Kushan Incident 鼓山事件, also raised tension. Yao Kuo-chien 姚國建, a Mainlander Village Head from a village inhabited by the military and their dependents, could not even speak a sentence of Hokkien.[4] He had been out with Chiu Sheng-hsiung 邱勝雄 in trucks announcing the next day's rally. Near the Kushan police station, they were arrested and both were severely beaten. They were then taken to the Southern District Taiwan Garrison Command Headquarters. When Su Chih-fen 蘇治芬, daughter of political prisoner Su Tung-chi 蘇東啓 and later County Executive of Yunlin County, saw Yao and Chiu, she said, "Their faces had been so beaten that they had changed shape and swollen up. I almost could not tell which was Yao Kuo-chien and which was Chiu Sheng-hsiung."[5] The police beating angered the *Formosa Magazine* workers and made the demonstration the next day a certainty.[6]

The *Formosa Magazine* had filed several applications in November to get permission to have an indoor rally in Kaohsiung on December 10. These were repeatedly rejected. On December 3, Huang Hsin-chieh applied to hold the rally in Kaohsiung's Rotary Park, one long block south of the *Formosa Magazine's* Kaohsiung Office.[7] Again, the application was rejected, but on the basis of previous experience the *Formosa Magazine* expected that last minute permission would be given.[8]

When the *dangwai* leaders began to arrive in Kaohsiung during the afternoon of December 10, they were met with a message from the Commander of the Southern District Taiwan Garrison Command, General Chang Chih-hsiu 常

---

2 *The Kaohsiung Tapes*, pp. 5–6. Zhang Fuzhong 張富忠 and Qiu Wanxing 邱萬興, *Lüse niandai I*, 1, p. 91.

3 Zhang Fuzhong 張富忠 and Qiu Wanxing 邱萬興, *Lüse niandai I*, 1, p. 91. Pingtung is the county directly south of Kaohsiung.

4 Ibid., p. 92.

5 Ibid., p. 93. A detailed account was given during the demonstration on the night of December 10 by Chou Ping-teh 周平德, *The Kaohsiung Tapes*, pp. 11–14.

6 Zhang Fuzhong 張富忠 and Qiu Wanxing 邱萬興, *Lüse niandai I*, 1, p. 93.

7 A clear map appears in Zhang Yanxian 張炎憲 and Chen Chaohai 陳朝海, *Meilidao shijian 30 zhounian*, p. 55.

8 *The Kaohsiung Tapes*, p. 6.

持琇: "You can give speeches indoors, but you can't march and you can't hold torches."⁹

When Huang Hsin-chieh arrived at the Kaohsiung Train Station about 6 PM, he was met by General Chang Chih-hsiu, who repeated that there could be speeches, but no marching. Chang took Huang Hsin-chieh to the Kaohsiung Office of the *Formosa Magazine* in his car. When Huang discussed this with Yao Chia-wen 姚嘉文 and Shih Ming-teh 施明德, the latter said that General Chang's statement was a lie as the Garrison Command had already surrounded the Rotary Park.¹⁰

The demonstrators had initially gathered outside the Kaohsiung Office of the *Formosa Magazine* at the corner of Chungshan First Road 中山一路 and Tatung Second Road 大同二路. (Chungshan is the main north-south road in Kaohsiung. Tatung First Road runs southwest off Chungshan.) Shih Ming-teh and Yao Chia-wen made the decision to take the approximately 1,000 demonstrators north about two blocks to the great Kaohsiung Circle 圓環 where they would have speeches.

The *Formosa Magazine* could have stayed at the Office and held speeches. General Chang had already given permission, though the *Formosa Magazine* leaders may have felt insecure considering the large numbers of security forces in the area. This decision of Yao Chia-wen and Shih Ming-teh to march, however, did escalate the situation as a fluid march is much more difficult for the organizers to control than a static demonstration. One could argue that the decision to march was one of many unfortunate errors that took place that night.

At the Circle, there were a number of speeches. While the speeches were underway, Shih Ming-teh and Yao Chia-wen went into the police station at the Circle to negotiate with the police. During the speeches, the demonstrators saw riot control vehicles coming from the east along Chungcheng Third Road 中正三路. In addition, the demonstrators discovered that the security forces had surrounded the Circle. One of the riot control vehicles let off some type of gas and people started to yell, "Tear gas! Tear gas!"

Tear gas is used to disperse crowds, but the marchers were surrounded and found it difficult to escape. The security ring was thinnest to the southwest and many demonstrators escaped in that direction along Chungcheng Fourth Road 中正四路. It was there that the first conflict took place between demonstrators and security forces. Later that night, after real tear gas had been used, several

---

9 Zhang Fuzhong 張富忠 and Qiu Wanxing 邱萬興, *Lüse niandai I*, 1, p. 93.
10 Ibid. During the court trial, Shih Ming-teh said that he was not present at that time and Huang then said he must have told Yao, *Zhongguo shibao* 中國時報, March 26, 1980, p. 3.

demonstrators realized that the gas released from the riot control vehicles was not tear gas. This release of a gas at a time when the demonstrators were surrounded at the Circle was another unfortunate error. Possibly this error occurred because the security forces were not familiar with their new riot control vehicles.

The demonstrators who had broken out through the security cordon went southwest along Chungcheng Fourth Road and then turned southeast along Chunghua Third Road 中華三路 until they reached Minsheng Second Road 民生二路 where they again turned northeast until they reached Chungshan First Road. There, they turned to the north and returned to the Kaohsiung Office of the *Formosa Magazine*. It was at the Kaohsiung Office of the *Formosa Magazine* that most of the speeches were given.

Clearly emotions were at a high pitch. Such organizers as Shih Ming-teh, Chang Chun-hung 張俊宏, Lu Hsiu-lien 呂秀蓮 and Yao Chia-wen repeatedly asked the demonstrators to remain non-violent and said that the Taiwanese demonstrators and the Taiwanese soldiers were from the same family and should not fight.[11] Perhaps the main speaker on the night was Lu Hsiu-lien who, with breaks, spoke for an extended period.[12] Kang Ning-hsiang, a *dangwai* legislator, spoke only a very short time,[13] while Provincial Assemblyman Lin I-hsiung, who in the end suffered the most, did not speak at all.[14]

About 10 PM, riot control vehicles that were more frightening than the riot control vehicles at the Circle earlier that evening moved from the south along Chungshan First Road toward the crowd. Now real tear gas was used in substantial quantities that dispersed very slowly. It was in this context of heightened "emotions of fear and anger" that conflict broke out between the security forces and the demonstrators.[15]

The next morning the daily press reported that the *Formosa Magazine* demonstrations had led to many injuries among security personnel. The *United Daily* opened its story with the following lines:

> Even though the *Formosa Magazine* did not obtain permission from relevant government agencies, it still held its human rights demonstration. The security units sent men to control traffic, but the magazine's people still gathered to give speeches and to march. In addition they beat the

---

11   For example, *The Kaohsiung Tapes*, pp. 29–33, 35–36.
12   Ibid., pp. 26, 32, 36–46.
13   Ibid., pp. 47–49.
14   Ibid., p. 47.
15   Zhang Fuzhong 張富忠 and Qiu Wanxing 邱萬興, *Lüse niandai I*, 1, pp. 93–94.

security people who were maintaining order and more than twenty people were injured.[16]

The report continued that the security personnel maintained an attitude of high tolerance: "when hit, they did not respond with their hands; when abused, they did not respond with their mouth 打不還手，罵不還口."[17] The *Central Daily News* had a similar report except that it said forty security personnel were injured.[18]

The following day, the newspapers were filled with the "violence" (*baoli* 暴力) of the Kaohsiung demonstration. The number of security personnel injured escalated many times to 182 security personnel in the *Central Daily News*.[19] As part of the anti-violence rhetoric, the *United Daily* editorialized, "If one moves the mouth, then when must be lenient; if one moves the hand, then one most definitely cannot be lenient!"[20] The newspapers were filled with pictures of injured security personnel.

About 5 PM on December 12, several *Formosa Magazine* leaders held a press conference in the magazine's Taipei headquarters to give their side of the story, which about one hundred domestic and foreign reporters attended. Huang Hsin-chieh explained that the Commander of the Southern District Taiwan Garrison Command, General Chang Chih-hsiu, had given permission to hold the rally in the Rotary Park. Afterwards, Shih Ming-teh and Yao Chia-wen had made an on-the-spot decision to hold the rally at the Great Circle on Chungshan Road. About 8.30 PM, some of the demonstrators began to have conflicts with

---

16 "Baotu zai Gaoxiong qunji zishi ... 暴徒在高雄麇集滋事 ... [Violence in Kaohsiung Gathers to Disturb the Peace ...]," *Lianhebao (Guowai hangkongban)* 聯合報（國外航空版）[*United Daily News (Overseas Edition)*] December 11, 1979, p. 2.

17 Ibid.

18 "'Meilidao' zazhi zai Gaoshi zishi ... '美麗島'雜誌在高滋事 ... ['Formosa' Magazine Creates Disturbance in Kaohsiung City ...]," *Zhongyang ribao (Guoji hangkongban)* 中央日報（國際航空版）[*Central Daily News (International Edition)*] December 11, 1979, p. 2.

19 "Kong Lingsheng shuoming baoli shijian jingguo ... 孔令晟說明暴力事件經過 ... [Kung Ling-sheng Explains the Experience of the Violent Incident ...]," *Zhongyang ribao (Guoji hangkongban)* 中央日報（國際航空版）[*Central Daily News (International Edition)*] December 12, 1979, p. 2. The *Lianhebao (Guowai hangkongban)* 聯合報（國外航空版）[*United Daily News (Overseas Edition)*], December 12, 1979, p. 2 stated that 183 persons were injured, but did not say that they were all security personnel.

20 "Shelun: dong kou, ying jia kuanrong; dong shou, jue bu ying kuanrong! 社論：動口，應加寬容；動手，絕不應寬容！[Editorial: If one moves the mouth, then when must be lenient; if one moves the hand, then one most definitely cannot be lenient!]," *Lianhebao (Guowai hangkongban)* 聯合報（國外航空版）[*United Daily News (Overseas Edition)*] December 12, 1979, p. 1.

the military police and the leaders realized that "non-Formosa Magazine people controlled the situation."[21] It was then that more than a hundred people were unfortunately injured.[22] Huang also denied that the demonstrators carried "wooden clubs 木棍", but they did carry torches as torches are the symbol of human rights.[23] According to this account, in addition to Huang Hsin-chieh, Yao Chia-wen, Lu Hsiu-lien, Chang Chun-hung, Shih Ming-teh, Chou Ping-teh and Lin I-hsiung all spoke, but the newspaper article has very little additional content.[24] A modern DPP account has even less information on the press conference than the *United Daily*.[25] A bit more information about the press conference, including that the violence was started by the security forces, is in two documents transmitted at the time by telephone to the United States.[26]

While the authorities and the press played up the "violence" of the Kaohsiung Incident, comparatively very little violence actually occurred. No one was killed and apparently none of the injuries to either security personnel or demonstrators proved permanent. In contrast, six months later at the Kwangju Massacre of May 18–27, 1980 in South Korea, the suppression of the democratic demonstrators by the Korean military government officially left 191 people killed and a further several thousand injured, though other estimates go considerably higher.[27] During the December 1987 presidential campaign, Kim Dae-jung, basing himself on statements by the American Ambassador to South Korea, William H. Gleysteen, said that one thousand had been killed in the suppression of Kwangju.[28]

---

21 "Huang Xinjie zuo shuoming Gaoxiong shijian jingguo ... 黃信介昨說明高雄事件經過 ... [Yesterday, Huang Hsin-chieh explained what happened in the Kaohsiung Incident ...]," *Lianhebao (Guowai hangkongban)* 聯合報（國外航空版）[*United Daily News (Overseas Edition)*] December 13, 1979, p. 2.
22 Ibid.
23 Ibid.
24 Ibid.
25 Zhang Fuzhong 張富忠 and Qiu Wanxing 邱萬興, *Lüse niandai 1*, 1, p. 94. This source also has the wrong time for the press conference. The next source makes clear that the time in the *United Daily* is correct.
26 Zhang Yanxian 張炎憲 and Wen Qiufen 溫秋芬, *Gaoxiong shijian*, pp. 144–149.
27 Young Whan Kihl, *Transforming Korean Politics: Democracy, Reform, and Culture* (Armonk, N.Y. and London: M.E. Sharpe, 2005), p. 78.
28 Kim Yong-taek, *5.18 Kwangju minjung hangjaeng* [*The May 18 Kwangju Uprising*] (Seoul: Tonga Ilbosa, 1990), p. 307. Later, Gleysteen estimated that around two hundred had been killed. See William H. Gleysteen, *Massive Entanglement, Marginal Influence: Carter and Korea in Crisis* (Washington, DC: Brookings, 1999), p. 131.

The Arrests

On the very same day as the Kaohsiung Incident, the Kuomintang (KMT, Nationalist Party) began a major annual meeting of the Party's leadership. The Fourth Plenum of the Eleventh Central Committee met five days from December 10 to December 14 at Yangmingshan. Of course, during the course of this meeting senior KMT leaders met to discuss how to deal with the *Formosa Magazine*. Clearly, the debate took two days and, except for Shih Ming-teh and Chang Chun-hung, most of the *Formosa Magazine* leadership was optimistic.[29] But the conservative hardliners, under the leadership of General Wang Sheng 王昇, the Director of the General Political Warfare Department, won the arguments and massive arrests took place during the early morning of December 13, more than fifty hours after the Kaohsiung Incident had ended.

Fourteen people were arrested in the first wave of arrests.[30] Shih Ming-teh 施明德 escaped capture. According to Article 74 of the Republic of China Constitution, members of the legislature may not be arrested without permission of the legislature. Thus, the government wrote to the legislature requesting permission to arrest Huang Hsin-chieh, a member of the legislature since 1969.[31] No such restriction protected the two provincial assemblymen arrested, Chang Chun-hung 張俊宏 and Lin I-hsiung 林義雄.[32]

Interviews with family members one or two months later suggested significant differences in the manner of arrests. In some cases, the arresting officers were curt. In other cases, they were quite polite saying such things as "Teacher, we have to take you away for a while. You should prepare pajamas and a toothbrush and you should say goodbye to your family."

The differences in manner of arrests and the apparent different treatment of the prisoners while incarcerated suggests that different security agencies had responsibility for particular prisoners. A recent document found in the Bureau of Investigation by Professor Chen Yi-shen validates this hypothesis. The Bureau of Investigation of the Ministry of Justice 司法行政部調查局 sent this document, dated December 20, 1979 and labeled "most rapid transmission

---

29   Zhang Fuzhong 張富忠 and Qiu Wanxing 邱萬興, *Lüse niandai I*, I, p. 27.
30   These were Chang Chun-hung 張俊宏, Yao Chia-wen 姚嘉文, Wang Tuoh 王拓, Chen Chu 陳菊, Chou Ping-teh 周平德, Su Chiu-chen 蘇秋鎮, Lu Hsiu-lien 呂秀蓮, Chi Wan-sheng 紀萬生, Lin I-hsiung 林義雄, Chen Chung-hsin 陳忠信, Yang Ching-chu 楊青矗, Chiu I–pin 邱奕彬, Wei Ting-chao 魏廷朝 and Chang Fu-chung 張富忠. List taken from *Lianhebao (Guowai hangkongban)* 聯合報（國外航空版）[*United Daily News (Overseas Edition)*], December 14, 1979, p. 1.
31   Ibid.
32   Ibid.

最速件," to Department of Security of the Taiwan Garrison Command 警備總司令部保安處, the Department of Intelligence of the Military Police Command 憲兵司令部情報處 and the Detective Bureau of the Department of Police 敬政署刑事警察局. This document directed the three recipient organizations on how to interrogate the defendants.³³

While awaiting the legislature to give approval for his arrest, Huang Hsin-chieh gave an interview with the *United Daily News*. While the interview appears edited, two questions were especially relevant:

Q: Do you believe Taiwan has the conditions for revolution?
A: No. Taiwan does not have the conditions for revolution. Revolution is that eighteenth century method for changing the political regime. In Taiwan, that is especially impossible.
Q: What is your evaluation of the current government?
A: ... Now everyone has food to eat and clothes are cheap. It's not bad, but no matter how good things are, people seek even better...³⁴

The next morning the legislature approved the arrest of Huang Hsin-chieh. Although there were over one hundred people outside his house, "order was excellent 秩序良好" and Huang was arrested at 9.32 AM.³⁵ On December 15, five more people were arrested³⁶ and the American wife of Shih Ming-teh,

---

33   Chen Yishen 陳儀深, "Taidu panluan huo minzhu yundong? Meilidao shijian xingzhi jiexi 台獨叛亂或民主運動？美麗島事件性質解析 [A Taiwanese Independence Rebellion or A Democratic Movement? An Analysis of the Nature of the Formosa Incident] " in *Meilidao shijian 30 zhounian yanjiu lunwenji* 美麗島事件 30 周年研究論文集 [*Compendium of Research Articles on the 30th Anniversary of the Formosa Incident*], ed. Zhang Yanxian 張炎憲 and Chen Chaohai 陳朝海 (Taibei 臺北: Wu Sanlian Taiwan shiliao jijinhui 吳三連臺灣史料基金會, 2010), pp. 100–101.

34   Huang Nian 黃年 and Chen Xiuling 陳秀玲, "Qie ting Huang Xinjie zenme shuo! 且聽黃信介怎麼說 [Let's Hear What Huang Hsin-chieh has to Say!]," *Lianhebao (Guowai hangkongban)* 聯合報（國外航空版）[*United Daily News (Overseas Edition)*] December 14, 1979, p. 2.

35   *Lianhebao (Guowai hangkongban)* 聯合報（國外航空版）[*United Daily News (Overseas Edition)*], December 15, 1979, p. 2.

36   These were Provincial Assemblyman Chiu Lien-hui 邱連輝, County Assemblyman Chiu Mao-nan 邱茂南, Fan Cheng-you 范政祐, Tsai Chui-ho 蔡垂和 and Lin Hui-chen 林慧珍. Lin was allowed to return home. According to the report, 101 people had been investigated. *Lianhebao (Guowai hangkongban)* 聯合報（國外航空版）[*United Daily News (Overseas Edition)*], December 16, 1979, p. 2.

Linda Arrigo, was deported.[37] The next day, Provincial Assemblyman Chiu Lien-hui was released, but an additional person was arrested.[38]

On December 21, 1979 a leading member of the Youth Party announced that Kuo Yu-hsin 郭雨新, a Youth Party member, had engaged in treasonous behavior against both the party and the government and decided to punish him.[39] Kuo, a leading *dangwai* member whose case is discussed in the previous chapter, was already overseas and safe from prosecution, but the Youth Party's action demonstrated the authorities were very concerned with anyone who had questioned the contemporary system. The Youth Party's Central Standing Committee met on December 27 and decided to investigate Kuo.[40]

The United States had announced that it would break diplomatic relations with the Republic of China on January 1, 1979. However, it abided by Article 10 of the Mutual Defense Treaty between the United States of America and the Republic of China signed on December 2, 1954 which provided for one year's notice before the Treaty would terminate.[41] Thus, despite the absence of diplomatic relations, the United States still had promised to defend Taiwan in 1979. However, with the beginning of 1980, Taiwan was no longer protected under the Mutual Defense Treaty. Thus, the government began to emphasize that 1980 was "Self-Strengthening Year 自強年."[42] This became a constant theme for 1980.

Shih Ming-teh, who had escaped capture on December 13, was finally arrested on January 8, 1980 in Taipei. Shih had been on the run for 26 days. The concerned authorities raised the reward for information leading to his detention from an initial NT$500,000 (US$13,888) to about NT$3 million (US$83,333). In order to hide, Shih had undergone some plastic surgery on his chin. Two other people, Lin Hung-hsuan 林弘宣, who later became one of the eight major defendants tried in the military court trial, and Tsai Yu-chuan 蔡有全, a defendant in the civilian court trial, were arrested with Shih.[43] Four additional

---

37 *Lianhebao (Guowai hangkongban)* 聯合報（國外航空版) [*United Daily News (Overseas Edition)*], December 16, 1979, p. 2.

38 This was Chen Po-wen 陳博文, *Lianhebao (Guowai hangkongban)* 聯合報（國外航空版) [*United Daily News (Overseas Edition)*], December 17, 1979, p. 2.

39 *Lianhebao (Guowai hangkongban)* 聯合報（國外航空版) [*United Daily News (Overseas Edition)*], December 22, 1979, p. 2.

40 *Taiwan lishi nianbiao (1979–1988)* 台灣歷史年表 [*Chronology of Taiwan History*], vol. III (Taibei: Guojia zhengce yanjiusuo ziliao zhongxin, 1990), p. 36.

41 Text available at <http://www.taiwandocuments.org/mutual01.htm>.

42 *Zhongyang ribao* 中央日報 [*Central Daily News*], January 21, 1980, p. 1.

43 *China Post (International Airmail Edition)*, January 9, 1980, p. 1.

people were also arrested on January 8 in connection with helping Shih according to an announcement two days later.[44]

On January 22, 1980, Kang Ning-hsiang, a legislator as well as one of the very few *dangwai* leaders not arrested, interpellated the Cabinet during question time in the legislature. Making a request for "our democratic future 為我們民主前途," Kang asked that the investigation of those who had not been directly and positively involved in the Kaohsiung Incident be concluded quickly and that they be released on bail. He also asked that the other suspects be tried soon. Kang demanded that any military court trial be open and that family members, friends as well as persons from international justice organizations be allowed to attend.[45] Kang also emphasized that the people arrested had all grown up on Taiwan under the Republic of China and that their starting point was "love 愛心" and "concern for the future 對未來命運的關心," not "hate 仇恨." He urged the government to use "love" to deal with the prisoners.[46] After the Kaohsiung Incident, many asked why Kang was not arrested. Clearly, his being a member of the legislature helped, though if the security forces desired, they could have arranged for the legislature to approve his arrest as in the case of Huang Hsin-chieh. Secondly, Kang had long held discussions with Chiang Ching-kuo and it is possible that Chiang wanted Kang out of prison to maintain contacts with the *dangwai*. Among many of the *dangwai*, Kang's staying out of prison was seen as a black mark against him.

The Taiwan Garrison Command announced on February 1, 1980 that the authorities had detained sixty-one suspects. Of these, fifty-three were imprisoned for treason 叛亂, while eight were held for hiding a criminal 藏匿人犯. The Taiwan Garrison Command noted that investigation normally should not take more than two months.[47]

Two news reports on February 5, 1980 suggested that the government might be taking a softer approach. The first report suggested that most defendants "might possibly 可能" be tried in a civil, and not a military, court.[48] The second report noted that the military court investigation of the two defendants in the Kushan Incident of December 9, 1979, Yao Kuo-chien 姚國建 and Chiu Sheng-hsiung 邱勝雄, found that there was insufficient evidence to convict the two.[49]

---

44   *China Post (International Airmail Edition)*, January 11, 1980, p. 1
45   *Lianhebao* 聯合報 [*United Daily News*], January 23, 1980, p. 2.
46   *Taiwan shibao* 臺灣時報 [*Taiwan Times*], January 23, 1980, p. 3.
47   *Lianhebao* 聯合報 [*United Daily News*], February 2, 1980, p. 1.
48   *Lianhebao* 聯合報 [*United Daily News*], February 5, 1980, p. 3. The same newspaper had a similar report four days later, *Lianhebao* 聯合報 [*United Daily News*], February 9, 1980, p. 3.
49   *Taiwan shibao* 臺灣時報 [*Taiwan Times*], February 5, 1980, p. 3.

THE KAOHSIUNG INCIDENT

On February 7, 1980, the Taiwan Garrison Command announced the release of three more individuals connected to the Kushan Incident. With the two defendants released on February 4, the total number imprisoned owing to the Kaohsiung Incident was now fifty-six.[50]

A substantial report on February 9, 1980 tried to assure readers that the prisoners were well. For example, readers learned that Su Ching-li 蘇慶黎 liked to eat corn, while Chen Chu 陳菊 enjoyed singing.[51] The report did not say that Lin I-hsiung had been tortured.

Contrary to the previous reports, on February 11 the two people who had been beaten severely in the Kushan Incident, Yao Kuo-chien 姚國建 and Chiu Sheng-hsiung 邱勝雄, were now indicted in a civil court on the charge of beating police.[52] Another report stated that now some twenty people would be indicted before the military court.[53] On February 12, 1980 three more people were released on bail, leaving fifty-three in prison.[54]

February 16, 1980 was Lunar New Year. Newspapers ran shortened holiday versions with little news. For example, under the picture of a busty "Blue-eyed blonde," one newspaper ran a wire service story about an eighteen-month old Australian girl who killed a venomous snake by biting off its head.[55] More relevant to Taiwan's politics, two key newspapers ran headline stories that Taiwan's delayed central elections would take place in late 1980.[56]

For those in Taiwan concerned about the fate of those detained after the Kaohsiung Incident, the nine weeks following the arrests were filled with tension. Would the authorities execute the defendants? No one outside of the security agencies could answer this question.

The Indictment

Nine weeks after the initial arrests, on February 20, 1980, the Taiwan Garrison Command published an indictment of eight key defendants who would be tried in a military court on charges of *"panluan* 叛亂," a term that means

---

50 *Lianhebao* 聯合報 [*United Daily News*], February 8, 1980, p. 3.
51 *Taiwan shibao* 臺灣時報 [*Taiwan Times*], February 9, 1980, p. 3.
52 *Lianhebao* 聯合報 [*United Daily News*], February 12, 1980, p. 3.
53 *Lianhebao* 聯合報 [*United Daily News*], February 12, 1980, p. 3.
54 The three were Su Chiu-chen, Su Ching-li, and Chiu I-ping, *Lianhebao* 聯合報 [*United Daily News*], February 13, 1980, p. 3.
55 *China News*, February 19, 1980, p. 3.
56 *Lianhebao* 聯合報 [*United Daily News*], February 20, 1980, p. 1; *Zhongguo shibao* 中國時報 [*China Times*], February 20, 1980, p. 1.

"rebellion" or "sedition."⁵⁷ The eight defendants in the order listed in the indictment were: Huang Hsin-chieh 黃信介, Shih Ming-teh 施明德, Yao Chia-wen 姚嘉文, Chang Chun-hung 張俊宏, Lin I-hsiung 林義雄, Lin Hung-hsuan 林弘宣, Lu Hsiu-lien 呂秀蓮 and Chen Chu 陳菊. The cases of thirty-seven other detainees were shifted to the civilian courts as the authorities did not believe the evidence would support charges of "rebellion."

Two aspects of the indictment are worth noting. First, the indictment listed the home addresses of all eight defendants. This would become relevant a week later.

Second, the indictment fit the structure outlined in the document of December 20, 1979, mentioned above, which the Bureau of Investigation of the Ministry of Justice sent to the Department of Security of the Taiwan Garrison Command, the Department of Intelligence of the Military Police Command and the Detective Bureau of the Department of Police. This document outlined three different types of "rebellion" including (A) "Communist Bandits," (B) "Taiwanese Independence," and (c) those who had hidden Shih Ming-teh during his escape. Of the eight defendants, only Huang Hsin-chieh was listed as working with the "Communist Bandits." Five of the others were listed as "Taiwan Independence": Yao Chia-wen, Lin I-hsiung, Chen Chu, Chang Chun-hung and Lu Hsiu-lien. No names were listed under helping Shih Ming-teh hide during his escape.⁵⁸

The existence of this document helps explain the bizarre beginning of the first main section of the indictment, "Criminal Facts 犯罪事實":

> In March 1979, Huang Hsin-chieh directed Hung Chih-liang (indicted December 22, 1979, on a charge of sedition) to ship eel fry from the Chinese mainland to Taiwan via Japan for an extraordinary profit. Huang planned to subvert the government and was prepared to use the profits for seditious activities...

According to the indictment, Hung Chih-liang⁵⁹ went to China under Huang Hsin-chieh's orders and met Yang Side 楊斯德, deputy secretary-general of the

---

57 The full text of the indictment is available in *Zhongguo shibao* 中國時報 [*China Times*], February 21, 1980, p. 3; *Zhongyang ribao* 中央日報 [*Central Daily News*], February 21, 1980, p. 3; and *Taiwan shibao* 臺灣時報 [*Taiwan Times*], February 21, 1980, p. 3. An English translation of the full text appears in *China Post*, February 21, 1980, pp. 12, 11.

58 Chen Yishen 陳儀深, "Taidu panluan huo minzhu yundong?," pp. 100–101.

59 Hung Chih-liang 洪誌良 was the publisher of a magazine called *Fubao zhi sheng* 富堡之聲 [*Demo-Voice*].

Chinese People's Political Consultative Conference, who passed a message back to Huang Hsin-chieh, "Hope to carry out peaceful reunification. If this succeeds, Taiwan will be made an autonomous district 自治區. Agree to appoint Huang the governor." The indictment then slips from saying that Huang Hsin-chieh cooperated with the Chinese Communists to "Huang Hsin-chieh attempted to collaborate with both the Chinese Communists and elements of the Taiwan Independence Movement in carrying out his conspiracy to overthrow the government by illegal means."[60]

Without missing a beat, the indictment then moves to Shih Ming-teh, outlining how Shih was sentenced in 1959 for seditious activities, but released on July 16, 1977. According to the indictment, Yao Chia-wen was influenced by Peng Ming-min, also "a seditious element," while Chang Chun-hung and Lin I-hsiung were influenced by Chang Chin-tse 張金策, "another seditious element." During trips to the United States, Lin Hung-hsuan, Lu Hsiu-lien and Chen Chu all

> maintained close communications with either Chang Tsan-hung 張燦鍙, president of the "World United Formosans for Independence" or with Chang Fu-hsiung 張富雄 and his wife, Yang Yi-yi 楊宜宜. Their treasonable intentions were fanned up by these contacts and they began to advocate overthrow of the government by violent means.[61]

According to the indictment, in March and April 1979, Huang Hsin-chieh ordered Shih Ming-teh, Yao Chia-wen, Lin I-hsiung, Chang Chun-hung and Hsu Hsin-liang "to study plans to subvert the government. After accepting this directive, the five met several times..."[62]

The indictment said, the purpose of these meetings was to

> formulate "long-range and short-range power-seizure plans" in their subversive campaign. The so-called "long-range power-seizure plan" called for use of *Formosa* magazine as a center to sponsoring various activities to attract sympathizers and augment their strength so that they could wield decisive influence in seizing political power. The so-called "short-range power-seizure plan" called for using the masses of the people, rallies, parades and demonstrations to escalate the level of violence and

---

60   Three quotes from *China Post*, February 21, 1980, p. 12.
61   *China Post*, February 21, 1980, p. 12.
62   *China Post*, February 21, 1980, p. 12. The indictment notes that Hsu Hsin-liang's case has been handled separately.

quickly overthrow the government. They did not hesitate even to engage in bloody conflict with government troops...[63]

The indictment goes into detail about how *Formosa Magazine* set up its offices and organization. According to the indictment,

> They planned to set up service offices under the name of the magazine to develop their organization and sponsor mass activities. In August of 1979, the *Formosa* magazine began publication. After that they sponsored a number of mass activities, including rallies, lectures, parades and demonstrations, to provide a seemingly legitimate cover for their illegal activities in keeping with their established plan. They made radical statements to besmirch the government, undermine solidarity, make trouble and engender conflict by shouting false slogans about human rights, democracy and freedom. In so doing, they attempted to carry out their goal of overthrowing the government by illegal means through simultaneous implementation of the "long-range and short-range power-seizure plans."[64]

According to the indictment,

> On December 6, 1979, Yao Chia-wen formulated five guiding principles based on the past activities of the magazine. These principles were (1) the principle of indirect approach, (2) the principle of flexibility, (3) the principle of concentration, (4) the principle of solidarity and (5) the principle of strength. The so-called principle of strength was a preparation for resort to violence. They did not hesitate to resort to violence... so they could attain the goal of overthrowing the government.[65]

The indictment next moved to the details of December 10, 1979, World Human Rights Day. According to the indictment, "Shih Ming-teh hoped to escalate a mass rally to the stage of violence as a step in carrying out the so-called 'power-seizure plan' to attain the final goal of subverting the government." After detailing the various applications for the rally and their rejections, the indict-

---

63   *China Post*, February 21, 1980, p. 12.
64   *China Post*, February 21, 1980, p. 12.
65   *China Post*, February 21, 1980, p. 12.

ment claimed, "Shih Ming-teh reiterated his hardline position and his determination to defy the prohibition and the rally."[66]

The indictment then discussed the Kushan Incident of December 9, 1979. According to the indictment, Yao Kuo-chien and Chiu Sheng-hsiung

> drove a public address car along the streets, openly broadcasting propaganda to inflame the people and persuade them to participate in the next day's illegal gathering. When police officers of the Kushan Sub-district Police Bureau 警察分局 were sent to the scene and tried to stop the illegal operation of the sound truck, Yao and Chiu resisted and *beat up the policemen* [emphasis added]...[67]

The distortions in the indictment continued. The next day, i.e. December 10, "At 6.10 PM more than 200 torch carrying hoodlums had assembled in front of the magazine's office in preparation for a parade along Chungshan 1st Road..."[68] According to the indictment, at the Circle,

> Shih Ming-teh, Yao Chia-wen, Lin Hung-hsuan and others incessantly broadcast their message of "Charge! Fight!" Rioters attacked the security forces with torches, placards and sticks (the nails protruding where the placards had been torn away made them vicious weapons), clubs stocked on the propaganda vehicles, steel bars pulled from the barricades of traffic safety islands and brickbats...[69]

The next substantial section of the Indictment was "Evidence and Articles of Law Violated 證據並所犯法條." This section basically reiterated the "Criminal Facts," though it also included sworn statements from witnesses and some further details. Section 4 of "Evidence and Articles of Law Violated" summarized the indictment:

> All of the defendants... have harbored seditious schemes. They used *Formosa* magazine as a legal cover for carrying out their so-called "power-seizure plan." They instigated the Kaohsiung incident in an

---

66   *China Post*, February 21, 1980, p. 12.
67   *China Post*, February 21, 1980, p. 12. After police beat citizens, their classic response around the world is to charge the citizens with beating up the police.
68   *China Post*, February 21, 1980, p. 12.
69   *China Post*, February 21, 1980, p. 11.

attempt gradually to escalate illegal mass violence in order to subvert the government and, in effect, they have begun to carry out their plan.[70]

The indictment then enumerated the laws which the defendants had transgressed. It then asked that "the more severe penalties laid down for seditious cases should be meted out in accordance with the law" including confiscation of property. However, the indictment then included the following contradictory passage, "Since their arrests, they have admitted their mistakes and shown repentance. It is therefore requested that commutation of their sentences be considered to show leniency."[71]

This strange conspiracy concocted by Taiwan's security agencies fell apart under questioning in the military court trial that followed. Yet, the "facts" in the indictment were used to convict the defendants.

The next day the spokesman for the Taiwan Garrison Command made a number of statements. First, the military court trial would be open to reporters and visitors. Second, the military court trial might start in early March. Third, the spokesman emphasized that the military court system was independent and impartial.[72]

On February 26, 1980, two newspapers reported that the lawyers of the defendants were not being allowed to photocopy materials. As the Taiwan Garrison Command believed the materials to be "top secret 機密," they were only allowed to copy statements by hand. It was also reported that the lawyers would see the defendants on February 27, but that these visits would be limited to forty minutes. Direct relatives of the defendants would also visit on February 27, but these visits would be for only fifteen to thirty minutes and would be limited to five persons.[73]

In the legislature, Wu Chu-jen 吳鑄人, Hsu Chung-chi 徐中齊, Huang Shun-hsing 黃順興 and Hsu Shih-hsien 許世賢 raised a number of questions concerning the Kaohsiung Incident.[74] In response to another question in the legislature, Premier Sun Yun-suan 孫運璿 stated that Taiwanese Independence

---

70 *China Post*, February 21, 1980, p. 11.
71 *China Post*, February 21, 1980, p. 11.
72 *Lianhebao* 聯合報 [*United Daily News*], February 22, 1980, p. 3. Similar comments can be found in *Zhongguo shibao* 中國時報 [*China Times*], February 22, 1980, p. 3.
73 *Lianhebao* 聯合報 [*United Daily News*], February 26, 1980, p. 3; *Zili wanbao* 自立晚報 [*Independence Evening Post*], February 26, 1980, p. 2.
74 *Lianhebao* 聯合報 [*United Daily News*], February 27, 1980, p. 3. See also *Zhongguo shibao* 中國時報 [*China Times*], February 27, 1980, p. 3.

organizations attempt to destroy the nation's political system and thus are illegal.⁷⁵

On February 27, some of the defendants had some visits from relatives. Huang Hsin-chieh saw his wife, younger brother and daughter for thirty minutes. Lin Hung-hsuan saw his wife and older brother, Yao Chia-wen his wife, and Shih Ming-teh his older brother, each visit also being for thirty minutes. The number of visitors for each visit was limited to three persons. In the afternoon, visits from family members of Chang Chun-hung, Lin I-hsiung, Lu Hsiu-lien and Chen Chu were scheduled. The wives of Chang and Lin planned to visit. Lu Hsiu-lien's older sister and Chen Chu's father also planned to visit.⁷⁶ The defendants and their visitors could only see each other through thick, sound-proof glass and had to speak through telephones. No personal contact was allowed.⁷⁷

Following the visits, newspapers suggested the health of the defendants varied. Huang Hsin-chieh was reported in good health as was Shih Ming-teh. On the other hand, Yao Chia-wen's health "seemed comparatively poorer 似乎較差" and "his facial coloring was pale 面色較爲蒼白." Chang Chun-hung's blood pressure had risen and his wife hoped he could go to a hospital. Lin I-hsiung was visited by his mother and wife. When Lin asked his mother if Lunar New Year went well, his mother burst into tears.⁷⁸ The *Central Daily News* quoted Huang Hsin-chieh as saying "We truly were wrong! 我們卻是錯了！"⁷⁹

The same newspaper also reported that Tao Pai-chuan 陶百川 and Wu San-lien 吳三連, two important liberals at the time, had successfully applied for seats to the military court trial. According to the report, the court had 120 seats. Sixty of these seats were reserved for the foreign and domestic press. The remaining sixty were for family members of the defendants and others who applied.⁸⁰

---

75 *Lianhebao* 聯合報 [*United Daily News*], February 27, 1980, p. 1; *Zhongguo shibao* 中國時報 [*China Times*], February 27, 1980, p. 1; *Zhongyang ribao* 中央日報 [*Central Daily News*], February 27, 1980, p. 1.
76 *Zili wanbao* 自立晚報 [*Independence Evening Post*], February 27, 1980, p. 2.
77 John Kaplan, *The Court-Martial of the Kaohsiung Defendants* (Berkeley: Institute of East Asian Studies, University of California, Berkeley, 1981), p. 24.
78 *Lianhebao* 聯合報 [*United Daily News*], February 28, 1980, p. 5.
79 *Zhongyang ribao* 中央日報 [*Central Daily News*], February 28, 1980, p. 3.
80 *Zhongyang ribao* 中央日報 [*Central Daily News*], February 28, 1980, p. 3.

The Murder of Lin I-hsiung's Mother and Twin Daughters

During the morning of Thursday, February 28, 1980, Fang Su-min was visiting her husband, Lin I-hsiung, in prison. Before she returned home, someone had stabbed Lin's mother and their six-year-old twins to death and left their nine-year old daughter critically injured. This was the first and only time in Taiwan that family members of political prisoners had been killed. The murders horrified Taiwan's society.

To date, the murders remained unsolved. Hypotheses about the murderer(s) ranged from the security agencies in Taiwan, to agents sent in from China, to a crazy person in Taiwan angered by the negative press reports about the Kaohsiung Incident. As noted earlier, the indictment had given widespread publicity to the home addresses of the defendants. In addition, Lin I-hsiung's home opened directly on the street and thus was easily accessible. On the other hand, many people argued that the house would have been under constant surveillance, though the writer, who is not an expert in such matters, never noticed any obvious surveillance. On the other hand, we now know that Lin's phone was tapped by the security agencies.

In addition, we know that Lin I-hsiung suffered considerable torture while in detention from his controlling agency, the Department of Security of the Taiwan Garrison Command 警備總司令部保安處. Some have argued that this agency killed his family because they were angry that Lin did not deny being tortured to his family, who then passed the news overseas. Despite repeated official reports since democratization, we still do not know who killed Lin's family.[81]

That afternoon, the Taiwan Garrison Command gave permission for Lin I-hsiung to be bailed out of prison to take care of his family. The next day, Antonio Chiang 江春男, a well-known *dangwai* journalist, wrote a moving column in the *Independence Evening Post* in which he noted that many *dangwai* leaders had called home and told relatives to protect their children. Chiang concluded:

> On February 28, this most bitter day for the Chinese people, this matter has unexpectedly exploded like a bomb. The explosive power of its wounds with respect to Taiwan politics and society is truly difficult to anticipate.

---

81 According to the police at the time, the writer became "involved 有關係人" in this case. This "involvement" is discussed in Part 2 of this book.

Such a thing could only have been done by a wild animal. Of all the words in the dictionary, none can describe the deep hate in my heart.⁸²

在二二八這個中國人最痛苦的日子，竟然爆發這種事，像一枚炸彈一樣，其對臺灣政治社會的炸傷力，實難逆料。
這是祇有禽獸才幹的出來的事，字典上的所有的字，均不足以形容我心中的痛恨。

Antonio Chiang's mention of February 28 as "this most bitter day" referred to the February 28, 1947 massacres of Taiwanese when Chiang Kai-shek's military systematically killed over 20,000 Taiwanese.⁸³ The Taiwan dictatorship under Chiang Kai-shek and Chiang Ching-kuo had banned discussion of this topic in Taiwan. Thus, Antonio Chiang had not only raised the forbidden topic of February 28, 1947 in a published article, he had linked it to a new, horrible event, the murder of Lin I-hsiung's family members on the very anniversary of this sensitive date.

During the next several days, press coverage concentrated on the murder case and upon "clues 線索" distributed by the police. Lin I-hsiung and Fang Su-min stayed at the hospital, under guard, with their daughter. On March 6, Lin and Fang held a short press conference with "traces of tears on their faces 兩人臉上也都有淚痕." They distributed a letter, signed by themselves and their daughter, thanking President Chiang and compatriots from the whole nation for their concern.⁸⁴ On March 15 the bodies of Lin's mother and twin daughters were temporarily placed in a Taipei funeral parlor 殯儀館.⁸⁵

On March 11, Yao Kuo-chien and Chiu Sheng-hsiung, the two men severely beaten by the police on December 9 in the Kushan Incident, were convicted. Yao was sentenced to three years and Chiu to two years and six months for beating police and destroying a police vehicle.⁸⁶

On March 10, the Taiwan Garrison Command announced that the military court trial of the eight defendants would begin on March 18.⁸⁷ The next day,

---

82 Sima Wenwu 司馬文武, "Qi'er, zhengzhi he lishi 妻兒，政治和歷史 [Family, Politics and History]," *Zili wanbao* 自力晚報 [*Independence Evening Post*] February 29, 1980, p. 2.

83 For the best account on the February 28, 1947 Incident, by an American eyewitness with many years experience in Taiwan, see George H. Kerr, *Formosa Betrayed* (Boston: Houghton Mifflin, 1965).

84 The full hand-written text appears in *Zhongguo shibao* 中國時報 [*China Times*], March 7, 1980, p. 3. See also *Lianhebao* 聯合報 [*United Daily News*], March 7, 1980, p. 3.

85 *Dahua wanbao* 大華晚報 [*Great China Evening News*], March 15, 1980, p. 3.

86 *Lianhebao* 聯合報 [*United Daily News*], March 12, 1980, p. 3 and other press of the day.

87 See afternoon press of March 10, 1980 and morning press of March 11, 1980.

the Taiwan Garrison Command announced that all 120 seats for the trial were taken. Forty seats were allocated to the local press, twenty seats to the foreign press and two seats for family members of each defendant.[88] Using the trial transcript and other materials, the next chapter discusses and analyzes the military court trial.

---

88 *Lianhebao* 聯合報 [*United Daily News*], March 12, 1980, p. 3.

CHAPTER 3

The Military Trial of the Eight Key Defendants

The military court trial of the eight key defendants served in many ways as the climax of the whole Kaohsiung Incident. To an extent, the trials were "open" and outsiders, including human rights organizations, attended. Furthermore, at least some of the reporting of Taiwan's Chinese-language media also proved relatively open.

In addition, we have two key documents. The Chinese-language newspaper, the *China Times* (*Zhongguo shibao* 中國時報), provided a full transcript of the trial. The *China Times* had two seats at the trial. The newspaper had its reporters write transcripts as the trial took place. When the reporters became tired, replacements were sent in. Each morning, the newspaper would print a transcript of the previous day's trial.[1]

At the time of the trial, the writer was in police "protection" (see Part 2). Each evening after the trial, I would telephone several people including both foreign correspondents and Taiwan reporters to ask about the key events of the trial that day. The next day, without fail, every one of the sensitive aspects appeared in the transcript. Thus, because of this transcript, we know exactly what happened during the trial's sessions.

Secondly, the late John Kaplan, a law professor at Stanford University, attended the trial for a human rights organization and wrote a monograph about the trial and related legal and human rights matters. Although Kaplan had no background in Taiwan or Chinese law, his work provides an important understanding of the trial in the contexts of both Taiwan and international law and international human rights regimes.[2]

Taiwan's judicial system is based primarily on continental law rather than on the common law familiar to most English speakers. In the common law

---

1 At the end of the trial, the *China Times* announced that its publishing arm, Shibao wenhua chuban gongsi 時報文化出版公司, would shortly publish a full transcript of the trial entitled *Gaoxiong baoli shijian dashen shilu* 高雄暴力事件大審實錄 [*The True Transcript of the Trial of the Violent Kaohsiung Incident*]. See *Zhongguo shibao* 中國時報 [*China Times*], March 29, 1980, p. 2. The following day, the *China Times* published more information about this book. It would be published on April 15 and cost NT$220 in hard cover and NT$180 in paperback. A savings was offered for pre-publication orders, *Zhongguo shibao* 中國時報 [*China Times*], March 30, 1980, p. 3. However, this book never appeared because the government prohibited its publication.
2 Kaplan, *Court-Martial*.

system, a judge listens to the prosecutors and defense attorneys present evidence. After this conflict of evidence, either a jury of lay people or the judge himself delivers a verdict. In the continental legal system the judge investigates. In the Taiwan system in 1980, the judges conducted the interrogations with the prosecutor, and defense attorneys had much smaller roles.

The transcript makes very clear that the defendants had met the five judges in court earlier. These sessions had occurred in secret without any defense attorneys present. These sessions were used to sign confessions or written records of investigation. Whether or not these confessions truly represented the opinions of the defendants became a central issue in the trial, which—unlike the earlier court sessions—was open in that the defendants had defense attorneys present and outside observers including the press as well as relatives of the defendants were also in court.

The trial transcript makes clear that many defendants had signed written records. The writer too had to sign such written records (see Part 2). These invariably simplified statements and could not accurately reflect complex issues. Yet, the judges repeatedly referred to such records. It should be noted that Chinese law has made use of confessions for several centuries. This pattern has also appeared in the People's Republic as well as in the authoritarian period of Chiang Kai-shek and Chiang Ching-kuo on Taiwan.

Another key issue relates to whether or not torture was used to obtain the confessions. Clearly, Lin I-hsiung was tortured. Whether or not the other defendants were physically tortured remains unclear. However, they clearly were deprived of sleep. In the words of John Kaplan, "almost all the defendants asserted that they were simply kept awake and questioned by police in relays until, under what is called *fatigue bombing*, they were willing to say and agree to anything that the police wanted. Indeed, at the trial Huang Hsin-chieh testified that he had been kept awake so long at the time he confessed that he would rather have died than have the questioning continue."[3] The writer had similar experiences (see Part 2), though as a foreigner the questioning was limited to only twenty-four hours and he was not physically beaten or threatened.

Day 1 of the Trial: Tuesday, March 18, 1980

The military trial began on Tuesday, March 18, 1980 at 9.50 AM with the oral examination of Huang Hsin-chieh. The presiding judge repeatedly asked

---

3   Ibid., p. 29.

Huang Hsin-chieh if he had formed a "Five-Person Committee" composed of Yao Chia-wen, Lin I-hsiung and Shih Ming-teh on December 25, 1978. Huang repeatedly answered that he had formed an informal group to discuss issues, but he never ordered the setting up of such a group in writing.[4]

According to the transcript, Huang became distressed by this repeated questioning. He stated to the court, "The confessions gained during the interrogations while in prison had doubtful aspects... Under questioning, death was preferable to continued living. In order to reduce the punishment, he wrote several confessions. He never expected that these confessions would become evidence.... [After] being [held] in the Bureau of Investigation for more than fifty days... I admitted everything."[5]

The presiding judge asked Huang about the objective in establishing the *Formosa Magazine*. Huang responded, "As I said, it had an anti-Communist standpoint and it pushed democracy, freedom, human rights. The *Formosa Magazine* asked its relevant units to send people to look at our draft articles. We were willing to work like this... *Formosa Magazine* never broke the law, not even once."

The presiding judge responded, "On February 21, when being investigated, you said the objective of *Formosa Magazine* was to make Taiwan Independent." Huang responded, "That was said at the Bureau of Investigation. It was not my original meaning."

After the presiding judge repeatedly referred to the signed confessions, Huang's defense lawyer, Chen Shui-bian 陳水扁, raised his hand and asked to speak saying that he had a "procedural question 程序問題". Chen cited a Supreme Court ruling that stated using "violence, cheating and coercion 強暴，詐欺，脅迫" ... Interrupted by the presiding judge, Chen continued and used the word "torture 刑求." This brought the Prosecutor to his feet. Then Yao Chia-wen's defense attorney, Hsieh Chang-ting 謝長廷, stated that the Prosecutor himself was not accused of torture. Yao's other defense lawyer, Su Tseng-chang 蘇貞昌, stated that Huang Hsin-chieh had not said he was tortured, only that he was questioned for fifty to sixty hours. "This is not a normal method and the strength of the evidence for the confessions needs to be investigated."[6] Later, the presiding judge asked, "Do you mean to say that the [facts] you admitted in the written records are all not true?"[7] Huang responded, "Yes."

---

4 *Zhongguo shibao* 中國時報 [*China Times*], March 19, 1980, p. 3.
5 Ibid.
6 Ibid.
7 Ibid.

Huang also denied sending Hung Chih-liang anywhere. He said Hung was not under orders. He said that he doubted that Hung had gone to Communist China, but that if he had, he should give himself up to the government.[8]

Two other noteworthy events occurred on the first day of the trial. First, Lin I-hsiung, accompanied by his wife, Fang Su-min, and his two lawyers, Chang Cheng-hsiung 張政雄 and Chiang Peng-chien 江鵬堅, appeared in the court at 11.20 AM and asked to be tried together with his seven co-defendants. This request was denied.[9] Tao Pai-chuan 陶百川, the great liberal, wrote a letter to the *China Times* saying that the newspaper's report that he had received a ticket to attend the trial was not correct. Tao stated that had applied for a ticket to the trial twelve times, but that he had not received permission to attend.[10]

Day 2 of the Trial: Wednesday, March 19, 1980

The second day of the trial was devoted to interrogating Lin Hung-hsuan and Lu Hsiu-lien. The presiding judge's first questions focused on whether or not Lin Hung-hsuan knew particular people overseas. Lin had studied for his doctorate in New Jersey during 1977–1978 and had met Chang Tsan-hung 張燦鍙 (George), then chairman of the World United Formosans for Independence (WUFI), once or twice and that he had seen Chang Chin-tse in the course of a Taiwanese Association 臺灣同鄉會 meeting. He readily admitted frequently meeting Chang Fu-hsiung 張富雄 and his wife, Yang Yi-yi 楊宜宜. Chang had been his classmate at university and lived nearby in New York. Lin said they frequently went to church together on weekends.[11]

Lin Hung-hsuan said that he only met Shih Ming-teh after joining the *Formosa Magazine* in late September 1979 when Shih came to the Tainan Theological Seminary and thereafter only saw him once every two months. The Presiding Judge asked, "Did you ever talk about opinions like Taiwan Independence?" Lin replied, "No, he only talked about *dangwai* activities."[12]

In July 1979 Lin Hung-hsuan returned to the United States to confirm his doctoral studies and to seek monetary donations for the *Formosa Magazine*. The presiding judge also spent a great deal of time asking about these funds,

---

8   Ibid.
9   Ibid.
10 Ibid.
11 *Zhongguo shibao* 中國時報 [*China Times*], March 20, 1980, p. 3.
12 Ibid.

which totaled US$5,000 given to Lin by Chang Fu-hsiung on behalf of the Taiwanese Association.[13]

Later, the Presiding Judge asked Lin, "Did you not say, when being questioned at the Bureau of Investigation on February 22, 1980, that the *Formosa Magazine* situation was to build strength and that its joint objective was to make Taiwan Independent. Is this true?" Lin replied, "I didn't say it that clearly."[14]

The *Formosa Magazine* also asked Lin to arrange the location for the Kaohsiung demonstration. Lin testified that he had applied to the Kaohsiung stadium, but did not receive permission. He had later applied to the local police dispatch station for permission to hold the demonstration in Rotary Park, but again permission was denied.

The Presiding Judge asked, "In your confession did you not say Shih Ming-teh had said that the purpose of *Formosa Magazine* was to cause Taiwan Independence?" Lin replied, "This is what Shih Ming-teh said." The Presiding Judge responded, "On February 12, 1980 I asked you, and you said that in addition to this, you also wanted to use the magazine to unite friends, increase strength and reach the objective of overthrowing the government. Is that correct?" Lin replied, after reading the record of investigation, "At that time I was unemployed. I only wanted to find work. I certainly did not have the idea of overthrowing the government."[15]

Several lawyers for the defendants then made statements. Chen Shui-bian said, "'Taiwan Independence' is a political term; it is not a legal term. Its concept is not clear. Can you allow the defendant to explain more clearly how he understands the Taiwan Independence?" Chang Chun-hsiung added, "With respect to understanding Taiwan Independence, the human rights proclamation of the Presbyterian Church, 'A New and Independent Country,' most definitely did not advocate violence. It also did not want Taiwan to decline and become a locality in the Communist Bandit regime. I request that the Presiding Judge examines this clearly." Yu Ching 尤清 added another point, "When interrogating the defendant, could the Presiding Judge allow the defendant himself to speak slowly. It would be best if the Presiding Judge did not give cues in order to avoid influencing the truth of the case." The Presiding Judge responded, "The defendants have already personally signed the written record [of investigation]. There is no need to have any doubts about its truth."[16]

---

13   Ibid.
14   Ibid.
15   Ibid.
16   Ibid.

Later, the Presiding Judge asked Lin Hung-hsuan whether his written record of investigation for January 30, 1980 was completely true. Defense lawyer Li Sheng-hsiung 李勝雄 intervened to request that the Presiding Judge ask Lin whether or not the entire written record was correct or only partly correct. Asked if the written record was correct, Lin replied, "Those parts of the written record which are comparatively clearly not truthful relate to using violence to overthrow the government. The defendant, with respect to this, has always advocated opposition to the use of force and has favored using peaceful methods to reform society."[17] In response to another question, Lin said, "The defendant participated in the *Formosa Magazine* to gain employment. I most certainly did not say it was to form power to overthrow the government."[18] Lin also denied that he was a member of WUFI or that he was doing any work for them. And he denied that he was assigned the work of overseas liaison.[19]

Asked what his overall position on the Kaohsiung Incident was, Lin replied, "From the time of my arrest on January 7 until the present, the defendant does not know what is called rebellion. At the same time, the defendant in advocating Taiwan Independence has always opposed violence and has advocated peaceful reform. The defendant from the time of studying in primary school right through to university has never heard it said that Taiwan Independence thought is the thought of rebellion. The defendant believes that if the government really has this belief, it ought to use newspapers, television, radio etc. to make this clear to the masses."[20]

The morning session ended with several of the defense lawyers making requests of the Presiding Judge. In response to a request from Chang Cheng-hsiung, the Presiding Judge said that Lin Hung-hsuan's unemployed status and his personal friendship with Chang Fu-hsiung were not related to the case. With regard to Li Sheng-hsiung's request to consider how the confessions were obtained, the Presiding Judge said that the court would give consideration to the issue. The morning session concerned with Lin Hung-hsuan adjourned at 12.20 PM.[21]

The afternoon session, during which Lu Hsiu-lien (Annette) was questioned, began at 2 PM. The Presiding Judge immediately focused on whether Lu knew Chang Tsan-hung and Chang Chin-tse. She admitted meeting them. When the

---

17   Ibid.
18   Ibid.
19   Ibid.
20   Ibid., p. 4.
21   Ibid.

Presiding Judge asked, "Did you approve of violence?," Lu responded, "I did not approve. I also did not approve of 'Taiwan Independence.'"[22]

The conditions of Lu's incarceration after her arrest came up. The Presiding Judge asked, "In your written record, you said in January 1978, after you participated in Taiwan Independence activities, that this even more deepened your Taiwan Independence consciousness." Lu responded, "This was not my true consciousness." After a few more questions, the Presiding Judge returned to the topic, "Did anyone ask you to return to Taiwan, to run in the elections for representative in order in order to preach 'Taiwan Independence'?" Lu replied, "No. I have never preached 'Taiwan Independence.' I have only preached 'Taiwan consciousness'."[23]

The Presiding Judge asked if in her February 1980 written record whether she had said that she had basically accepted the idea of "Taiwan Independence." Lu replied that at the time she had been incarcerated for fifty days, that she had been asleep and suddenly awoken when she appeared in court and that she had not completely awoken. She agreed that the same five judges were in court, but that she had not fully awoken when she signed the written record.[24]

After a while, Lu Hsiu-lien's defense attorney, Lu Chuan-sheng 呂傳勝, raised some questions: "I have two points for the Court to investigate. One, the defendant underwent more than fifty days of questioning and she has said that in her mind she had fear. Mentally, she had obstacles. Please ask her about this fear and these obstacles. Two, the defendant, when I saw her had said that, when she was arrested, she was interrogated night and day. She was punished by being forced to stand for two days. The investigator wanted her to write in accord with what he read aloud. When she did not write in accord with what he said, he made her look at frightening photographs and he also said that her situation was very close to the photographs."[25]

The prosecutor intervened and asked the Presiding Judge to ascertain whether Lu Hsiu-lien had been tortured. She stated that she had not been tortured, but she started to sob and said, "What I said was not limited to torture. In addition to torture, there were still other inappropriate methods. There were still more clever methods…" The Prosecutor intervened, but Lu was allowed to continue. "(Crying) Thank you, Presiding Judge. No one tortured. Once the written confessions were finished, then they were very polite. They even gave tea. They were very polite. But I have thought in detail about these

---

22 Ibid.
23 Ibid.
24 Ibid.
25 Ibid.

two days. In the more than fifty days, more than four hundred hours, they had four methods of interrogation. The first was 'the method of disintegration of the personality'...[26]

The Presiding Judge cut her off, but she continued, crying even more loudly, "I'll give you an example: they first hypothesized I was CIA, they hypothesized I was Taiwan Independence. With this premise, they insulted and taunted. They used this kind of interrogation attitude. If I only said that I did not remember, they said that in here there is no not remembering... They said that coming to the Bureau of Investigation was like taking off all one's clothes. We can see very clearly. I don't know how many times they showed me Wu Tai-an's[27] picture. They also read to me the prayers used in a funeral parlor. Several times I was punished by being forced to stand from six o'clock in the morning after breakfast until 9 o'clock at night... I had nothing to eat..." After an interruption, Lu continued, "During the interrogation, they mixed violent activities with their hypotheses.[28] My confession became their confession."[29]

The session closed at 4.45 PM after some more legal arguments from several defending attorneys and the prosecutor.

Day 3 of the Trial: Thursday, March 20, 1980

The third day of the trial, which began at 8.30 AM, was devoted to interrogating Shih Ming-teh. The Presiding Judge began questioning Shih about his record. Shih said in 1962 he had been convicted of sedition (*panluan zui* 叛亂罪) and released in June 1977. He had only known the other defendants from November 1978 to August-September 1979. The purpose for publishing *Formosa Magazine* was that the *dangwai* needed an official newspaper (*jiguan bao* 機關報).[30]

After more questions, Shih expanded upon the purpose of *Formosa Magazine:* "We felt after the United States and the [Chinese Communist] Bandits established diplomatic relations, in order to resist Chinese Communist unification, that we must awaken Taiwan's more than eighteen million people. For more than thirty years, Taiwan has already been independent, especially since the

---

26   Ibid.
27   Wu Tai-an 吳泰安, also known as Wu Chun-fa 吳春發, was sentenced to death on April 16, 1979 in connection with the Yu Teng-fa case discussed in Chapter 1.
28   The original Chinese in this sentence of the transcript is not clear.
29   *Zhongguo shibao* 中國時報 [*China Times*], March 20, 1980, p. 4. In the final sentence Lu has engaged in wordplay on the word "confession."
30   *Zhongguo shibao* 中國時報 [*China Times*], March 21, 1980, p. 3.

United States and China..." After the Presiding Judge asked Shih to slow down, Shih continued: "When the United States and the Bandits established diplomatic relations, the government propounded five principles. It said that the United States must work from the standpoint of government to government. This explains that Taiwan was in fact already independent, that internationally it had obtained [the status of] an independent, sovereign country. Across the Taiwan Strait on one side there is the 'People's Republic of China', while on this side there is the 'Republic of China.' In law, Taiwan is already independent. Our purpose in running the magazine was to request the government to improve such questions as the living situation of the people and democratic politics. This included the prohibition on political parties, the prohibition on newspapers, martial law and the 'Ten-Thousand Year Parliament'."[31]

Again, after being told to slow down, Shih continued, "Okay, I feel that in the past thirty years of no re-election of the 'Ten Thousand Year Parliament,' the Taiwan people have become indecisive with respect to the political system. Especially with the prohibition on political parties, one cannot fully realize democratic politics. I used the authority as General Manager of *Formosa Magazine* to push for the establishment of service centers in various locations in order to organize and develop a political party without the name of a political party, to plan a foundation and to promote marches."[32]

The Presiding Judge expressed surprise, "Do you mean that at the beginning the motivation was not simply to run a magazine?" Shih replied, "Correct, running a magazine was a method to promote democracy."[33]

The Presiding Judge asked if the leadership of the magazine discussed Taiwan Independence. Shih replied, "I've already expressed this in the written record. For the past thirty years, Taiwan has already been independent in fact. In May, we restarted [a campaign] for Taiwan to re-enter the United Nations with the name Republic of China and not Taiwan. In law, we use Republic of China. Privately we call it Taiwan. The dividing line is very clear. The independence of Taiwan is the independence of the Republic of China... In the indictment, the [Prosecutor] did not say modify the political system. He only said subvert the government."[34]

The Presiding Judge asked, "You talk about promoting democracy, how did you cause violence?" Shih answered, "That was an accidental matter. For the past thirty years Taiwan has not changed the parliament, it has not rescinded

---

31 Ibid.
32 Ibid.
33 Ibid.
34 Ibid.

martial law, the prohibition on political parties or the prohibition on newspapers. Is this democracy?"[35]

The Presiding Judge asked, "Did you discuss how to grasp power in the future?" Shih responded, "The so-called long and short-term plan for the grasping of power is what the Bureau of Investigation said… Our idea was to promote a political party that did not have the name of a political party." The Presiding Judge asked if this was illegal. Shih answered, "It was not illegal. It contravenes martial law and it contravenes the publication law."[36]

Asked about the overseas organizations with which he maintained contact, Shih replied the Taiwan Association 台灣同鄉會, the Voice of Taiwan 台灣之音 and international human rights organizations. Asked if there were any other organizations, Shih replied, "I repeatedly maintained my position. We never had interaction with the Chinese Communists. And we had no liaison with Taiwan Independence. This is my proclamation for responsibility for this work." Asked if he had liaison with the Voice of Taiwan, Shih responded, "Yes, that is the [Taiwan] Association."[37]

The issue of violence came up again. The Presiding Judge said, "You have said you wanted to use peaceful methods, yet you said at the Investigation Session you spoke about violent methods." Shih responded, "That is not called violence. It is a manifestation of determination to proceed."[38]

Shih said, "In the past, when we applied for various kinds of activities, initially we were always refused, but on the day we obtained permission. The security agencies did not want to have too many people participate. The security agencies were step-by-step also walking towards democratization."[39]

The session adjourned for lunch from 12.05 PM to 2 PM.

After lunch some matters were re-hashed. In response to an assertion by another witness in the written record, which the Presiding Judge quoted, Shih answered, "This was created by the Prosecutor and is the only witness who says I led the violence. But, to the present, I still have not cross-examined this person. Why am I not allowed to cross-examine this person? What he says is completely unreasonable. He says I told him to attack. Will the police fire their guns? When I came out of the Police Branch Bureau, the vehicles were already

---

35 Ibid.
36 Ibid.
37 Ibid.
38 Ibid.
39 Ibid.

moving. How could I tell him these things? I have all along wanted to cross-examine him. Please, let the Court understand, what he says is false."[40]

Shih Ming-teh proved a feisty defendant. He pointed to contradictions in the questions of the Presiding Judge and he pointed out where witnesses had made errors and how at least one "witness" was not present in Kaohsiung. In one response, Shih even pointed out that a so-called "fact" was not used in the indictment because it was wrong.[41]

In response to one picture that the Presiding Judge said showed the hitting of military police, Shih responded, "That police did not respond by hitting is true, but they used gas." After looking at another picture, Shih said, "In the Police Branch Bureau, I told the Deputy Commander that moving was not as good as staying calm. If they moved, we had no way to control." Shown pictures with blood, Shih replied, I am very sorry about this." The Presiding Judge then said, "Look at these. They are all police. The [Formosa Magazine] Service Center had not one person who was injured." Shih replied, "The Service Center did have [people who were injured].[42]

Shown the name list of the 183 injured security personnel, Shih said, "That day's [events] occurred unexpectedly. I have already said that they all occurred at the entrance to the Service Center. This was incited when the crowd was attacked with gas. Only after more than an hour's conflict did such injuries result."[43]

Later, the Presiding Judge asked what he thought about the events now. Shih replied, "From the beginning, we only wanted to have speeches in Rotary Park. We had no intention to create a disturbance, otherwise I could have turned the demonstration at Juiyuan Road. This was our approach."[44]

Shih also complained that he had written two letters from prison to his defense lawyer, but that neither had been received. He also reiterated his request to cross-examine five of the court's witnesses.[45]

In response to requests from the defense lawyers, the Presiding Judge asked Shih Ming-teh some questions. Asked about *Formosa Magazine* people who were injured, Shih answered, "I don't remember their names, but there were at least two people. One, with blood flowing all over his head, ran to the podium. I called a person to give him a few thousand NT dollars so he could leave on his

---

40   Ibid.
41   Ibid.
42   Ibid.
43   Ibid.
44   Ibid.
45   *Zhongguo shibao* 中國時報 [*China Times*], March 21, 1980, p. 4.

own. In addition, a person was injured because of the tear gas attack. For example, the girlfriend of Chiu Chui-chen 邱垂貞 was sent to the hospital because of this. Right until the time we were arrested, she was still in the hospital."[46]

Asked about the "Theory of the Brink of Violence 暴力邊緣", Shih said, "This occurred at a meeting following the Tide Incident. Hsu Hsin-liang said that the *dangwai* should consider the use of violence. The Kuomintang arrests people at any time. With respect to this, the *dangwai* cannot have no resistance. But all of us did not express any support for his idea. We felt the [two alternatives] of either doing nothing or responding to violence with violence were not good. So, we advocated the Theory of the Brink of Violence to express our determination to run activities. That was all."[47]

Asked if Lin I-hsiung arrived late and whether or not he spoke, Shih said, "Whether or not Lin I-hsiung got up on the podium and spoke, I can certainly say that on that day Lin I-hsiung arrived very late. When he arrived, the gas had already been set off. Furthermore, at the location [people] were being beaten terribly. He arrived together with Kang Ning-hsiang. Afterwards, I know that Kang Ning-hsing got on the podium and spoke. I don't know whether Lin I-hsiung got on the podium or not."[48] Later, in response, Lin I-hsiung's lawyer, Chang Chun-hsiung, said that they had obtained a copy of the tape of the evening's events. Chang said, "The result of our having repeatedly listened to the tape is that we most definitely did not hear Lin I-hsiung speak. Someone only introduced him on the stage…"[49]

In response to a question about Hung Chih-liang and Huang Hsin-chieh, Shih said, "As to the relationship between Huang Hsin-chieh and Hung Chih-liang, according to what I know, the two of them did not have a deep relationship. Furthermore, last year when Hung Chih-liang was arrested, that night at about 11 PM I learned this news and I rang Huang Hsin-chieh to ask for instructions on how to deal with the matter. Huang Hsin-chieh said that Hung Chih-liang was from the unificationist camp and that we should not to get involved in the matter as we are opposed to the Communist Party ruling Taiwan… In 1978, when Huang Hsin-chieh organized the *Dangwai* Election Assistance Group, at that time Hung Chih-liang ran in the third electoral dis-

---

46   Ibid.
47   Ibid.
48   Ibid.
49   Ibid.

trict and Huang Hsin-chieh from the very beginning refused to support his campaign."[50]

The session ended at 4.30 PM.

Day 4 of the Trial: Friday, March 21, 1980

The fourth day of the trial, which lasted seven hours, began at 8.30 AM and was devoted to the interrogation of Yao Chia-wen. The Presiding Judge began his questioning by asking whether or not Yao knew Peng Ming-min 彭明敏. Yao answered that he had met him when he was a law student and Peng was a professor at National Taiwan University. The Presiding Judge honed in on his key question, "Did you ever discuss the question of Taiwan Independence?"[51] Yao replied, "No. He had one sentence that left a deep impression on me. He said, the name of the nation and the national flag were small matters. One does not need to change the name of the nation or the national flag to implement political reform... He advocated using the present situation as a foundation to engage in political reform... In my confession, I wrote this point very clearly."[52] The Presiding Judge asked Yao whom he had met in the United States and again returned to Peng Ming-min, but gained no further information.

The Presiding Judge moved to the "Five-Person Committee," which Yao said was first mentioned on December 25, 1978. Yao said it met in various homes eight times. When asked, "Did you ever discuss a plan for the seizure of power?", Yao replied, "No. We never used that word... [When] the Presiding Judge says plan for seizure of power, he is using a term added by the Bureau of Investigation... We talked about how to increase the *dangwai's* momentum. At the time in the Bureau of Investigation, I discussed this point with them for a very long time. I finally was forced to agree and they also agreed to say this was not overthrow [of the government]."[53]

The Presiding Judge asked about the use of "concept" in his confession. Yao replied, "In writing my confession, I first wrote, I remember, we 'discussed.' Afterwards, the Bureau of Investigation changed this to 'concept.' In the end they said 'plan.'"[54]

---

50 Ibid.
51 *Zhongguo shibao* 中國時報 [*China Times*], March 22, 1980, p. 3.
52 Ibid.
53 Ibid.
54 Ibid.

The questioning between the Presiding Judge and Yao became increasingly tense. Despite Yao's making clear that the term "long and short term plan to seize power 長短程奪權計劃" came from the Bureau of Investigation, the Presiding Judge repeatedly used the term in his questions. Yao responded, "Would the Presiding Judge please not use that term again?"[55] A little later, Yao said, "About the *Formosa Magazine*, I've talked about this a great deal in the Bureau of Investigation. The Presiding Judge should go and look it up. Don't ask again." The Presiding Judge responded, "This is the power of the Presiding Judge." Yao responded, "Besides power, there is also law."[56]

Asked if Huang Hsin-chieh had issued instructions when setting up *Formosa Magazine*, Yao responded, "Yes. I can sum up in two features. First the magazine cannot have 'unification' ideas. Second, this magazine should belong to everyone in the *dangwai*. It should not belong only to Huang Hsin-chieh." So Huang declared in an editorial meeting that "the content must have an anti-Communist standpoint and it must publicize free and democratic thought."[57]

In answer to questions, Yao said that they had decided in August to set up service centers in order to better sell the magazine and to provide a place to make activities more convenient. The Presiding Judge asked if this was to build an organization, but Yao replied, "It was not to develop an organization. It was to increase momentum…" The Presiding Judge asked, "Did you approach this by expanding the organization?" Yao replied, "This is a conclusion. I only stated the facts. Different people have different views about [your] conclusion."[58]

A lot of the questioning concerned whether or not the *Formosa Magazine* had a principle of violence. Yao responded, "We most definitely did not have a principle of violence. It was the indictment that raised the 'principle of violence.'[59]

In his testimony, Yao Chia-wen explained why the demonstrators marched. First, even though they had not obtained permission, in the past they had subsequently been given permission. Another factor was anger over the destruction of the Pingtung office on December 8. A third factor was anger at the beating of Yao Kuo-chien and Chiu Sheng-hsiung on December 9. Furthermore, on December 10 the newspapers said that the police had not beaten the men. Finally, on the day, holding a rally with just speeches was difficult. So Shih Ming-teh made two proposals: (1) that they march, but not too far and (2) that

---

55   Ibid.
56   Ibid.
57   Ibid.
58   Ibid.
59   Ibid.

they end the rally after the speeches. They did not agree to proposals that they march to the Third Police Branch Bureau after the speeches to protest. The actual decision to march still had not been made by 3 PM on December 10. It was only made about 5 PM.[60]

Clearly, the Kaohsiung Incident had a lot of last-minute decision-making. Yao Chia-wen told Shih Ming-teh that the original plans to go to Rotary Park could not be implemented as the park was surrounded by security personnel. Holding speeches there was difficult and marching would be even more impossible. In discussing with the police if the rally could be cancelled, Yao said that it was important for the police to apologize for beating the two people the previous night.[61]

Yao said that he and Shih received no response from the police and continued to study the issue of marching. They discovered that the area outside the Hsin-hsing Police Branch Bureau, where they had held discussions with the police, was large and was not blockaded by security forces. In addition, it was not far from the *Formosa Magazine* office. They began marching about 6.30 PM. Shih Ming-teh was the General Commander 總指揮, while Yao Chia-wen was March Leader 遊行引導 as well as a speaker. This work as March Leader did not involve any announcement; Yao simply led the march from the front.[62]

About 6.30 PM, the marchers arrived at the Circle near the Hsin-hsing Police Branch Station. They put out the torches, sang songs, and then the speeches began. About 7 PM, just as Huang Hsin-chieh was beginning to speak, the Circle was surrounded by security forces. The demonstrators were told that they did not have permission to speak at the Circle. Yao and Shih went into the Hsin-hsing Police Branch Bureau to discuss to situation. When they came out, riot control vehicles had surrounded the demonstration and the situation was already quite chaotic. Yao got up to speak and read the letter about the Kushan Incident to the citizens of the entire nation. He also asked the riot control vehicles to back up a bit and not to continue advancing. Apparently, at this time, there were also 20,000 people waiting at the Rotary Park, but neither group could get to the other because of security blockades. At the Circle there were five or six thousand people. Then, about 8 PM, Yao and Shih again went to the Police Branch Bureau for discussions.[63] In the next hour or so, they moved away from the Circle. The road there was not blockaded.[64]

---

60 Ibid.
61 Ibid.
62 Ibid.
63 Ibid.
64 *Zhongguo shibao* 中國時報 [*China Times*], March 22, 1980, p. 4.

When they returned to the *Formosa Magazine* office, they decided to have more speeches. This was an effort to calm things down as some were calling for more marches. About 10 PM there were four or five thousand people listening to speeches at the *Formosa Magazine* Service Center and more than 20,000 a bit further away. Then the riot control vehicles came north along Chungshan Road.

In response to a question from the Presiding Judge, did the security forces hit people, Yao responded, no they did not hit people, but they used electric cattle prods to shock them. Some people dispersed, but others did not. Then smoke was used and then gas.[65]

Yao Chia-wen raised considerable questions about the confessions. He said they had to copy them and that they were shortened and that items were changed.[66]

Yao said, "The Bureau of Investigation wanted me to write a sentence that the Kaohsiung Incident was to overthrow the government. I did not go along, so they crossed out the first line. The [confession] sent to the Prosecutor began with the second page."[67]

Yao said, after Hsu Hsin-liang went overseas in October, the Five-Person Committee met very rarely. "The Bureau of Investigation continuously wanted us to acknowledge that all of the activities were planned by the Five-Person Committee." The Presiding Judge showed Yao Lin I-hsiung's confession. Yao replied, "This is not true. That passage is completely from the Indictment. I don't know how Lin I-hsiung signed that!"

In conclusion, Yao noted several places where the indictment had quoted testimony of various people incorrectly. The session ended at 6 PM. The next session would begin at 8.30 on March 24 after the weekend.

Day 5 of the Trial: Monday, March 24, 1980

The fifth day of the trial was devoted to questioning Chang Chun-hung and Chen Chu. The morning session began at 8.30 AM with questioning of Chang Chun-hung. After asking about Chang Chin-tse 張金策, the Presiding Judge zeroed in on the Five-Person Committee asking what responsibilities it had. Chang replied that it took care of *dangwai* matters. Asked if they had studied activities to oppose the government, Chang replied that they had not and, in

---

65   Ibid.
66   Ibid.
67   Ibid.

answer to a question, said that the six or seven meetings of the Five-Person Committee were mainly to plan the magazine.[68] The Presiding Judge asked, "Did you ever research a so-called plan for the seizure of power?" Chang replied, "I honestly say, absolutely not." After a few more questions, the Presiding Judge asked, "Was the long or short plan raised?" Chang replied, "With regard to this, I again honestly say, absolutely not."[69]

Again, the Presiding Judge returned to the topic of the *Formosa Magazine* attempting to overthrow the government, "Did you use the magazine offices as assembly points, to develop organization and excite the emotions of the masses to overthrow the government?" Chang responded, "Using assembly points to promote the magazine is a fact. Exciting the emotions to overthrow the government is not a fact."[70]

The issue of the confessions came up again in the questioning of Chang Chun-hung. The Presiding Judge exclaimed, "But you said this in the Investigation Court!" Chang responded, "From the beginning I have said that the confessions were not obtained under normal conditions. At the time, the court said to speak in this way was not beneficial to me." The Presiding Judge questioned, "At the time, the court didn't say that?" Chang responded, "I still believe that in creating a critical magazine, it must have criticism. This is a most basic aspect of democratic politics, and it is not vilifying or sowing discord.[71]

In answers to the Presiding Judge, Chang said that when he got to the Circle at 7.30 PM, things were calm. He said the police had controlled the traffic. The Presiding Judge asked how Yao Chia-wen could ask for the resignation of Kung Ling-sheng 孔令晟 and Chang responded that it was because of the Kushan Incident the night before. Asked, how things changed, Chang replied, "At Chungcheng Road there was a puff of white smoke. At the time, some people yelled that they had set off tear gas. The masses then became agitated and one-by-one protected themselves." After some more questions, Chang continued, "The masses were at the Circle. They [Yao Chia-wen and Shih Ming-teh] got on the first leading vehicle. All around was a line blockading [the Circle]. There was no way to move."[72]

The Presiding Judge asked, "How many times were there beatings?" Chang answered, "Two times, on Chungcheng Fourth Road and on Juiyuan Road

---

68   *Zhongguo shibao* 中國時報 [*China Times*], March 25, 1980, p. 4.
69   Ibid.
70   Ibid.
71   Ibid.
72   Ibid.

while turning when returning to the Service Centre. Because the military police had blockaded, the people had no exit, so conflicts occurred."[73]

The Presiding Judge asked Chang Chun-hung what happened after they returned to the Service Center. Chang replied, "The microphone was originally with Wang Tuoh. He gave it to me. The whole area was a sea of torches. It was very bright. I was afraid that the fires could cause an even greater disaster, so I thought about how to extinguish them. I yelled, 'Tonight we are already victorious. Everybody please extinguish the torches.' I yelled this three times and then the entire place extinguished them. At the time, my thought was the disaster has already occurred, but we cannot have an even great disaster. This language was in my confession, but the Prosecutor did not believe it."[74] Chang testified that people had calmed down after extinguishing the torches. The Presiding Judge asked, "Was this the time when military police were beaten?" Chang replied, "At about 11 o'clock, a very large riot control unit came from the direction of Rotary Park. It was at that time that beating occurred again." After another question, Chang continued, "The last time only occurred after the riot control unit came and set off tear gas and white smoke. The Indictment said I got up on the rostrum and spoke to incite [the people]. This is not true."[75]

The Presiding Judge again raised statements in the confession. Chang responded, "These words were written entirely while being interrogated for a confession. Let me again declare that the confession under interrogation was not in accord with my free will. It was not in accord with the facts. The Five-Person Committee discussed the magazine and not long and short term plans. It did not discuss overthrowing the government or seizing power." The Presiding Judge then asked, "Was the written record in accord with your free will? Is it true?" Chang replied, "From the beginning [things that] I have repeatedly declared have not gone into the record. I have been in detention for 102 days. Today is the one and only one time I have spoken in accord with my free will."[76] Chang's lawyer tried to get the court to listen to how the written records were obtained, but the court did not pursue this. The Presiding Judge again read from the written record and Chang again stated that these statements were gain by abnormal means.[77]

In conclusion, Chang Chun-hung said, "The Kaohsiung Incident was a very unfortunate incident. I only participated from midway and used my greatest

---

73   Ibid.
74   Ibid.
75   Ibid.
76   Ibid.
77   Ibid.

effort to reduce the calamity. All of the articles used by *Formosa Magazine* were to defend against traitors and prevent harm. A critical magazine in a democratic country is very important. What it says may not all be correct just like what the government says may not necessarily be all correct. The final decision is made by the readers. We just offered different opinions to enable society to progress more quickly and to allow local government to establish roots in Taiwan. The Bureau of Investigation people said this was Taiwan Independence thought. In fact, this is what our government has been implementing for thirty years and it is the significance of elections."[78] The morning session ended at 12.50 PM.

The afternoon session, which focused on questioning Chen Chu, began at 2.30 PM. The questioning began with the Presiding Judge trying to ascertain the effects of Chen Chu's relationship with Kuo Yu-hsin on her. (She had been Kuo's secretary for ten years.) The Presiding Judge also asked about her relationship with other Taiwanese in the United States. Although one of the Taiwanese, Chang Chin-tse 張金策, had advocated violence, Chen Chu maintained that she did not agree with him.[79]

Asked if the government had given permission for the Kaohsiung demonstration, Chen replied, "No. The understanding of the defendant is that every time we ran activities, we usually did not obtain permission, but in the end after mediation with the security organs we regularly obtained permission. Because of this, the defendant believed that we would obtain permission after mediation."[80]

The Presiding Judge asked if the meeting on December 7 decided to buy wooden clubs? Chen responded, "This was not decided on the 7th. After the defendant returned to Taiwan, over time people had invaded and wrecked various service centers and the home of Huang Hsin-chieh. Because of this, the defendant understands that the central office [of the magazine] wanted each service center to prepare wooden clubs so, on the small chance there was any event, they could defend themselves. So, each place apparently had prepared wooden clubs before the 7th."

The issue of the accuracy of investigation came up again. The Presiding Judge asked Chen Chu whether she was in charge of liaison with overseas. Chen responded, "It was only after the defendant saw the Indictment that I knew this."[81]

---

78   Ibid.
79   *Zhongguo shibao* 中國時報 [*China Times*], March 25, 1980, p. 3.
80   Ibid.
81   Ibid.

The afternoon session closed at 6.05 PM.

Day 6 of the Trial: Tuesday, March 25, 1980

The sixth day of the trial began at 8.30 AM. Lin I-hsiung entered the court holding hands with his wife, Fang Su-min, and asked that his wife be allowed to sit next to him. The Presiding Judge granted this request. The Presiding Judge told Lin he could sit, but Lin said he would stand to show respect for the court. He did, however, request that he be allowed to take ginseng since his body was weak. The interrogation of Lin began.[82]

The Presiding Judge asked Lin if he knew Chang Chin-tse and Kuo Yu-hsin. Lin replied that he had known Chang since 1975. He said that while in Taiwan Chang had given no evidence of opposing the government or having Taiwan Independence thoughts. Lin said that he had had no interaction with Chang after Chang went overseas, but that when he went back to Ilan, Lin went to see Chang's mother, wife and daughter.[83]

The Presiding Judge asked about Kuo Yu-hsin. Lin replied that Kuo Yu-hsin was the elder generation in Ilan and he respected him like he respected all older people in Ilan. Even though he had been Kuo's legal adviser in the 1975 legislative election, he and Kuo had not had much contact. Before he went overseas, Kuo said that he had a lot of friends who could help Lin in an election. Lin met these and some did help him in his campaign for provincial assemblyman. In September 1979, when Lin went to the United States, he did not intend to see Kuo, but Kuo learned he was in Washington and came to see him and invited him to a meal. Lin said that Kuo talked about his current situation.[84]

Lin also said that he had seen Chang Chin-tse on his American trip. Chang had called from New York and insisted on coming down to see Lin in Washington. Chang said that he had left the "Taiwan Independence Alliance" 台獨聯盟. "I saw that he was very lonely and we did not discuss politics." They only talked about mutual friends and family. When Lin returned to Taiwan, he gave Chang's mother NT$5,000 and Chang's wife NT$10,000, saying the money came from Chang, but in fact it was Lin's own money because Lin saw that they had no funds.[85]

---

82 *Zhongguo shibao* 中國時報 [*China Times*], March 26, 1980, p. 4.
83 Ibid.
84 Ibid.
85 Ibid.

Lin's trip was sponsored by the American Institute in Taiwan (AIT). As part of this trip, Lin met many congressmen and civil rights activists. At their request, he had a meal with Peng Ming-min and others from Taiwan, who took him touring around many Washington tourist sites including the White House. "We didn't talk about political matters."[86]

The Presiding Judge asked Lin about his stop in Japan on the way back to Taiwan. "The written transcript of the Department of Security [of the Taiwan Garrison Command] says there was a Japanese woman called 'Daisy.' I don't know. My wife is called 'Daisy.' When I sleep, I often call her name. The Department of Security people thought it was this Japanese 'Daisy.'"[87]

Asked about his political thought, Lin replied, "My thought is that Taiwan's future must be decided by Taiwan's 17 million people. The so-called 17 million people includes Taiwanese and Mainlanders. This is a natural conclusion in accord with democratic thought. We 17 million people could decide to counter-attack the Mainland immediately."[88]

When asked why the *Formosa Magazine* established "Service Centers," Lin answer that he did not know. Lin said that Shih Ming-teh was the General Manager and that he decided. This was not something decided jointly by the so-called Five-Man Committee.[89]

The Presiding Judge asked Lin if Yao Chia-wen had mentioned his Brink of Violence Principle? Lin replied, "I had never heard this term. It was only after I arrived at the Department of Security that I heard it."[90]

The Presiding Judge asked, "Lin I-hsiung, have you advocated using violence to respond to violence, using strength to respond to strength?" Lin responded, "I have said this sentence. Before and after I said it, my state of mind was not so simple. I will tell it again to allow the Presiding Judge to consider [the question]. At that time I considered that Hsu Hsin-liang was a county executive elected by the people. If he performed badly, it should be the voters who recalled him, and not a decision of the Public Functionary Disciplinary Sanction Commission. I believe this is not a phenomenon which democracy ought to have, so I proposed two lines. One was to use violence to respond to violence and to use strength to displace strength. The other was to become silent and to leave the Kuomintang to its own fate. This is the opinion that I presented in the *dangwai*. Afterwards, Chen Wan-chen 陳婉貞 wrote this in

---

86   Ibid.
87   Ibid.
88   Ibid.
89   Ibid.
90   Ibid.

Tide. I felt she shouldn't have written this, but she is a journalist. I said she could write it, so I did not blame her. At that time a Mr Li at National Chengchi University wanted to sue me. I arranged to see him in a restaurant. The *China Times* reporter, Tang Kuang-hua 唐光華 was also there. I told him my state of mind that let me make that statement. According to my personality, I would become silent and I would not be able to act in this way [using violence to respond to violence]. When Chen Po-wen 陳博文 was arrested, I felt apathetic. Later I felt acting this way was not good, so I took the initiative to ask Kang Ning-hsiang to find a person responsible for liaison in the Kuomintang to mediate. I said the Yu Teng-fa matter is a government policy and a state of mind with respect to the *dangwai*. The Chen Po-wen matter is relatively small. If the government is lenient, it can demonstrate the government's leniency. Afterwards, Chen Po-wen's case was dealt with and one can see that my efforts were not wasted."[91]

The Presiding Judge asked Lin if a statement in his response was correct. Lin said it was correct, and proceeded to read: "I believe Hsu Hsin-liang was a county executive elected by the people. If he performs badly, he should be recalled by the voters, and not lose his position on a decision by the Public Functionary Disciplinary Sanction Commission. This acts against the will of the people. In a democratic country, the people are the masters, they are the emperor(s). To act against the will of the people is to act against the emperor. To act against the emperor is to rebel, so the Kuomintang government is a seditious organization. At the time, I had generated a psychology of hopelessness with respect to Taiwan's democratic future, so I said these words. Later, I felt that I should not have done so and my actions were not like that. The government did not pursue this and I am very grateful."[92]

The Presiding Judge asked Lin I-hsiung about the Kaohsiung Incident and when he arrived. Lin said, "On the tenth, Kang Ning-hsiang came to find me. He said the riot control troops had already started moving and that we should go and see if we could separate them a bit.[93]

Lin said that he got a taxi in Taipei about 5 PM and arrived in Kaohsiung about 10 PM. He explained that about 4 PM Kang Ning-hsiang came to find him and said that something had happened in Kaohsiung. The riot control troops had already started moving and there could be conflict. Kang wanted

---

91   Ibid.
92   Ibid.
93   Ibid.

Lin to go south with him to see if they could make an effort to prevent the occurrence of conflict.[94]

The Presiding Judge asked Lin about several comments made in February 1980 by another defendant. Lin answered, "I don't know under what circumstances he made that kind of statement."[95] Shown a record of interrogation, Lin responded by telling the Presiding Judge of several errors in the transcript.

Before the morning session ended, the Presiding Judge gave the defense lawyers an opportunity to raise issues. Lin I-hsiung's lawer, Chiang Peng-chien 江鵬堅, asked the Presiding Judge to listen to the tape of the Kaohsiung Incident speeches. Chiang said that it would be easy to check that Lin I-hsiung did not speak from listening to the tape. There was no need to seek such other proof as witness statements. Chiang also noted on February 25 that Lin I-hsiung had made a statement about how the confession was obtained in the detention center. Lin was ready to take legal responsibility for this statement. Another lawyer, Chang Chun-hsiung 張俊雄, said that the indictment stated the court had evidence including photographs and tapes that Lin I-hsiung had gotten up and spoken. But court case only had the words of witnesses and lacked any other evidence. Chang asked for the prosecutors to explain. Secondly, with respect to the Five-Man Committee and the issue of Long and Short Term Plans to Seize Power, the indictment has only the defendant's confession as evidence. Is there any other evidence?[96]

The main news report of the *China Times* on page 2 headlined, "Answering questions, Lin I-hsiung denies his former written confession."[97] Another article lower on the page had the headline, "The Bureau of Investigation responds to the Presiding Judge, there was absolutely no torture during the examination."[98]

At 12.50 PM, the court session recessed and resumed at 2.30 PM. The unofficial transcript tells us that two rows of eight mandarin oranges had been laid out as the eight defendants entered the court. This purpose of this session was to give the defendants an opportunity to cross-examine.

The Presiding Judge began with Yao Chia-wen, who requested that all of the written records of all of the defendants including confessions be made available to all of the defendants. In answering the Presiding Judge, Shih Ming-teh stated that the Five-Man Group met seven or eight times, but never discussed any plan for seizing power. Lin I-hsiung told the Presiding Judge, "I believe

---

94 Ibid.
95 Ibid.
96 Ibid.
97 *Zhongguo shibao* 中國時報 [*China Times*], March 26, 1980, p. 2.
98 Ibid.

when a person is excessively tired, if you keep repeating the same question and it is clear that this event did not occur, if you are asked for long enough, you can feel it is real."[99]

Yao Chia-wen's defense lawyer, Su Tseng-chang, noted that the Presiding Judge had given Lu Hsiu-lien the opportunity to speak about her confession. Su asked that Yao Chia-wen also be given this opportunity.

In response to questions from his defense lawyer, Chen Shui-bian, Huang Hsin-chieh asserted that he was anti-communist and he stated that he did not ask the Five-Man Committee to overthrow the government.[100]

The Presiding Judge asked Huang Hsin-chieh if he was questioned when fatigued. Huang replied, "In addition to be questioned for fifty to sixty hours, I was also deceived. When I was arrested, I did not know legal procedure and legal provisions. They wanted me to admit everything."[101]

The Presiding Judge responded, "Are you saying that the Bureau of Investigation written record is not true?"[102]

Huang replied, "Some is true and some is not true. Because of this, I want to explain about the Prosecutor's Indictment."[103]

The Presiding Judge asked, "Do you feel this is questioning when fatigued?"[104]

Huang responded, "Yes. In addition to questioning when fatigued, I was also deceived. They said they only wanted me to admit [guilt] and to be honest, then they could change it to a 'Article 9, Clause 1' verdict. In order to reduce the penalty, I admitted everything."

The Presiding Judge then asked Chang Chun-hung, "Are the Investigation Written Records from January 20 and January 22 all true?"[105]

Chang answered, "The majority are all not true."[106]

At this stage, Chang's defense lawyer, Kuo Chi-jen 郭吉仁, asked the Presiding Judge to ask Chang which portions of the written record were not true.

Chang responded, "The reasons for being not true are the same as for Huang Hsin-chieh."[107]

---

99 *Zhongguo shibao* 中國時報 [*China Times*], March 26, 1980, p. 3.
100 Ibid.
101 *Zhongguo shibao* 中國時報 [*China Times*], March 26, 1980, p. 2.
102 Ibid.
103 Ibid.
104 Ibid.
105 Ibid.
106 Ibid.
107 Ibid.

THE MILITARY TRIAL OF THE EIGHT KEY DEFENDANTS 67

The Presiding Judge then asked, "Did they beat you?"[108]

Chang responded, "They did not use torture implements. But using questioning when fatigued is even more dangerous than using torture implements because [after] fatigue questioning for close to a hundred hours, they then said Huang Hsin-chieh and Yao Chia-wen had individually come across. They said that they had admitted everything and it is not okay for you not to admit it."[109]

The Presiding Judge then asked Shih Ming-teh, "Are your Investigation written records of January 18 true?"[110]

Shih Ming-teh responded, "Some is not true. At the very end, they used recordings of Huang Hsin-chieh and Chen Chu in talking to me. The recording of Huang Hsin-chieh said, 'I am Huang Hsin-chieh. I engaged in Taiwan Independence...' etc."[111]

The Presiding Judge then asked, "Did you suffer violence?"[112]

Shih responded, "No, they showed me the written records of others and said they had all already spoken [confessed]. If I didn't speak [confess], then they couldn't go back."[113]

The Presiding Judge then asked, "But were not your written records different?"

Shih replied, "They were not identical. Because of this, I don't know the meaning of 'they all mutually supported each other's words'?"[114]

At this point Chen Chu stood up and explained, "When I was in the Bureau of Investigation, there was a senior officer. One day he said that soon he would find a very high officer and ask him to listen. But I did not know that I was being taped for Shih Ming-teh to listen."[115]

In response to the Presiding Judge, Lu Hsiu-lien answered: "During fifty days [of interrogation], an investigator frequently said, 'Coming here is like taking all of your clothes off to sleep. You must say everything very clearly.'"... The Presiding Judge asked if her statements of January 22 and 23 were accurate. She responded, "Not completely. Some parts were accurate."[116]

---

108   Ibid.
109   Ibid.
110   Ibid.
111   Ibid.
112   Ibid.
113   Ibid.
114   Ibid.
115   Ibid.
116   Ibid.

The Presiding Judge then asked Lin Hung-hsuan if his written records and confessions of January 22nd and 24th were accurate. Lin responded, "In the main, they were not accurate."[117]

The Presiding Judge asked Lin in which ways were they inaccurate? Lin replied, "The most important part was that part in the indictment that said we used violence to overthrow the government, etc."

The Presiding Judge asked Lin, "At the Bureau of Investigation, did you receive any wrongful methods?"

Lin answered, "No. When I was at the Bureau of Investigation, a high-level leading official often asked me this question. I felt it was very strange."

The Presiding Judge asked if there was any other treatment. Lin responded, "In the beginning there was no sleep for seventy or eighty hours. After was arrested on the 7th I did not sleep until the 10th."

In response to questions from the Presiding Judge, Lin said that he had food and water and that he was not tortured.[118]

After the Presiding Judge asked Yao Chia-wen the same questions, Yao spoke at length until the Presiding Judge cut him off: "This defendant has repeatedly thought about this. If I speak up in this way, then it will not be good for either me personally or for the nation. But, since everyone else have all spoken up. I will also speak. In the past, I privately told the Military Prosecutor that the Presiding Judge had said that he had no way to investigate this kind of matter. Since the beginning when I was arrested on the 13th, one could investigate and gather the nearly 100,000 characters I wrote on the mountain of confessions. My written records are in three booklets. One booklet is small and basically is irrelevant. On the cover of one booklet they put that they did not agree, so it did not go through. All my written records were written by them. Every day they made a journal of the examination. Every day they had four teams. Each team had two individuals who rotated. They all had journals which they had to give their superior officers to criticize. We requested the esteemed persons to pay attention to the whole text and not emphasize the use of particular words. I said to them, if you use the crime of sedition to arrest me, then I am very sad as it will hurt my reputation. When I went in [to custody], they constantly discussed the Kaohsiung Incident with me. After I left the Military Law Detention Center, each day I slept only two or three hours. In the middle of the night, when I went to the toilet, I could see them still examining. Because in the past I often stayed up late, this didn't matter. There is also the matter of being cheated. Because they discovered our situation was not serious, so they told

---

117   Ibid.
118   Ibid.

me to change 'political reform' in my written record to 'Taiwan Independence thought'...."[119]

The Presiding Judge interrupted Yao, "You say you were cheated?"

Yao answered, "Yes. They told me that Shih Ming-teh had already told everything. So, they told me to copy a section. So I then copied it. Only later did I know that at that time Shih Ming-teh had still not come in. They also still wanted me to say that the magazine which we ran wanted to overthrow the government. I did not agree with this. There are examination journals about all this."[120]

The Presiding Judge asked Yao if he had been tortured. Yao responded, "There was a person who threatened me, but there was no torture." About the written record, Yao said, "During it [the interrogation], there were no questions, there were no answers. It was copied." Asked if the written record was accurate, Yao responded, "It is not completely inaccurate. They said they just wanted me to cooperate and then everyone could go out. I even told them that Shih Ming-teh should also come out."[121]

Chen Chu's defense lawyer, Kao Jui-cheng 高瑞錚, had a question to ask Chen Chu about the written record, but the Presiding Judge said that the time for such question was already over. At the request of his defense lawyer, Chiang Peng-chien, Lin I-hsiung made a short statement: "If the Presiding Judge believes it is necessary, I will announce it. I originally decided not to announce in consideration of the benefits to the nation and individuals. I only want to tell the other defendants, you are too fortunate."[122]

After the prosecutors and defense attorneys had some argument about the validity of the written records, Lin I-hsiung stood up. He said, "I request the Prosecutor look at me, I request the Prosecutor discuss this with me face-to-face." According to the transcript, Lin spoke agitatedly, "I am a defendant. He is the Prosecutor. I want to ask him why, after one interrogation, I was sent to the the Department of Security [of the Taiwan Garrison Command] for forty days? After the Department of Security returned me to the Military Court, why did they still allow Department of Security people come to see me? After I was indicted, when I was supposed to see my family, why did the examination people still come to look for me to warn me not to speak irresponsibly?"[123]

---

119 Ibid.
120 Ibid.
121 Ibid.
122 Ibid. This could have two meanings. First, the other defendants were not tortured. Second, the other defendants did not have their families murdered.
123 Ibid.

A Prosecutor rose and said that the Department of Security has the status of judicial police and that sending him there was legal. At this moment, Lu Hsiu-lien's defense lawyer, Lu Chuan-sheng 呂傳勝, spoke: "The second day after her arrest, Lu Hsiu-lien was sent to the Bureau of Investigation for forty or fifty days just in order to get a confession. If they wanted a confession, they could have used an occasion like this to get a clear confession. Why did they want to go to such a secret place? Lu Hsiu-lien has already said with tears that this was worse than torture. In her confession, would she say such words as overthrow which could lead to a death penalty?"... The Presiding Judge interrupted, "You cannot use this kind of attacking words!"

Lu Chuan-sheng responded, "The Presiding Judge has a conscience. The reason I am like this is because this is a question of human rights."[124]

At that point, Chiang Peng-chien, Lin I-hsiung's defense lawyer, spoke: I have the same attitude as the defendant. I don't want to harm the nation. If it wasn't for the court's encouragement, everyone would still mince their words. On February 28 Lin I-hsiung submitted a memorandum, I ask the Court to give a copy to the Prosecutor. I will read aloud from section which explains why he wrote the memorandum. 'On the day of December 10, if Kang Ning-hsiang had not asked me to go, I most definitely would not have gone to Kaohsiung. I now don't know if I can physically survive this fatal catastrophe. Can my will endure this agony? I apologize to my family members. There are many reasons that have caused me to be like this today. I don't want to be persecuted. I only wish that the people of this world could return to me my original appearance. I am not willing to be considered as a virtuous official. I am also not willing to be considered a traitor. I am an ordinary person. I only hope for a society which has progress and therefore hope. It is for this that I have dedicated myself and for which I have sacrificed. This is the only asset that I have to give to my three daughters.'[125]

At this point, Yao Chia-wen stood up to speak, "Now, everyone's heart is filled with grief. Do not believe that we all admit the crime of treason. The Prosecutor in the indictment said that I have under Peng Ming-min's spell. Some people believe we now are overthrowing our confessions and because of this are withdrawing the confessions here in Court. In fact, it isn't like this. To say I was under Peng Ming-min's spell, to say that Huang Hsin-chieh directed us to run a magazine in order to overthrow the government is all a misunderstanding. That day, I went to eat dinner before returning. The

---

124 Ibid.
125 Ibid.

THE MILITARY TRIAL OF THE EIGHT KEY DEFENDANTS   71

indictment said that I knew everything had failed 什麼情知事敗. This is all a misunderstanding."[126]

The Presiding Judge then said, "With respect to the confessions and with this Court having asked each of the defendants, each defendant feels he or she was not subject to methods using threats of violence, but there were circumstances of interrogation while fatigued and being cheated. With respect to the Lin I-hsiung portion, this court will consider how to handle it." The Presiding Judge then cited a series of documents that he said proved in each instance (except Lin I-hsiung) that there "absolutely was no use of threats, torture, violence or any other improper rmethods used to obtain confessions." He stated, "This is the conclusion of my investigation. Are there any opinions?"

Yu Ching, Chang Chun-hung's defense lawyer, immediate stood up and said, "This kind of investigation is not fair. There are many reports that are available and can be consulted about whether fatigue interrogation is threatening or not."[127]

There was a bit more argument, but the Presiding Judge cut off Yao Chia-wen. At 6.20 PM the session ended. Lin I-hsiung continued on his bail, while the other defendants were incarcerated.[128]

Day 7 of the Trial: Wednesday, March 26, 1980

The trial recommenced at 8.30 AM on Wednesday morning, March 26, to begin the oral arguments (言辭辯論).[129] Then, the Prosecutor and the defendant's lawyers read their oral statements.[130] The Prosecutor basically argued that the defendants had vainly attempted to engage in illegal activities, repeatedly used violence in order to overthrow the government and institute their traitorous goal of "Taiwan Independence." They established the Five-Man Committee to plan the seizure of power. They colluded with overseas traitors to advocate Taiwan Independence. They used the *Formosa Magazine* to develop their organization. They met illegally to pressure the government and they incited thugs to beat the military police.

---

126   Ibid.
127   Ibid.
128   Ibid.
129   *Zhongguo shibao* 中國時報 [*China Times*], March 27, 1980, p. 3.
130   The complete text of Prosecutor's statements and some of the defendant's statements are available in *Zhongguo shibao* 中國時報 [*China Times*], March 27, 1980, p. 2.

After the Prosecutor's statement, defense lawyer Yu Ching on behalf of all eight defendants raised some important points. He noted that several legal scholars argued, according to the spirit of Articles 154 and 301 of the Code of Criminal Procedure,[131] a confession cannot be the only evidence in a conviction. In addition, if "there is doubt in the evidence, the benefit must go to the defendant" 罪證有疑，利於被告.[132] The Presiding Judge responded, "Just now the Court has already announced the beginning of the oral arguments. Because of this, your presentation of this request now is not appropriate."[133]

Of the defendants, Huang Hsin-chieh spoke first. He told the Presiding Judge that he could not write essays, so he would speak orally. The Presiding Judge asked him to speak slowly so that the court stenographers could record his statement.[134]

Huang began concisely: "Did we commit crimes? The main evidence is the confessions and the records from the Bureau of Investigation. I have already spoken with respect to these. They used fifty to sixty hours of fatigue interrogation. Because of this, it is not reliable. In addition, I have raised the indictment. At that time on the 20th, that day and that night three people came from the Bureau of Investigation. They told me to confess. They said if I did that this would reduce my penalty. Because of this, I finally confessed on the 22nd. They did not use torture, but I was incarcerated. At that time it felt that living was worse than death. Because of this, one could confess anything..."[135]

Huang then denied the accusations about Hung Chih-liang saying he knew nothing about eel fry, that he knew no one in Japan sympathetic to the Chinese Communists, that he knew no one among the Communist Bandits and that he was anti-Communist. Huang also said the indictment stated the defendants had conspired with overseas Taiwan Independence elements. Huang asked, "Can you tell me with which overseas treasonous element I have had contact? One telephone call? One letter?"[136]

Huang completely denied that he wanted to overthrow the government and stressed *Formosa Magazine* had a completely anti-Communist stance and pursued freedom and democracy. Huang stressed that he cooperated with the government in running *Formosa Magazine*. "After we started *Formosa*

---

131 For the texts of these articles, see Tao Bai-chuan (editor) 陶百川 (編), *Zuixin liufa quanshu* 最新六法全書 [*The Most Recent Complete Six Legal Codes*] (Taipei 台北: San-min shuju 三民書局, 1980), pp. 330, 336.

132 *Zhongguo shibao* 中國時報 [*China Times*], March 27, 1980, p. 3.

133 Ibid.

134 *Zhongguo shibao* 中國時報 [*China Times*], March 27, 1980, p. 2.

135 *Zhongguo shibao* 中國時報 [*China Times*], March 27, 1980, p. 3.

136 Ibid.

Magazine, the Director of the Taipei Government Information Office, Huang Lao-sheng 黃老生, and the Chief Secretary came to look for me. I told them to send some people to help us look at manuscripts. When the Taiwan Garrison Command sent people, I also invited them to send people to help us. If they found problems with articles, I would deal with it. Even though *Formosa Magazine* criticized the government, this was still completely done from friendship. There was no evil intent. Please let the Presiding Judge consider the situation of the defendant."[137]

Huang concluded, "Among security personnel, one or two may be bad, but this does not mean that all security personnel are bad. Civil servants are the same. Because of this, in the past we may have been a bit too fiery. This defendant did hope to increase the strength of the opposition. We hoped to make a democratic government…"[138] Huang finished by noting he had little education. His junior high school was under the Japanese and it was only at university that he received the education of the fatherland, though his Mandarin Chinese was poor.

Following Huang's statement, one of his two defense lawyers, Chen Shui-bian, took seventy minutes to read a twenty-five page document totaling about 20,000 characters in defense of Huang which questioned the materials about Hung Chih-liang, the Five-Man Committee and other matters.[139] Chen also raised some important questions about the "Records of the Investigation of Hung Chih-liang" 洪誌良調查筆錄. First, the copy was a photocopy. The table of contents for the original did not fit the contents of the photocopy. Secondly, the records were not the original records. The original had sixteen pages, but the court only gave us seven or eight pages to read, while eight or nine pages were missing. In addition, the number of columns per page was also short of the customary amounts. Third, the content of the Records was also unclear. The dates of the records also differed from what is normal. Thus, this raises questions about Hung Chih-liang's testimony. Chen Shui-bian also raised many other issues. He concluded asking the court "to judge the defendants not guilty, in order to protect human rights, and furthermore, for our democratic rule of law to allow it to blossom radiantly, so that our nation is fortunate and our people are fortunate!"[140]

---

137 Ibid.
138 Ibid.
139 *Zhongguo shibao* 中國時報 [*China Times*], March 27, 1980, p. 2.
140 *Zhongguo shibao* 中國時報 [*China Times*], March 27, 1980, p. 3.

When Chen concluded, the Presiding Judge said, "Your oral argument is exceedingly verbose. Do you request the court to consult it?" Chen replied, "Of course, I do."[141]

Another defense lawyer for Huang, Cheng Ching-lung 鄭慶龍, raised questions about the indictment and the procedures used in the case. After considerable discussion of the relevant laws, Cheng concluded, "From the foregoing, we know even if we could be sure of the capability of the evidence and the power of the proof in the defendant's confession as raised by the indictment, still it would not prove the criminal behavior of the defendant, Huang Hsin-chieh. We request in accord with the law that he be judged not guilty."

Huang Hsin-chieh's young brother, Huang Tien-fu 黃天福, also made a presentation. He concluded, "From the above facts, the defendant could not possibly have wanted to join with the Bandits and even more so did not have any intention to overthrow the government. This supporter hopes the Presiding Judge, in accord with the principle of 'not guilty if there are doubts about the crime,' will employ discerning wisdom and professional conscience to give the defendant a judgment of not guilty."[142]

The Prosecutor then responded to three items. The first related to the "voluntary nature" 任意性 of the confession. The Prosecutor argued that the confessions were freely given. The second related to the reliability of Hung Chih-liang's confession. The Prosecutor maintained the accuracy of Hung's confession. Finally, he argued that Huang Hsin-chieh was responsible for the violence in Kaohsiung.[143]

At the invitation of the Presiding Judge, Huang Hsin-chieh responded: "When the Prosecutor asked me, I was still at the Bureau of Investigation. How could I dare speak? Just now the Prosecutor spoke of my Taiwan Independence point of view. That was when we were discussing things, but there was no plan. With respect to Hung Chih-liang, at the time I urged him to turn himself in. He certainly did! He surrendered to the authorities. With respect to the check for the eel fry, how is it so easy to borrow money? Just make a phone call and borrow the money? The Prosecutor has probably never engaged in business. As to political capital, Presiding Judge and Prosecutor, our *Formosa Magazine* in one month had a net income of a bit more than NT$1,000,000. If the money was more, there was still no place to use it! I told them to contact Japanese trading companies. If the government permitted fish fry to come in, then even if it was illegal, it became legal. Legal or illegal, the only question was whether the gov-

---

141   Ibid.
142   Ibid.
143   Ibid.

ernment would permit it. With respect to saying I wanted to negotiate with the government, politics has always been negotiations! When I was meeting in the Legislature I was negotiating. Because both sides did not understand, everyone needed to negotiate. When negotiating, if you know you are not correct, you can compromise. If you say negotiating with the government is overthrowing it, this is not correct. We wanted to make a mass movement, to expand political power. Politics has always been like this. We wanted to expand our political power to counter-attack the mainland. Is this breaking the law?[144]

Both of Huang's lawyers again argued against the case of the Prosecutor. The court adjourned for lunch about 12.20 PM.

When the court resumed at 2 PM, Lin Hung-hsuan presented his oral argument, which made two key points. The first related to the confessions and the records of the questioning in the Bureau of Investigation. Lin said that after his arrest on January 7, 1980, he was subject to fatigue interrogation for long periods of time. He said that he "lost his ability to defend himself and his ability to resist."[145]

The second point related to the indictment. Lin quoted a portion which stated that in August 1977 he had worked with several people in the United States in order to "overthrow the government" 推翻政府. Lin said these assertions were "only conjectures without proof" 推測而沒有證據. Lin also raised several other issues concerning the accuracy of the allegations in the indictment.[146]

One of Lin's lawyers, Lin Sheng-hsiung 李勝雄, then raised some "procedural" 程序 matters. He noted the defendant had received the indictment at 5 PM on January 20, but neither he nor his family was permitted to appoint a defense lawyer despite Article 73 of Military Justice Law 軍事審判法.[147] Furthermore, on January 22 there was a secret court investigation session. This was against the defendant's right to defense counsel. Li also noted that Article 53 of the same law requires all sessions of the Military Justice Court to be open unless matters of National Defense or the Reputation of the Military are involved.[148] Li noted that these provisions did not apply in this case.[149]

---

144   Ibid.
145   *Zhongguo shibao* 中國時報 [*China Times*], March 27, 1980, p. 4.
146   Ibid.
147   For the text of this article, see Tao Bai-chuan (editor) 陶百川（編）, *Zuixin liufa quanshu*, p. 562. Article 73 says, "After an indictment, the defendant must at any time appoint defence counsel" (被告於起訴後，得隨時選任辯護人).
148   Ibid., p. 561.
149   *Zhongguo shibao* 中國時報 [*China Times*], March 27, 1980, p. 4.

Li Sheng-hsiung said that the day after Lin's arrest on January 7, interrogations began. During this period, the defendant did not confess to any crime, yet on January 22 a confession of more than 6,000 characters suddenly appeared stating in detail his traitorous intentions and behavior. In looking for records of these interrogations, we lawyers have been unable to find any records from January 9th until January 22nd. Furthermore, when defense counsel finally saw the defendant on March 5th from 2.50 PM to 3.20 PM, he told us that he had been continuously interrogated for 70–80 hours a session. Only after the confession, starting on January 24 do we have any records of interrogation. Thus, the court may not use any evidence produced by such illegal means.[150]

Lin's second defense lawyer, Chang Chun-hsiung 張俊雄, also raised issues in defense of Lin Hung-hsuan. He noted, for example, that Lin had never joined any Taiwan Independence organization. The indictment provides no evidence that Lin had any "treasonous intentions" 叛亂意圖 to "overthrow the government" 顛覆政府.[151]

Following the statements of Lin's two lawyers, Lin's wife, Lin Li-ching 林黎琤, also made a tearful statement. Although life with Lin Hung-hsuan had been impoverished 清苦, they had not lacked anything because of their shared ideals 共同追求理想. Mrs Lin concluded, "I believe the government will impartially and fairly take all into account while passing judgment and will right a wrong and restore his innocence and allow him to obtain his freedom one day. His daughter, his old mother, his brothers and sisters will all be grateful for the government's honesty and justice and the concern of the judges in this case." After finishing, as Mrs Lin walked past her husband, she put out her hand and stroked his face, then she trembled and collapsed 深處洲祖模他的臉，然後搖搖欲墮.[152]

The Prosecutor then made a statement concentrating on a passage in a letter Lin Hung-hsuan had written to Chang Tsan-hung. According to the Prosecutor, this letter demonstrated the relationship between Lin and Chang was not "innocent" 單純.[153]

Lu Hsiu-lien was the next defendant to present an oral statement. As she did not have a prepared written statement, she spoke for about half an hour. Lu stated she wished to raise five points: (1) the indictment, (2) her activities overseas, (3) her relationship with the *Formosa Magazine*, (4) her relationship with the Kaohsiung Incident and (5) her speech on the day in Kaohsiung. Beginning

---

150 Ibid.
151 Ibid.
152 Ibid.
153 *Zhongguo shibao* 中國時報 [*China Times*], March 27, 1980, p. 2.

THE MILITARY TRIAL OF THE EIGHT KEY DEFENDANTS   77

with the indictment, Lu noted that, when she received the indictment on February 20, she knew nothing of many matters raised including Lin Hung-hsuan's supposed activities, the Hung Chih-liang case, the so-called preparation of wooden clubs and the "five-man committee." Yet, all of the defendants were accused of these actions.[154]

Lu spent some time discussing her speech in Kaohsiung. Originally, when Wang Tuoh introduced her, she refused to speak. She said she only spoke about how those listening and the security agencies were all our compatriots and then she got down from the platform. At the time there were many people calling for more speeches and some were shouting her name. So she hurriedly prepared an outline and went on the platform to speak. She talked about freedom of speech and about peace. She noted that in the past she had emphasized women's issues, but as international issues had come to the fore, she had paid attention to them. "However, Taiwan Independence has not influenced me. The quality of Taiwan Independence journals is too low." She noted that when studying at Harvard she was most influenced by November 1977 testimony of Professor Chiu Hungdah 丘宏達 to the United States Congress, where he argued if the United States and the Chinese Communists established diplomatic relations, the Republic of China had several options including declaring Taiwan independent, developing nuclear weapons and establishing relations with the Soviet Union. Lu noted that Professor Chiu had been her professor at National Taiwan University and was well known as "extremely loyal" 非常忠貞 to the government.[155]

Lu said that in the Bureau of Investigation people were labeled as "close to the Communists" 親共 or "opposed to the Communists" 反共. As I was opposed to the Communists, I was labeled as Taiwanese Independence. However, when I was overseas, I never once said "Taiwanese are not Chinese" 台灣人不是中國人. Lu also said that since the indictment she had been reading the Six Law Codes and raised several legal issues.[156]

Lu's lawyer, Lu Chuan-sheng 呂傳勝 also raised several legal points about confessions. He quoted the Article 156 of the Criminal Procedure Law,[157] which requires confessions to be taken through "upright" 正 and "legal" 法 means, otherwise they cannot be used as evidence. Furthermore, confessions cannot be the sole evidence for conviction.

---

154   Ibid.
155   Ibid.
156   Ibid.
157   For text, see Tao Bai-chuan (editor) 陶百川 (編), *Zuixin liufa quanshu*, p. 330.

Lu Chuan-sheng noted that after Lu Hsiu-lien was arrested on December 13, 1979, the record of her interrogation by the Prosecutor said, "I only participated in the commemoration ceremony. I only went with everyone else. I did not beat up security personnel and I did not participate in planning." She denied any criminal behavior. According to her lawyer, on January 22, 1980, forty days after her arrest, Lu Hsiu-lien suddenly wrote a confession and admitted to the complete list of criminal behaviors.[158]

Lu Chuang-sheng noted that fourteen defendants including Lu Hsiu-lien were sent to the Bureau of Investigation on December 15, 1979, three days after their arrests. They were returned to the military court's jurisdiction on February 8, 1980. Lu Hsiu-lien's confession was dated January 23, 1980, so it was prepared at the Bureau of Investigation. In addition, the indictment was put forward on January 19, 1980. Lu was appointed defense lawyer on January 21, 1980, but he was not notified that a court session was being held. This breaks Article 273 of the Criminal Procedure Law, which states the defense lawyer must be present at the first court session.[159] In addition, Article 168 of the Military Justice Code requires some further evidence in addition to a confession which demonstrate whether or not the charge corresponds with the facts.[160] In Lu's case, there is no evidence which demonstrates any correspondence to the facts.[161]

The court recessed at 5.43 PM.[162]

Day 8 of the Trial: Thursday, March 27, 1980

Day 8 of the trial was particularly long, beginning at 8.30 AM and continuing until 7.50 PM. The day focused on the oral arguments of Shih Ming-teh, Yao Chia-wen and Chang Chun-hung. The day began, however, with statements from Lin Hung-hsuan's two defense lawyers, Chang Chun-hsiung and Li Sheng-hsiung, as well as Lin Hung-hsuan himself, raising questions about the prosecution's evidence and logic.[163]

Shih Ming-teh stated that he wished to concentrate on two matters, the issues of treason and human rights. Shih began by saying that overthrow of the government 顛覆政府 was legal as one can overthrow the government through

---

158   *Zhongguo shibao* 中國時報 [*China Times*], March 27, 1980, p. 2.
159   For text, see Tao Bai-chuan (editor) 陶百川 (編), *Zuixin liufa quanshu*, p. 335.
160   For text see ibid., p. 567.
161   *Zhongguo shibao* 中國時報 [*China Times*], March 27, 1980, p. 2.
162   *Zhongguo shibao* 中國時報 [*China Times*], March 27, 1980, p. 3.
163   *Zhongguo shibao* 中國時報 [*China Times*], March 28, 1980, p. 2.

elections. "Since coming out of prison, I have written many things, but the Prosecutor has never said these are related to overthrowing [the government]. Because of this, when the indictment says I have the intention to be treasonous, it is completely without any factual basis ..."[164]

Shih went on to make another important claim. "The indictment again says the reason the defendant(s) established *Formosa Magazine* was to engage in Taiwan Independence, but this defendant must point out that this defendant has all along believed in the past thirty years that Taiwan has an independent status." Shih emphasized that Taiwan Independence was not a final status for Taiwan. After Shih finished, his defense lawyer, Yu Ching also made several legal points.[165]

After the court reconvened at 2.30 PM, two Prosecutors responded to Shih's oral argument. Most of the time was spent stating that Taiwan has not been independent for thirty years. The Prosecutor also stated that he has received a phone call from Dr Li Tchong-Koei 李鐘桂 denying that she had said "Taiwan's status is still undecided" 台灣地位未定論.[166]

Next, Yao Chia-wen made his oral statement. He noted that many people had told him that if he participated in *dangwai* political activities, sooner or later he would be arrested. Yao noted that he believed that as long as his political activity was within the law, he was safe. Now, he asked, what could he tell his wife and friends? Yao then raised several questions concerning the indictment's accusations. He noted that the confessions were neither impartial nor fair. When they were copied, very long sections were shortened and cut, some places totally lacked continuity and conclusions became facts. Concerning the Five-Man Committee, this was to study how to run the work of the Magazine, but in the indictment this became planning the seizure of power. Yao again said that the term Five-Man Committee was simply an abbreviation. In fact, usually only two or three people met at a time. Furthermore, the discussion was very disorganized. What the Prosecutor put in the indictment about the Five Principles was very different from what was in Yao's confession. The terms "principle of strength" 實力原則 and "brink of violence" 暴力邊緣 came from [John Foster] Dulles' 杜勒斯 term "The Brink of War" 戰爭邊緣. Yao conceded that he had made two conceptual errors in his analysis. First, he had been excessively afraid that the Kuomintang would surrender to the Communists.

---

164   Ibid.
165   Ibid.
166   *Zhongguo shibao* 中國時報 [*China Times*], March 28, 1980, p. 3.

Secondly, he was excessively concerned that the government would go a step further in implementing military rule.¹⁶⁷

Hsieh Chang-ting, Yao Chia-wen's defense lawyer, continued the oral argument. Hsieh raised some questions about the legitimacy of martial law. He also said that the indictment only discussed the "criminal intent" 犯罪意圖 of the defendant, but provided no evidence. The indictment does not emphasize facts nor does it emphasize evidence. It only emphasizes propaganda. The indictment mentions Yao Chia-wen's "treasonous thought" 叛國思想, but it uses several different words such as "treasonous consciousness" 叛國意識, "treasonous ideas" 叛國意念, and "treasonous intent" 叛國意圖. The indictment starts with ideas, then consciousness becomes intent. This is simply "writing cleverness" 文字技巧. Hsieh also discussed the concept of the "brink of violence" stating that it was not violence. The concept not only is not violent, it rejects the idea of violence.¹⁶⁸

At 5.05 PM, the court took a five-minute break after which Yao's second lawyer, Su Tseng-chang spoke. Su noted that the indictment claimed that Yao had shouted "charge" 衝 and "strike" 打, but that several witnesses had stated in their testimony that they did not hear Yao say any such things. The indictment simply ignored all such evidence.¹⁶⁹

Chang Chun-hung was the next defendant. He stated that the "long and short term plan to seize power" 長短程奪權計劃 was a central element of his confession, but Chang stated that this confession was not freely given. He only signed because he was threatened that his wife and younger sister could be charged because they were also at Kaohsiung. Because of this threat, he signed everything. Chang noted at Chungcheng Fourth Road that there was some smoke. Some people thought that tear gas had been used and people panicked. In such circumstances it was difficult to control the situation. Chang noted that he had consistently urged that Taiwanese and Mainlanders should be united and that he had consistently opposed violence. He noted that he had never used such language as "seizure of power" 奪權.¹⁷⁰

Kuo Chi-jen 郭吉仁, Chang Chun-hung's defense lawyer, then spoke. He raised the issues of the confession not being freely given and the use of the term "riot" 暴動 in the indictment. He asked what in Kaohsiung constituted a "riot"? Chang's second defense lawyer, Yu Ching, then also raised some issues. He wished to raise three issues which would take about 90 minutes, but it was

---

167   Ibid.
168   Ibid.
169   Ibid.
170   Ibid.

already almost 7.30 PM. At the request of the court, he summarized his points and presented written statements. He noted, for example, that "confessions which are not true cannot be used as evidence" 自白之非真實者固然沒有證據能力.

The day's session adjourned at 7.50 PM.

Day 9 of the Trial: Friday, March 28, 1980

The final day of the trial began at 8.30 AM when the lawyers for Chang Chun-hung continued to present their arguments from the previous day. Then two family members, Chang Chun-hung's eldest brother and his wife, Hsu Jung-shu 許榮淑, both made comments. Hsu noted that she had lived with Chang for over ten years and testified that he was a person in favor of "moderate reform" 溫和改革 and was always opposed to violence.[171]

Chen Chu was the seventh defendant to present oral arguments. She began by addressing the issue of the confessions and told the Presiding Judge that she had "a psychological pressure of fear" 心理上的恐懼壓力. Thus, when asked several days ago whether the confession was true, she had said it was. She felt the court has used the statement resulting from her "negative mentality" 消極心態 to the disadvantage of the other defendants. Now she wished to make clear that "My confession was most certainly not true" 我的自白並不真實. Chen's two lawyers also made several points.[172]

Lin I-hsiung, the final defendant to present his oral argument, spoke next. Lin noted that the prosecutor had said that the "witchcraft" 蠱惑 of Chang Chin-tse had influenced Lin, who thus had a "treasonous consciousness" 叛國意識. Lin responded, "But Chang Chin-tse, no matter in cultivation of personality or in learning ability, has not in the slightest way influenced me" 但張金策無論在人格修養、學識能力上沒有一點足以影響我. Lin also said that in all his years of studying law, he had never seen the two characters "witchcraft" 蠱惑 and he also said that he did not understand the "legal significance" 法律意義 of these two characters.[173]

When in the Department of Security 保安處, Lin said that he had repeatedly emphasized that he did not know that Huang Hsin-chieh had appointed a Five-Man Committee and, furthermore, that Huang Hsin-chieh did not have the standing to designate others into position. Furthermore, the so-called

---

171 *Zhongguo shibao* 中國時報 [*China Times*], March 29, 1980, p. 3.
172 Ibid.
173 Ibid.

Five-Man Committee never discussed any "long and short term plan to seize power" 長短程奪權計劃.[174]

On the night of the Kaohsiung Incident itself, Lin only accepted the invitation of Kang Ning-hsiang to go to Kaohsiung and settle the dispute 化解糾紛. But, when they arrived, the incident had already occurred and they were "powerless" 無能爲力. "In addition, I did not get on the podium and speak" 也沒有上台說話. These facts are clear. The indictment has been "negligent" 疏忽.[175]

Lin explained that during his forty days in the Department of Security, but before he was returned to the military court, he was forced to write a "letter of guarantee" 保證書 stating that he would not tell anyone about his interrogation in the Department of Security or else he would be "responsible" 負責. He asked the prosecutors and court to tell him for what he would be responsible as a result of such an illegal document?[176]

In the afternoon session, Lin's defense lawyer, Chiang Peng-chien, made several comments. Chiang noted calling the Kaohsiung Incident "treasonous" had caused him to laugh. For example, Yao Chia-wen's daughter cannot even speak Taiwanese, yet her father is actually considered a Taiwan Independence element 台獨份子. In the past several days, Chinese and foreigners have evaluated the Presiding Judge well saying the trial is open and fair. Chiang noted that he had still reserved his evaluation since a trial also includes the verdict.[177]

Chiang noted that some people distinguish between national security 國家安全 and individual security 個人安全 with national security having priority. But Chiang noted that in fact the two worked in tandem. If individual security suffered, then national security was also shaken 動搖. Peng Ming-min was a National Taiwan University professor of international law, one of Taiwan's ten most prestigious youths and a member of the delegation to the United Nations. Chang Chin-tse had been elected Township Executive 鄉長 of Chiao-hsi Township 礁溪鄉. Both of them knew many people. If just having some contact with them is evidence that one has treasonous intentions, then Mainlander compatriots living here must fear that they will be accused of dealings with the Bandits regime because of their relatives on the mainland.[178]

Chiang proceeded to criticize the process of the case. "Yesterday in his oral argument, Shih Ming-teh said, first arrest the criminals, then find the evidence. The prosecutor later responded that there is a reasonable doubt [about what

---

174 Ibid.
175 Ibid.
176 Ibid.
177 Ibid.
178 Ibid.

THE MILITARY TRIAL OF THE EIGHT KEY DEFENDANTS   83

Shih said]. The response of this defense lawyer is: This case is not only first arrest people and then find evidence. It is fundamentally a "set of interlocked rings". The accusations against the eight defendants have been put together. Because of this each individual has been dealt with in the same manner. In all cases, first have an interrogation and then have a confession. Because of this, this defense lawyer with respect to the so-called first arrest people and then find evidence also raises "reasonable doubts".[179]

While conceding that the Kaohsiung Incident trial has been a great improvement over the trial of Lei Chen in 1960, Chiang said there were still many things which he did not understand. The Prosecutor issued the indictment on the 19th, but it was only given to the defendants on the 20th. Why, before the defendants had an opportunity to choose defense lawyers, had the court already held its first investigation session on the 21st? How could the court determine whether or not the confessions were given through free will? Because of this situation, Chiang asked the Presiding Judge not to make the confessions, the records of interrogation and the first meeting of the court as the main criterion 準. Rather, you "must use facts and truth which have been discovered as the main evidence because this is after all a major case that concerns human lives!"[180]

The Presiding Judge asked Lin I-hsiung's wife, Fang Su-min, if she wished to speak, but she declined.[181] Then the Prosecutor stated that national law did not allow violence. The Presiding Judge responded that the judges had been under considerable pressure to be accountable to the prosecutors, the defense lawyers, the defendants and to society at large.[182]

The trial ended with final impact statements 最後陳訴. Huang Hsin-chieh denied the content of the confession, records of interrogation and the indictment which claimed he wanted to engage in Taiwan Independence and overthrow the government. Furthermore, he said, there was no evidence for this. Shih Ming-teh spoke at some length to explain why he had presented a laughing face in court. Until yesterday when Mrs Yao Chia-wen had testified, he had not been aware of the murder of Lin I-hsiung's mother and daughters. Now, of course, he cannot smile. Shih said, if it would help calm the resentment of the nation's people and if it would help unify the nation and create social harmony, he was quite willing for the Presiding Judge to sentence him to death. "I beg you! I beg you!" 我懇求！我懇求！ Defense lawyer Yu Ching then said, "Honorable Judge, please do not allow anyone to confuse you. Please

---

179   Ibid.
180   Ibid.
181   Ibid.
182   *Zhongguo shibao* 中國時報 [*China Times*], March 29, 1980, p. 2.

make a wise and farsighted judgment." According to the transcript in the *China Times*, "At this time many people in the front and the back of the court were sobbing" 此時，法庭前後多人出聲哭淚. The Presiding Judge called the court back to order.

At 5.10 PM, the court announced that it had completed hearing the evidence. Except for Lin I-hsiung, who continued to be released on bail, the defendants were retained in custody.

Question Time in the Taiwan Provincial Assembly and the Trial of Hung Chih-liang

On April 3, during question time at the Taiwan Provincial Assembly, Provincial Assemblyman Chou Tsang-yuan 周滄淵 asked, "Are Lin I-hsiung and Chang Chun-hung still members of the Taiwan Provincial Assembly? Why hasn't someone drawn committee assignments on their behalf? Their research expenses have also not been paid. This is not appropriate…" The Vice-Chairman of the Provincial Assembly, Wei Lun-chou 魏綸洲, who was presiding, explained that Lin and Chang had been arrested and could not exercise their duties as provincial assemblymen. Chou responded that both had still not been convicted, yet they could not have anyone draw their committee assignments on their behalf. However, severely ill provincial assembly persons have in the past been allowed to have people draw their committee assignments on their behalf.[183]

On April 3 the military court of the Taiwan Garrison Command announced it would begin the trial of Hung Chih-liang 洪誌良, the alleged conspirator whom Huang Hsin-chieh was supposed to have sent to China.[184] In fact, the military court trial of Hung Chih-liang was very short-lived. Hung pleaded guilty and the afternoon papers had the news. Hung testified that he had met with the Chinese official on the orders of Huang Hsin-chieh. Hung said that he only went into business to earn a bit of money and that he absolutely had no intent to overthrow the government.[185] Hung's admission of guilt at a public trial reinforced the guilt of Huang Hsin-chieh in the major military trial. Of

---

183 *Zhongguo shibao* 中國時報 [*China Times*], April 4, 1980, p. 3.
184 *Zhongguo shibao* 中國時報 [*China Times*], April 4, 1980, p. 3.
185 The most detailed report appears in *Zili wanbao* 自立晚報 [*Independence Evening Post*], April 11, 1980, p. 2. See also *China News*, April 11, 1980, p. 4; *Dahua wanbao* 大華晚報 [*Great China Evening News*], April 11, 1980, p. 3 and *Minzu wanbao* 民族晚報 [*Minzu Evening News*], April 11, 1980, p. 2. The newspapers the next morning also carried the story.

course, no evidence was provided that Hung had undergone a difficult "investigation." On May 9, 1980, the military announced that Hung Chih-liang had received a sentence of five years' imprisonment.[186]

The Verdict in the Military Trial

On April 18, 1980, three weeks after the conclusion of the trial, the judges in the military trial of the eight main Kaohsiung defendants delivered their verdict. Shih Ming-teh received a life sentence, Huang Hsin-chieh received a term of 14 years, while the remaining six defendants each received a term of 12 years. These were heavy sentences, especially in view of the evidence provided in the court, but at the time many feared that at least some of the defendants would be executed. In addition, all of the defendants' property, except that required to defray the living expenses of dependents, was confiscated.

The verdict itself was 24,000 Chinese characters and reprinted in full in Taiwan's Chinese-language newspapers.[187] In summary, the verdict was based on the "evidence" provided by the pre-trial interrogations and used in the preparation of the indictment. In other words, the verdict came directly from the indictment; it was as if no trial had taken place. The verdict makes reference upon reference to the pre-trial interrogation documents, but nowhere in the indictment is there a mention of the torture, the deprivation of sleep and the threats made against the defendants, all of which became clear during the trial. The fact that the pre-trial confessions were all denounced as not true by the defendants had no role in the verdict, though the second part of the verdict did briefly consider some of these issues like the confessions.

The *China Times*, which bravely printed the entire transcript of the trial, editorialized that "While maintaining legal discipline, [the court] clearly expressed leniency" 維持法紀, 表顯寬仁. [188] In the sense that none of the defendants was executed, this evaluation was correct. But the fact that the actual trial had little to do with the convictions, owed completely to the authoritarian political system then ruling Taiwan.

---

186   *Zhongguo shibao* 中國時報 [*China Times*], May 9, 1980, p. 3. The text of the verdict appears in *Zhongguo shibao* 中國時報 [*China Times*], May 10, 1980, p. 3.
187   *Zhongguo shibao* 中國時報 [*China Times*], April 19, 1980, p. 3; *Lianhebao* 聯合報 [*United Daily*], April 19, 1980, p. 3; *Zhongyang ribao* 中央日報 [*Central Daily News*], April 19, 1980, pp. 3, 6.
188   *Zhongguo shibao* 中國時報 [*China Times*], April 19, 1980, p. 2.

The famous reformer, Tao Pai-chuan 陶百川, who maintained access to President Chiang Ching-kuo,[189] made a much more pungent comment on the Kaohsiung trial the next day. Tao wrote: "Let us take the Kaohsiung Violent Incident as an example. Although this case has now entered the legal process, in its essence and intentions it is still a political incident comprising political opinions, political interests and political conflict…"[190] Of course, such perceptive comments were very rare in Taiwan's press at the time.

On April 28, 1980, the last day for an appeal, the eight defendants in the military trial filed an appeal. For two of the defendants, this had been done automatically because Huang Hsin-chieh had been a legislator while Shih Ming-teh had a life sentence. The appeal gave four main reasons for the verdict to be set aside. First, the appeal stated that the defendants should not have been tried in a military court. While the legal reasons were complex, basically the appeal said that the military court lacked jurisdiction over civilians who were not subject to military orders. Second, the main text of the verdict and the reasons for conviction had serious contradictions. Third, the facts, which the verdict accepts, are completely fabricated. This included such items as "the long and short-term plan to grasp power" and "to reach the objective of an independent Taiwan."[191] Finally, the verdict uses words from the confessions out of context. The appeal spends considerable space debunking the use of the confessions in the court's verdict. It also notes that the verdict starts with the defendants giving speeches and running a magazine, but then infers they were seditious.[192] The next day, the family members of the defendants also appealed to President Chiang Ching-kuo, requesting improvements in the conditions of their incarceration.[193]

The Kaohsiung Incident had two more important trials: the civil trial of thirty-three defendants and the military trial of those charged with concealing Shih Ming-teh from December 13, 1979 until his arrest on January 8, 1980. The next chapter discusses these two trials.

---

189   Tao's representations to Chiang Ching-kuo paved the way for the author to leave Taiwan after three months of "police protection" during this period. See memoirs in Part 2 below.
190   *Zhongguo shibao* 中國時報 [*China Times*], April 20, 1980, p. 2.
191   *Zhongguo shibao* 中國時報 [*China Times*], April 29, 1980, p. 3.
192   *Zhongguo shibao* 中國時報 [*China Times*], April 29, 1980, p. 5.
193   The full text appears in *Taiwan shibao* 臺灣時報 [*Taiwan Times*], April 30, 1980, p. 3.

CHAPTER 4

The Other Important Trials

In addition to the military trial of the eight key defendants and the rapid, related trial of Hung Chih-liang, the authoritarian regime conducted two other important trials. The first was a civil trial of 33 defendants, who were indicted for a variety of crimes including attacking the police, but were deemed not to have attempted overthrow of the government. The second trial, in a military court, judged whether Reverend Kao Chun-ming and nine other defendants were guilty of concealing Shih Ming-teh, who escaped arrest from December 13, 1979 until January 8, 1980. This chapter examines these two trials.

The Civil Trial of the 33 Defendants

Three days after the completion of the testimony in the Military Court trial, on March 31, 1980, the prosecutors issued an indictment for thirty-three more defendants. According to the indictment, none of the thirty-three defendants was aware that the demonstration was part of a plan to overthrow the government. This distinction enabled the authorities to try the case in a civil court rather than in a military court, a process which they hoped would give them some credibility with overseas governments and critics. According to a news report, an additional four persons were not indicted because there was insufficient proof of their crimes. One of the thirty-three was a juvenile less than eighteen years of age and his name was not completely released. Thus, the indictment named 32 persons, many of whom were already well-known—or would become well-known— in Taiwan's political and cultural circles.[1]

The indictment by the Taipei Municipal Procuracy is in three parts. The first part, "Facts of the Offenses" 犯罪事實, states that defendants all knew that the march in Kaohsiung on December 10, 1979 had not been approved and resulted in 183 security personnel and police being injured. This part of the indictment listed all thirty-three defendants, including the juvenile, briefly described their work, and outlined their purported crimes. The second part, "The Evidence" 證

---

[1] *Lianhebao* 聯合報 [*United Daily*], April 1, 1980, p. 1. The thirty-two names are: 周平德, 楊青矗, 邱茂男, 范政祐, 陳博文, 王拓, 張富忠, 陳仲信, 魏廷朝, 蘇振祥, 吳振明, 吳文賢, 許天賢, 蔡垂和, 傅耀坤, 邱明強, 戴振耀, 蔡有全, 紀萬生, 邱垂貞, 陳福來, 劉華明, 余阿興, 許淇潭, 鄭官明, 蔡精文, 劉泰和, 潘來長, 李長宗, 王滿慶, 陳慶智 and 李明憲.

據, asserted that Chou Ping-teh and five others participated in the demonstration, brought loudspeakers 擴音器, wore bright sashes 身被彩帶, and marched holding torches in their hands. In addition, they gathered to give speeches and loudly shouted slogans 高呼口號, one of which was "Kill the military police and the civilian police" 打死憲、警. Others defendants were accused of other actions. For example, Yang Ching-chu was accused of saying, "Taiwan's children must stand up and fight" 台灣的孩子起來打. According to the indictment, many of the statements were based on confessions given while in custody. "The Evidence" also asserted that the thirty-three defendants did not know of the plan to overthrow the government. Therefore, the Taiwan Garrison Command had found they were not guilty of sedition and sent the case to the Taipei Municipal Procuracy. The final part of the indictment, "The Transgressed Laws" 所犯法條, stated which legal provisions that defendants had purportedly violated.[2] According to an analysis in another newspaper, the maximum penalty according to these legal provisions was ten years imprisonment.[3]

The trial was held in two parts. The first part, held for three days during April 16–18, is referred to both as a "trial" (see the *China Post*), a 審理 or "trial" in the Chinese-language press, and as a "hearing" (see the *China News*). Later, this first part was also called an "investigation session." This first part received extensive coverage in Taiwan's press and is discussed here extensively. The second part, also referred to as a "trial" or as "a continuation of the trial" 再度開審,[4] was held during May 21–23, just as I was leaving Taiwan (see Part 2 below). As I did not have access to Taiwan's Chinese-language press at the time, I have resorted to using the *China Post's* International Air-Mail Edition for the second part of the civil trial.

The civil trial began in the Taipei District Court 台北地方法院 at 9.00 AM on April 16 with the first group of ten defendants brought into court handcuffed in pairs.[5] The day began with the defense lawyers requesting the Presiding Judge, Tsai Hsiu-hsiung 蔡秀雄, to recuse himself since he had been a KMT candidate in the central parliamentary elections in which some of the defendants had also been candidates. After about ten minutes of such procedural issues, Chou

---

2　The full text of the indictment appears in ibid., p. 3.
3　*Zili wanbao* 自立晚報 [*Independence Evening Post*], April 1, 1980, p. 2.
4　*Zili wanbao* 自立晚報 [*Independence Evening Post*], May 21, 1980, p. 2.
5　For pictures of the defendants handcuffed, see *China News*, April 16, 1980, p. 4; *Dahua wanbao* 大華晚報 [*Great China Evening News*], April 16, 1980, p. 3 and *Minzu wanbao* 民族晚報 [*Minzu Evening News*], April 16, 1980, p. 2. The afternoon papers of April 16 had news of the morning session of April 16, while the morning newspapers of April 17 had full coverage of the trial on April 16. I have used the *Zhongguo shibao* 中國時報 [*China Times*] reports as they have the most information as well as extensive quotations from the court proceedings.

THE OTHER IMPORTANT TRIALS 89

Ping-teh 周平德, the first defendant was brought forth and the remaining nine defendants were removed.⁶

According to a witness, someone said that if you hit a military policeman on the head with a club, his helmet would protect him and it would not hurt. According to the witness, Chou responded that you should hit him on the body. Chou denied that such a discussion had taken place.⁷

About 10.50 AM, the trial moved to the second defendant, Chen Po-wen 陳博文. In his testimony, Chen Po-wen said, "When arrested on December 16, I was taken by the investigators to an unknown place. Mentally, I was suffering from torture. The confession was copied; it was not true."⁸

The third defendant, Yang Ching-chu 楊青矗, was called about 11.40 AM. Yang noted that he was Chairman of the Kaohsiung Office of the *Formosa Magazine* in name only 掛名主任. A Kaohsiung person, he was employed during the day at low wages and in the evening at home he had a western clothes shop. In addition he liked writing. He noted that he had not been sent from Taipei and that Shih Ming-teh had sent Lin Hung-hsuan as General Manager with Chen Chu as his deputy. Thus, he was unaware of the demonstration on Human Rights Day and he had not participated in the planning. On December 10 he had been at work all day and only got to the demonstration at 8 PM. He also noted that Chen Chu had originally asked him to speak for ten minutes on the labor movement, but he said that at 8 PM the atmosphere did not seem right and he twice rejected Wang Tuoh's invitations to speak.

The presiding judge asked Yang if he knew that the demonstration had not received permission. Yang responded, "In the past all activities did not have permission. After discussions with the security agencies, they all received permission on the last day."⁹

In describing himself, Yang said he was the first worker-writer in 5,000 years of Chinese history. He also said he did not have a narrow conception of provincialism and that many of his friends were Mainlanders and even his sister's husband was a Mainlander. One of Yang's defense attorney's, Chiang Peng-chien 江鵬堅, noted that Yang had saved a military policeman, who either had given a statement or written to the court. Chiang asked the court to identify the military policeman.¹⁰

---

6   *Zhongguo shibao* 中國時報 [*China Times*], April 17, 1980, p. 3.
7   Ibid.
8   Ibid.
9   Ibid.
10 Ibid.

At 2 PM the afternoon session of the trial began with defendant Chiu Mao-nan 邱茂男, the director of the Pingtung County office of the *Formosa Magazine*. Chiu testified that he had not hired some named individuals. He did participate in the World Human Rights Day demonstration on December 10, but "he did not speak, he did not have the power to direct other people. This is what the investigative people wanted me to write, but it is not the truth."[11] He also denied yelling slogans.

Fan Cheng-yu 范政祐 appeared next. He responded that much of the record made in Taiwan Garrison Command was not true, but Fan said that in the military procuracy he did not dare offend them 得罪; otherwise he would be charged with subversion. He felt that the district court was the appropriate place to say this.

Wang Tuoh 王拓 was called to the court at 3.12 PM. The judge asked if he knew the demonstration had not received permission. Wang replied that Huang Hsin-chieh had obtained permission from the Commander of the Taiwan Garrison Command's Southern District at 6.30 PM. Wang said that before 6.30 PM he felt quite concerned, but afterwards felt quite relaxed. Asked if he had seen torches and wooden sticks, Wang answered that he had, but that he did not believe anyone wished to engage in violence. Wang stated that he believed, "Excessively radical action was not favorable to the *dangwai* and that it was also not favorable to the development of Taiwan's democratic politics."[12]

The Court asked Wang if he had the power to order violence? Wang replied that he was master of ceremonies 司儀 from 7 PM to 8.35 PM. This position had two roles: to introduce speakers briefly and to explain instructions to the crowd simply. This was not a position of being responsible for giving orders and during this period he gave no orders to anyone. Wang declared that he did not give a speech that night and denied the statement in the indictment that he had "made an agitating speech."[13]

Wang stated that the Taiwan Garrison Command had recorded every word he made as Master of Ceremonies. Furthermore, when he returned to the *Formosa Magazine* Office, he had gotten on a truck and spoken loudly, saying, "Everyone, don't hit [anyone], [they] are all our own brothers."[14]

Wang Tuoh made a point that I have made elsewhere, that the violence arose when the riot suppression vehicles let off some white-colored smoke and

11 Ibid.
12 Ibid.
13 Ibid.
14 Ibid.

people said it was gas. Also, violence only began when small numbers of riot suppression vehicles and crowd control police entered among the crowds.

At 4.42 PM the court began its cross-examination of Chang Fu-chung 張富忠, who said he was responsible for taking photographs. Chang said he took four rolls of film, all of which the Taiwan Garrison Command had confiscated. At 5.12 PM the court began its cross-examination of Chen Chung-hsin 陳仲信, the last defendant called on the first day of the trial. Chen stated that he felt that, unless the Ku-shan Incident was properly handled, a more intense opposition might appear.

On the second day of the trial, the day's first defendant, Wu Chen-ming 吳振明, raised the "old question" of torture. Wu asserted that his genitals had been tortured and showed his bloody pants as proof. According to a senior justice official with several decades of experience, as soon as a case involved national security, the methods for dealing with the case changed. "National Security was first. Sacrificing a few people for national security was permitted."[15]

Wu Chen-ming was a taxi driver. He had no relationship with the *Formosa Magazine* and denied carrying a torch. Wu said that he had been beaten for an hour and was sent to the Southern Headquarters of the Taiwan Garrison Command where he asked for treatment of his injuries, which was denied. On December 13th he was send to Bureau of Investigation in Taipei, where he was treated well. He continuously denied that he had thrown bamboo sticks at military police. He was subjected to ten rounds of rotating questioning, taken to a basement and frightened to such an extent that he tried to commit suicide. He was in despair and had lost hope and cried. Then he underwent another three or four days of interrogation. They asked him to sign and place his seal on records of interview in which he admitted that he had yelled out slogans and held a torch. He was very frightened and a Bureau of Investigation person said that he would be thrown into the sea if he did not admit his guilt. Wu stated that his confession was completed under conditions of compulsion.[16]

At 9.48 AM, the court began to question the second defendant of the day, Wu Wen-hsien 吳文賢. Wu stated that he had not been allowed to see his record of interrogation and that most of the record was not in accord with the facts. Wu also denied the statement of a witness that he had attacked a military policemen with a torch and rocks.

At 10.15 AM, Hsu Tien-hsien 許天賢, a Christian missionary who also worked in the Tainan office of *Formosa Magazine*, was called. He was arrested on

---

15   This paragraph is based on a special article about torture in this case: *Zili wanbao* 自立晚報 [*Independence Evening Post*], April 18, 1980, p. 2.
16   *Zhongguo shibao* 中國時報 [*China Times*], April 18, 1980, p. 3.

December 23, just before Christmas and was in the midst of preparing for Christmas celebrations. When arrested, the police said he could return as soon as he signed a confession. The police wanted him to admit he had assaulted a military policeman and, if he did not, he would be sent to the Taiwan Garrison Command. In addition, the police said those who admitted their crimes would be treated lightly and released. So, in order to have his Christmas celebrations and to be with his daughter, he signed the confession. He did not expect that after signing he would be sent to the Southern Headquarters of the Taiwan Garrison Command, fed on salted rice, and have his ankles fettered. He asked to see the accusing witness and noted that witnesses who made accusations had been taken on trips.[17]

Tsai Chui-ho 蔡垂和, called at 10.45 AM, denied the statement in his record of interrogation that he had said that the violent demonstration was planned. While admitting he carried a torch, he denied that he had been a leader of the demonstration.[18]

Tai Chen-yao 戴振耀 was called at 11.10 AM. Although he had admitted hitting a military policeman, he denied actually hitting one and in fact had been hit by a military policeman.[19] The final defendant in the morning session, Fu Yao-kun 傅耀坤, was a 47-year old taxi driver who could not speak much Mandarin and who answered questions in Taiwanese. Fu had taken one of the other defendants to the demonstration.[20]

The interrogation of the first defendant in the afternoon session, Chiu Ming-chiang 邱明強, began at 1.30 PM. The indictment said that Chiu "participated in the violent demonstration and beat a military policeman with a torch."[21] Chiu denied that he had even gone to Kaohsiung and denied the accusations in the indictment. Chiu's defense lawyer brought in a witness who had known Chiu for years and testified that they had been together in Pingtung on December 10.[22]

At 1.52 PM the court called Tsai Yu-chuan 蔡有全, who also stated that many things in the record of interrogation were not factual. He denied inciting the demonstators, denied any disputes with the police and denied beating a military policeman.[23]

---

17   Ibid.
18   Ibid.
19   Ibid.
20   Ibid.
21   Ibid.
22   Ibid.
23   Ibid.

Chi Wan-sheng 紀萬生 came to the stand at 2.57 PM and said that he came to Kaohsiung with his wife on a trip, not knowing about the Kaohsiung demonstration. He went to the Kaohsiung Office of the *Formosa Magazine* at 9.30 PM, so he was not present when the violence occurred. He requested that the court not believe the records of interview from the Taiwan Garrison Command.[24]

At 3.33 PM, the court called Yu A-hsing 余阿興, the final defendant of the second day of the trial. Yu denied that that he worked in the Tainan office of *Formosa Magazine*. Yu also said that his Mandarin was not good and requested to speak in Taiwanese. The court arranged an interpreter. When shown photographs, Yu asked if he was arrested because the police had seen him in photographs and the audience tittered. Yu also denied beating a military policeman. The day's session finished at 4.20 PM and the defendants remained in custody.[25]

On the third and final day of the first part of the civil trial, the last fifteen of the thirty-three defendants appeared before the court with ten defendants in the morning and another five in the afternoon. In addition, two military policemen, who were injured during the Kaohsiung demonstration, also testified.[26]

The first defendant on the third day, Hsu Chi-tan 許淇潭, testified that he had not gone to participate in the demonstration, but only to look for a friend. The court said that from photographs it looked like Hsu had held the microphone and stood near Huang Hsin-chieh and Wang Tuoh. He said he had used the microphone to find his friend. Hsu denied standing behind Yao Chia-wen when Yao gave a speech. Hsu replied, "When the military prosecutors asked me this, I had nothing to say. They punished me by making me half-squat, half-kneel."[27]

At 9.15 AM, the court called the next defendant, Cheng Kuan-ming 鄭官明. Cheng denied participating in the demonstration and said he was at least 100 meters from the *Formosa Magazine* office. The court asked why he had confessed to belonging to *Formosa Magazine* and shouting slogans. Cheng replied, "There, I was coerced to write [that]. I was not allowed to look at the records [of interrogation.]"[28] Cheng also said that he saved an injured military policeman, but when a defense lawyer offered to show evidence to the court, the

---

24 Ibid.
25 Ibid.
26 *Zhongguo shibao* 中國時報 [*China Times*], April 19, 1980, p. 4.
27 Ibid.
28 Ibid.

judge said that it was not necessary. In his article on the trial, the reporter noted that "the court's questioning proceeded very quickly" 庭訊進行的很快.[29]

The third defendant, Tsai Ching-wen 蔡精文, appeared at 9.40 AM. Tsai also denied participating in the Kaohsiung demonstration and said he was only trying to find a colleague who was lost. Tsai said the police arrested him, beat him and told him that he was helping Chou Ping-teh's election campaign. They wanted him to admit this and sent him to the Southern Taiwan Garrison Command. He was returned to the police who did not make records of interrogation, but who beat him and told him that if he did not cooperate, he was the enemy. They said they would hit his ears and break his ear drums and make him deaf. Only after he confessed were his shackles removed. He used the word "torture" 刑求.[30]

The next defendant, Liu Tai-ho 劉泰和, also denied participating in the demonstration and said he was only looking for his younger brother. Liu denied the testimony of a witness, who said he saw Liu, stating that the alleged witness was much too far away.[31]

Pan Lai-chang 潘來長 testified next. He admitted wearing a red banner, which said "World Human Rights Day Commemorative Meeting."[32]

Wang Man-ching 王滿慶 testified next, denying that he worked for the *Formosa Magazine*. He had attended one of their meetings and had met Chen Chu. She asked him if he could charge a bit less as a driver that evening and that is how he was at the *Formosa Magazine* office. He said that he had picked up a wooden club in self-defense after being beaten, but he denied hitting a military policeman.[33]

At 10.55 AM, the court called Li Chang-tsung 李長宗. He denied that he had carried a club and said that his confession, which was not true, was the result of torture.[34] Chen Ching-chih 陳慶智 then followed. He stated that he wore an armband 臂章 proclaiming human rights for only an hour.[35] Li Ming-hsien 李明憲 stated that in the military prosecutors office he had written as instructed and that it was not in accord with his own wishes.

The juvenile defendant, Hung X-fa 洪 X 發, was the only defendant to admit guilt. He said he had been pushed into a military policeman. The military

---

29 Ibid.
30 Ibid.
31 Ibid.
32 Ibid.
33 Ibid.
34 Ibid.
35 Ibid.

policeman had hit him, so he threw a cobblestone 鵝卵石 at the military policeman. Altogether he threw three stones at the military policeman, but none hit.[36]

In the afternoon, Wei Ting-chao 魏廷朝, one of the most famous defendants, was called first. Wei had been an assistant to Peng Ming-min 彭明敏 and helped him publish the famous "Declaration of Formosans" in 1964. Wei was sentenced the next year to eight years in prison. In 1971, Wei received another twelve years for "sedition," so Wei had spent considerable time in prison for political "crimes." In his testimony, Wei said that he had worked at the *Formosa Magazine* only to run a magazine and not for activities. In response to the court's question about records of interrogation taken by the military prosecutor, Wei answered, "I only remember that none of the records of interrogation made by the military prosecutors came from free opinions. Because of this, I simply never looked at the records and just signed them."[37]

Chiu Chui-chen 邱垂貞 began his testimony about 2.12 PM. Chiu had been invited to sing some of his folksongs and had prepared these. If he had been preparing for violence, why would he bring folksongs? He also denied yelling out "strike" 打 or carrying a torch. The judge asked about the records of interrogation and whether Chiu would like to see them? Chiu responded, "I don't need to see the records of interrogation. They are all forced confessions gathered under improper circumstances." Furthermore, he was not allowed to sleep for 45 days. Chiu said that the interrogators told him all he had to do was to sign and then he would have a lighter sentence and could return home by Lunar New Year. Chiu said that he did note hate his interrogators; he only wanted to tell the judge the circumstances of the records of interrogation. Chiu said that after he signed the records of interrogation that the interrogators gave him fruit, bought him snacks at night and let him read magazines. When asked about a witness who said that Chiu had broken a torch hitting a military policeman, Chiu said that the witness was lying and asked to cross-examine him.[38]

At 2.43 PM, Su Chen-hsiang 蘇振祥, who was accused of throwing rocks and dirt clods at military police, was called. Su said that his wife was working in a telecommunications office near the Circle and he went to pick her up about 10.20 PM. As they were leaving, a riot control vehicle sent out gas. As she was nine months pregnant, he told his wife to return to her office and he went to an island in the circle. Because of the gas, he was very angry and threw two clods of dirt. As he was about 100 meters from the riot control vehicles and 60–70

---

36 Ibid.
37 Ibid.
38 Ibid.

meters from the *Formosa Magazine* speech platform, neither of the clods hit anyone. Furthermore, he could not hear any of the speeches. At about 10.40, as he was going to get his wife, he was arrested. During the interrogations they constantly wanted him to say that he heard the speeches and that the speeches had incited him to throw rocks to attack the military police. In addition, they used torture 刑求. Two military police witnesses gave testimony which identified Su as the person who threw stones at military police. One of the witnesses said that Su was arrested an hour later and Su's defense lawyer asked the court to investigate and find out the actual time Su was arrested.[39]

Chen Fu-lai 陳福來, a janitor in the Kaohsiung office of the *Formosa Magazine*, was called at 3.39 PM. Chen stated that Shih Ming-teh had asked him to buy wooden sticks to make banners. He was not asked to buy torches and he did not stand on the leaders' car, though he did have some responsibility for the public address equipment. After the teargas was released, everyone ran in different directions and he returned alone to the office. He did not march with others. Asked by the court about the records of interrogation, Chen said that after he was arrested, the police beat him. In the Southern Taiwan Garrison Command and at the Bureau of Investigation, he was tortured. So, ultimately he wrote what they told him to write.[40]

Finally, at 4.16 PM, the final defendant, Liu Hua-ming 劉華明 was called. Liu said that he had marched and carried a torch, but denied carrying a wooden club or yelling "strike" 打. Liu also stated that the records of interrogation taken at the Taiwan Garrison Command had no truth and asked the court to investigate this. Asked about the interrogations, Liu said that he was tortured and also told that if he signed a confession, he could be bailed out of prison, but if he retracted his confession he could be charged with forgery.[41] The first part of the trial ended at 4.40 PM on the third day.[42]

As noted earlier, the trial continued for three days during May 21 to May 23. On the first day, sixteen defendants testified. Much of the ground seems similar to that of the first part of the trial. Yang Ching-chu denied shouting a slogan and denied speaking to the crowd or holding a microphone. A witness, Wu Wen-hsien, stated that he could not remember clearly and that his confession was made when he was extremely tired during the police interrogation. All of the defendants denied assaulting security personnel themselves or instigating

---

39 Ibid.
40 Ibid.
41 Ibid.
42 Ibid.

others to assault security personnel. They also stated that their "confessions" were not made of their own free will.[43]

On the second day, seventeen defendants testified. Chiu Ming-chiang stated that he remained home and, later, he was acquitted. Most of the defendants stated that their confessions were not made of their own free will. Most also denied attacking security personnel.[44]

The final court session lasted from 8.30 AM to 7.50 PM. Chou Ping-teh asserted that the accusations in the indictment were "invented" and he stated that the government should be held responsible because it had not drawn a clear-cut line between what was legal and what was not. The prosecutor replied that Chou statement was merely an excuse "because he should at least be aware that he was obstructing the police in performance of their duties then." Many defendants denied instigating the demonstrations and attacking the police. The prosecutors requested leniency for the juvenile, Hung X-fa, as he was too young to discern between right and wrong. The prosecutors also refuted the accusations of some defendants that they were tortured during the investigation, saying that all confessions and statements of the defendants were made of their own free will.[45]

Ten days later, the three judges issued their verdict on June 2, 1980. As noted earlier, one defendant, Chiu Ming-chiang, was acquitted. The other 31 adult defendants received sentences ranging from six years and eight months to ten months. The juvenile received a sentence of one year plus six months, though this appears to have been suspended. The sentences together with the names of the thirty-one adult defendants follow:

- Six years and eight months: Chen Po-wen.
- Six years and six months: Fan Cheng-yu.
- Six years: Chou Ping-teh, Yang Ching-chu, Chiu Mao-nan, Wang Tuoh, and Wei Ting-chao.
- Five years: Su Chen-hsiang, Wu Chen-ming, Wu Wen-hsien, Hsu Tien-hsien, Tsai Yu-chuan, Chi Wan-sheng, Chiu Chui-chen, Liu Hua-ming, and Yu A-hsing.
- Four years: Chang Fu-chung, Chen Chung-hsin, Tsai Chui-ho, Fu Yao-kun, Tai Chen-yao, and Chen Fu-lai.
- One year and five months: Pan Lai-chang.
- One year and four months: Li Chang-tsung.

---

43   *China Post* (International Air-Mail Edition), May 22, 1980, p. 1.
44   *China Post* (International Air-Mail Edition), May 23, 1980, p. 1.
45   *China Post* (International Air-Mail Edition), May 24, 1980, p. 1.

- One year and two months: Wang Man-ching and Chen Ching-chih
- Ten months: Hsu Chi-tan, Cheng Kuan-ming,, Tsai Ching-wen, Liu Tai-ho, and Li Ming-hsien.

In addition, all guilty defendants also lost their civil rights for an additional period of up to five years.[46]

The Military Trial of Reverend Kao Chun-ming and Nine Others for Concealing Shih Ming-teh

On April 24, 1980, the Reverend Kao Chun-ming 高俊明, the Executive Secretary of the Presbyterian Church, along with eight others, was arrested for hiding Shih Ming-teh.[47] On April 29 the military prosecutors indicted ten persons including Reverend Kao for the two crimes of "concealing traitors" 藏匿叛徒 and "knowing a bandit spy and not making a report" 明知匪諜而不告密檢舉. All ten of those indicted were members of the Presbyterian Church and, interestingly, the military prosecutor asked the military court to reduce their sentences.[48]

Kao and his fellow defendants had a one-day hearing on May 8 to examine the evidence in a military court at the Taiwan Garrison Command. Reporters were not allowed, so the press reports were relatively short. The hearing lasted from 9 AM until 4.50 PM and, according to reports, defendants were allowed to cross-examine witnesses. Shih Ming-teh testified that he was not a "traitor" 叛徒 and therefore the defendants should not be tried in a military court.[49]

Revered Kao and his fellow nine defendants had a very long one-day trial on May 16, which lasted from 8.30 AM until 8.50 PM with an hour's break at noon. The trial was open to the press. Lin Shu-chih 林樹枝, the first defendant called, said that at 6 or 7 in the morning on December 13, Shih Ming-teh went to his house in Taipei and asked Lin to hide him, which Lin did in his house. That night, Lin and Chao Chen-erh 趙振貳 took Shih to Wu Wen's 吳文 house in the Taipei suburb of Shih-pai 石牌. At that time, Lin said that he did not know that

---

46   *China Post* (International Air-Mail Edition), June 3, 1980, p. 1.
47   *Zhongguo shibao* 中國時報 [*China Times*], April 25, 1980, p. 3; *Lianhebao* 聯合報 [*United Daily*], April 25, 1980, p. 3.
48   *Lianhebao* 聯合報 [*United Daily*], April 30, 1980, p. 3. This article includes the full text of the indictment. The indictment is also available at *Zhongguo shibao* 中國時報 [*China Times*], April 30, 1980, p. 3.
49   *Zhongguo shibao* 中國時報 [*China Times*], May 9, 1980, p. 3.

Shih was wanted for sedition and only learned this the next day at noon when he read a newspaper.⁵⁰

Chao Chen-erh testified that during the evening of December 13, Lin Shu-chih had called him on the telephone twice and arranged to meet him personally. It was only then that he saw Shih Ming-teh. Chao said that he refused to hide Shih, but because "his heart could not endure" 心生不忍, he called Wu Wen and asked to meet him. Then Lin and Chao took Shih to Wu Wen's house. The next day, when Chao went to see Shih, Shih asked him to speak to Reverend Kao Chun-ming and ask him to use the church and powerful people in America to urge the government to release those detained because of the Kaohsiung Incident. Kao had replied, "We'll see." On the third day, the 15th, they told Shih that Lin Wen-chen 林文珍 was willing to receive Shih. That night, Chao and Wu Wen got Huang Chao-hui 黃昭輝 to drive them and Lin to Lin Wen-chen's house on Dunhua South Road. Chao believed that Shih was not seditious and he helped because he was sympathetic.⁵¹

Wu Wen testified that he saw Shih Ming-teh about 10 PM on December 13 with Lin and Chao. Chao said that his house could not hide Shih and asked Wu to hide him for one night. Wu, despite contradictions in his mind, agreed. On the second day, when Wu learned that Shih was wanted, he asked Shih to leave. Chao, Lin and Huang took Shih to someplace near Lin Wen-chen's house. Wu Wen said on the night of December 16, Shih asked him to call a Mr Cheng 鄭 to get the number of Hsu Ching-fu 許晴富. Mr Hsu was unwilling to have Shih live at his place because a female servant might not be reliable, but Mr Hsu was willing to see Shih. According to Wu Wen, Shih and Hsu seemed very close and on December 28 Hsu agreed to hide Shih. That night Hsu drove Shih to his house. (Hsu had dismissed the female servant). Wu emphasized that his feelings were quite complex, but that subjectively he did not believe that Shih Ming-teh was a seditious criminal who advocated the use of violence.⁵²

The fourth defendant questioned was Reverend Kao Chun-ming, the Executive Secretary of the Presbyterian Church in Taiwan. Kao said that he had asked Lin Wen-chen to consider Shih's living place and said that her behavior was in Christian love 愛心 and compassion 同情心. Kao said that he had had no interaction with Shih. Last December Chao Chen-erh had asked Kao to help arrange a place for Lin Hung-hsuan 林弘宣, Tsai Yu-chuan 蔡有全 and Shih Ming-teh to stay. Kao felt surprised by the request to help Shih, but he promised owing to his Christian love and compassion. Lin Wen-chen had a place in

---

50   *Zhongguo shibao* 中國時報 [*China Times*], May 17, 1980, p. 3.
51   Ibid.
52   Ibid.

Ilan that could be used. Kao said it could be dangerous, but Lin agreed to help. It was only on approximately December 17 that Kao learned that Shih was living near Lin's place in Taipei. The judge asked Kao why he didn't put Shih in his own house and Kao replied that his house was very unsafe because it was observed twenty-four hours a day. The judge also asked if Kao had seen the television and newspaper reports stating that Shih was wanted for sedition, but Kao replied that he was very busy and had not seen these reports. Kao also noted that he observed several teachings in the Bible such as "respect life" 尊重生命 and "love those in great distress" 愛困苦的人. On the basis of these beliefs, Kao stated, "I decided to sacrifice myself and not betray Shih Ming-teh." Kao said that he did not remember being asked to seek help from the American church or from Congressmen.[53]

Lin Wen-chen admitted that she had hidden Shih in her house for thirteen days, from December 15 to December 28, but it was only when she was incarcerated in the Department of Security that she knew that Shih was a seditious criminal. She said that on December 14 at 2 PM Chao Chen-erh had contacted her and asked her to save Shih Ming-teh's life. She replied that she would go back and pray and then call him back. At 7 PM she agreed to take Shih. On December 18 she had seen on television that Shih was wanted and tried to arrange a new place for Shih to hide, but this did not happen until December 28 when Wu Wen and Mr and Mrs Hsu Ching-fu came to pick Shih up. Lin said that she had asked Shih what would happen if he gave himself up. Shih replied he would receive the death penalty because he had a prior conviction and had run the Human Rights Day rally.[54]

Chang Wen-ying 張文鷹, a dentist, admitted that she had operated on Shih to fix false teeth, but she denied that she had operated to change his appearance. Furthermore, before the Kaohsiung Incident, Shih had been to see her before to fix his false teeth. She noted that she had operated in accord with the regulations of dentists to help those in need. The judge asked if Shih had requested a change of appearance and Chang replied that he had, but that she had only fixed his false teeth. The judge asked why Chang had cut his eyelids. Chang replied that Shih had not eaten for several days and that severing the eyelids was to induce Shih to eat. The operation was carried out at Hsu's house. Shih had insisted on fixing his false teeth, otherwise he would not be able to eat in prison. Chang said that she was present when Shih was arrested on January 8. She was not arrested and called the Bureau of Investigation to surrender.[55]

---

53   Ibid.
54   Ibid.
55   Ibid.

The first defendant to testify in the afternoon was Shih Jui-yun 施瑞雲, Reverend Kao's secretary. When Lin Hung-hsuan and Tsai Yu-chuan rang Rev. Kao, he was not in and she took the call. She later did not hear their conversation. The next defendant was Huang Chao-hui 黃昭輝, who drove the car on December 15 with Chao Chen-erh to get Shih Ming-teh. When Shih got in the car, Huang only drove the car and did not speak to Shih. In response to a question from the judge, Huang said at the time he did not know Shih was wanted and he only learned that later.[56]

Hsu Ching-fu 許晴富 was called next. Shih lived in Hsu's house from December 28 until his arrest on January 8. Originally, Hsu's wife opposed Shih's coming to their house. But Hsu dismissed their servant and took his wife to see Shih under the pretext of going to see the doctor. In answer to a query from the judge, Hsu said that he had been very busy with his film and that he did not know that Shih was wanted for sedition. He took Shih because his family and the Shih family had known each other well for over twenty years. Mrs Hsu, Chiang Chin-ying 江金櫻, the last defendant called, stated that she was opposed to Shih's coming to their house, but that she could not reject Shih after he personally asked her for help.[57]

At 4.05 PM the court moved to cross-examination. Reverend Kao noted that the indictment listed Lin Wen-chen as a principal main offender 共同正犯, but Kao noted that Lin had become involved only because Kao had contacted her. Kao expressed willingness to bear the entire punishments of Lin Wen-chen and Shih Jui-yun. He also expressed respect for all of the other defendants and hoped Taiwan's 17 million people would have democratic rule of law, freedom and contribute towards world peace. Lin Wen-chen stated that she did not believe religious love 宗教愛心 would be perceived as the public enemy of the people 人民公敵. Huang Chao-hui stated that he had been "insulted" 侮辱 while questioned in the Department of Security so that parts of his confession and records of interrogation were not true. The trial ended at 8.50 PM.[58]

Twenty days later, on June 5, 1980, the military court announced its verdict. All of the defendants were found guilty with Revend Kao Chun-ming and Hsu Ching-fu receiving sentences of seven years each and Lin Wen-chen a five-year prison term. The other seven defendants all received two-year prison terms, though four may have had their sentences suspended and three—Chao Chen-erh, Huang Chao-hui and Shih Jui-yun—were apparently released on bail

---

56   Ibid.
57   Ibid.
58   Ibid.

following the judgment. At least five of the defendants also lost their civil rights for an additional period.[59]

With the trial verdicts, the defendants began their long terms in incarceration despite the trials failing to prove guilt except in the trial of Reverend Kao and his fellow defendants. The next chapter considers how the Kaohsiung Incident contributed to Taiwan's eventual democratization.

---

59   *China Post* (International Air-Mail Edition), June 6, 1980, p. 1. *The New York Times*, June 6, 1980, p. 5, in a report from Reuters, lists the sentences of five of the defendants.

CHAPTER 5

How the Kaohsiung Incident Contributed to Taiwan's Democratic Movement

With the sentencing of the defendants to long prison terms, Taiwan's authoritarian regime appeared victorious. Taiwan then underwent at least three years of quite conservative and repressive rule under President Chiang Ching-kuo as well as General Wang Sheng 王昇, the director of the Political Warfare Department (the political commissars) in Taiwan's military and a close confidant of Chiang Ching-kuo dating back to 1939 when Wang worked under Chiang Ching-kuo in Jiangxi 江西 Province. Wang became particularly important at the Fourth Plenum of the KMT's Eleventh Central Committee, which met at the very time of the Kaohsiung Incident and the arrests, and remained very powerful until Chiang Ching-kuo believed he was setting up an alternative power center in the KMT. Wang finally lost power when he was exiled as ambassador to Paraguay on September 20, 1983.[1]

Taiwan's government had hoped that the opening of its trials to public scrutiny would demonstrate the validity of its legal system both domestically and internationally. However, as we have shown, this plan backfired. The so-called "violence" of the Kaohsiung Incident clearly came from the security forces, not the demonstrators. In addition, it also became clear in both Taiwan and overseas that the security forces had used deprivation of sleep and even physical torture to gain the "confessions" of the defendants. And, from the transcripts of the trials published in *The China Times* and some other newspapers, it became very clear that the government's cases against the defendants failed in all of the main military and civil trials, yet the verdicts took the "evidence" from the indictments—based on the forced confessions—and convicted the defendants without regard to what had transpired in court. Only in the case of Reverend Kao Chun-ming and his co-defendants, tried for concealing Shih Ming-teh, were the accused guilty as charged.

The defendants in the two main trials also had to serve long sentences, which were especially severe in that they were not guilty of any crimes. A good

---

1 An excellent biography of Chiang Ching-kuo is Jay Taylor, *The Generalissimo's Son: Chiang Ching-kuo and the Revolutions in China and Taiwan* (Cambridge, MA and London: Harvard University Press, 2000). For a good biography of Wang Sheng, see Thomas A. Marks, *Counterrevolution in China: Wang Sheng and the Kuomintang* (London and Portland, OR: Frank Cass, 1998).

comparison can be made with General Wang Hsi-ling 汪希苓, Director of the Intelligence Bureau of the Ministry of National Defense 國防部情報局. Wang had ordered the murder of Henry Liu 劉一良 (also known as Chiang Nan 江南), an American citizen living in the United States who was killed on October 14, 1984.[2] A military court sentenced Wang Hsi-ling to life in prison, but he was given a nice specially-built four-room house at the Ching-mei prison, where many of the Kaohsiung Incident defendants were kept in much harsher conditions. In addition, Wang had another small house where he could receive female visitors. Wang was released within a few years and was honored at a huge banquet for his eightieth birthday.[3]

Compared to South Korea, which eventually democratized with many parallels to Taiwan,[4] the Kaohsiung Incident was non-violent and its punishments relatively light. In the commensurate Kwangju Uprising, South Korea's military government killed 191 persons according to the official figures and estimates of the true numbers run much higher.[5]

Both the Kaohsiung Incident and the Kwangju Uprising were important to the later democratization of Taiwan and South Korea, though the former had a greater impact. In Taiwan, three different groups of people emerged from the arrests, imprisonment and trials associated with the Kaohisung Incident to contribute to Taiwan's democratic movement and later democratization.

The First Group: The Defendants

The first group, the defendants themselves, had all been leaders of the *dangwai* movement. Their convictions in the clearly unfair trials made them martyrs as well as important activists. After their imprisonment ended, many became active in democratic politics and played leading roles in Taiwan's democratization. These people included seven of the original eight defendants in the military court trial.

Huang Hsin-chieh 黃信介 later became the third chairperson of the Democratic Progressive Party (October 30, 1988–January 20, 1992). He won

---

2 See preface.
3 Jacobs, *Democratizing Taiwan*, pp. 60–61, 272.
4 J. Bruce Jacobs, "Taiwan and South Korea: Comparing East Asia's Two 'Third-Wave' Democracies," *Issues & Studies* 43, no. 4 (December 2007), pp. 227–260.
5 J. Bruce Jacobs, "Two Key Events in the Democratisation of Taiwan and South Korea: The Kaohsiung Incident and the Kwangju Uprising," *International Review of Korea Studies* 8, no. 1 (2011), pp. 50–51.

election from Hualien County to the first fully elected legislature in December 1992. When he died on November 30, 1999, he was mourned as one of the important leaders of Taiwan's democratic movement.

Shih Ming-teh 施明德 became the fifth chairperson of the Democratic Progressive Party (July 18, 1994–March 23, 1996). He won three terms as a legislator winning from Tainan County in 1992 and 1995 and Taipei Municipality in 1998. After winning election in 1995, he was the DPP's candidate for Speaker of the Legislature and tied with the KMT's candidate on the first vote, before losing on the second vote. Shih lost political clout after leaving the DPP in 2001.

Chang Chun-hung 張俊宏 won election to the legislature four times beginning in 1992 and serving there until early 2005. He then became Vice-Chairman of the Straits Exchange Foundation under the DPP government of President Chen Shui-bian.

Chen Chu 陳菊 won election to the National Assembly in 1991. She was appointed as Director of the Bureau of Social Affairs in the Taipei Municipal Government in 1995 under Mayor Chen Shui-bian and to the same role in the Kaohsiung Municipal Government in 1998 under Mayor Hsieh Chang-ting. In 2000, she gained a cabinet position as Director of the Council of Labor Affairs, a position she held until 2005. In 2006, as the DPP's candidate, Chen won election as mayor of Kaohsiung Municipality. In 2010 and 2014 she won election as the mayor of the new Greater Kaohsiung Municipality.

Lin I-hsiung 林義雄 became the sixth chairperson of the DPP (18 July 1998–20 April 2000), playing an important role in Chen Shui-bian's successful campaign for president. He has eschewed political office, but has campaigned for some DPP candidates. He has also been a leader in Taiwan's anti-nuclear movement.

Lu Hsiu-lien 呂秀蓮 won election as a legislator in 1992. She then won the position of County Executive of Taoyuan County in 1997. In 2000 and 2004 she won two terms as Vice-President of the nation.

Yao Chia-wen 姚嘉文 became the second chairperson of the DPP (December 20, 1987–October 30, 1988). He won election to the legislature in 1992, but failed to be re-elected in 1995 and 1998. In 2002, he was appointed Head of the Examination Branch in the central government, a post he held until 2008.

Some of the defendants in the civil trial also had political careers. Wang Tuoh 王拓, in addition to his writing, was elected to the legislature from December 1992 until January 2008. Following his defeat, President Chen Shui-bian appointed Wang the Minister of Cultural Affairs for the last months of his presidency. Yang Ching-chu 楊青矗 continued his writing including three volumes related to the Kaohsiung Incident.[6] Chang Fu-chung 張富忠 co-edited the important book, *Green Era*, cited in this monograph.[7]

The Second Group: The Defense Lawyers

The second group, the lawyers who defended the Kaohsiung Incident defendants, formed a second generation of opposition political leaders. One source mentions fifteen such lawyers[8] and about half have become politically prominent. Several of these lawyers appeared in both the military and civil trials. We examine the future political careers of these politically prominent defense lawyers in alphabetical order.

Chang Chun-hsiung 張俊雄 won election to the legislature three times in 1983, 1986 and 1989 prior to the removal of the "old thieves" and he won election to the new legislature in 1992, 1995 and 1998. In 2000, he was appointed Vice-Premier and then Premier, a position he held until 2002. During 2002–2005 he was Secretary-General of the DPP. In 2005 he again won election to the legislature and also served as Chairman of the Straits Exchange Foundation until 2007, when he again became Premier towards the end of Chen Shui-bian's presidency.

Chen Shui-bian 陳水扁 won a seat as a non-partisan member of the Taipei Municipal Council in 1981 and won re-election in 1985. In 1986 he was sentenced to prison for libel. From the founding of the DPP, Chen played an active role in the party. In 1989 he won a seat in the legislature. He also won a seat in the newly reformed legislature in late 1992. In 1994, Chen won a three-way race for mayor of Taipei Municipality. Running for re-election in 1998, Chen gained more votes, but lost in a two-way race to Ma Ying-jeou. In 2000 and 2004, running as the DPP nominee, Chen won two terms as President of the nation.

Cheng Sheng-chu 鄭勝助 did not become politically active, though he later acted as a lawyer for Chen Shui-bian both during his presidency and afterwards.

Chiang Peng-chien 江鵬堅 won election to the legislature in 1983 and again won a term in 1995. A founding member of the Democratic Progressive Party, Chiang was the DPP's first chairperson (November 28, 1986—December 20, 1987). He was appointed to the Control Branch in 1996 and remained a member until he died on December 15, 2000 at the age of 60.

---

6 Yang Ching-chu 楊青矗, *Meilidao jinxing qu* 美麗島進行曲 [*Songs on the Development of Formosa*], 3 vols. (Taibei 台北: Dunli 敦理, 2009).
7 Zhang Fuzhong 張富忠 and Qiu Wanxing 邱萬興, *Lüse niandai I*, 1.
8 Ibid., p. 106.

Hsieh Chang-ting 謝長廷 won two terms as a member of the Taipei Municipal Council in 1981 and 1985. In 1989 he won a term as a legislator and won another term in the reformed legislature in 1992. In 1996, in the first popular presidential election, Hsieh ran as vice-presidential candidate on the DPP ticket with presidential nominee Peng Ming-min. In 1998 and 2002, he won two terms as the DPP candidate for mayor of Kaohsiung Municipality. Hsieh served as premier for a year (February 1, 2005–January 25, 2006) and ran as the DPP's nominee in the 2008 presidential election, but lost to Ma Ying-jeou.

Li Sheng-hsiung 李勝雄 is a self-described human rights lawyer. He was involved with the DPP, but later became active in the Taiwan Independence Party 台灣建國黨. He has served as the lawyer for the wife of Chen Shui-bian, Wu Shu-chen 吳淑珍, and has also defended people who were on the government blacklist and refused entry to Taiwan in the late 1980s and early 1990s such as Chang Tsang-hung 張燦鍙, Wang Kang-lu 王康陸, Kuo Pei-hung 郭倍宏, Li Ying-yuan 李應元, Lo I-shih 羅益世 and Shih Ming 史明.

Lu Chuan-sheng 呂傳勝 is the older brother of Kaohsiung Incident defendant and former Vice-President Lu Hsiu-lien 呂秀蓮. After the Kaohsiung Incident trial, he appears to have devoted himself primarily to the law.

Su Tseng-chang 蘇貞昌 was elected to the Taiwan Provincial Assembly in 1981 and 1985. In 1986 he was a co-founder of the Democratic Progressive Party. In 1989 he won election as County Executive of Pingtung County. In 1995, he was elected as a legislator, but in 1997 he won election as County Executive of Taipei County, where he won re-election in 2001. In 2004, he left the County Executive's position to become Secretary-General of the Presidential Office under President Chen Shui-bian. He became Premier from January 25, 2006 to May 21, 2007, when he resigned to run for president. When he came in second to Hsieh Chang-ting in the DPP presidential primary, Su withdrew from the presidential race and ultimately ran as vice-presidential candidate with Hsieh Chang-ting in the losing 2008 presidential race. He lost an "unwinnable" race for Taipei Municipality mayor in 2010 and served as Chairman of the DPP from May 30, 2012 to May 28, 2014.

You Ching 尤清 won a six-year term as a member of the Control Branch in 1980, when the Control Branch was elected by the Taiwan Provincial Assembly. He then won election as a DPP member to the legislature in 1986. In 1989 and 1993, he won two terms as County Executive of Taipei County. He again won legislative terms in 2001 and 2004. In 2007 he became Taiwan's representative to Germany, a position he held until September 20, 2008.

The Third Group: Wives and Relatives of Defendants

The third group, wives and relatives of defendants, also became politically prominent. Originally, they ran for office to show support both for their husbands or relatives as well as the opposition political movement. In running for office at a time that their husbands or relatives were in prison, they showed great bravery. In addition, they became magnets for citizens who wished to express their support for their imprisoned husbands and/or for the democracy movement. In this section, we briefly mention three such wives and one other relative.

Fang Su-min 方素敏 and her husband, Lin I-hsiung, suffered grievously as a result of the Kaohsiung Incident. While in prison, Lin I-hsiung was tortured more than any of the other prisoners. In addition, on February 28, 1980, while Lin was in prison and Fang Su-min was visiting him for the first time since his arrest six weeks earlier, someone came to their house and stabbed to death Lin's mother and two twin daughters, then aged 6 years old. The killer also severely injured their nine-year old daughter, who miraculously survived after extensive surgery. In the election of December 3, 1983, Fang Su-min returned from the United States and ran for legislature from the electorate containing Taipei and Ilan counties and Keelung Municipality. She led the electorate with 121,204 votes, over 20,000 votes more than the second ranked candidate. Her campaign used such words as "Accept Bitter Sufferings, Save Taiwan 受苦難，救台灣" and "Return Lin I-hsiung to Taiwan 把林義雄還給台灣." Baited at a campaign rally, she responded, "My husband, I-hsiung, is innocent! ... Today, seeing so many people, proves that I-hsiung was correct in seeking his democratic ideals! 我的丈夫義雄是無罪的！... 今天看到這麼多人,就證明義雄所追求的民主理想是對的！"[9] She did not play a major role in Taiwan's politics, but her speech at Chen Shui-bian's election eve rally in 2000 was inspirational.

Chou Ching-yu 周清玉, Mrs Yao Chia-wen, ran for National Assembly from Taipei Municipality in the December 6, 1980 election when she won over 153,466 votes, about fifty per cent more votes than the person in second-place. In this election, one of her campaign leaflets said, "Walk with me 與我同行."[10] On December 6, 1986, Chou won re-election as a member of the National Assembly, again leading the Taipei Municipality electorate with 125,283 votes. Chou won a term as County Executive of Changhua County in 1989, but in fact the DPP had very little support in Changhua at that time and she defeated a

---

9   Ibid., p. 158.
10   Ibid., p. 114.

KMT candidate that even the police opposed. At that time, not one member of the County Assembly had joined the DPP.

Hsu Jung-shu 許榮淑, the former Mrs Chang Chun-hung, won election to the legislature in the December 6, 1980 election from the third electoral district (Taichung Municipality and County, Changhua County and Nantou County) winning 79,372 votes fairly evenly distributed between the three counties and one municipality.) On December 3, 1983, she won re-election with 118,898 votes, the highest in the electorate. On December 6, 1986, she again won re-election and again led the district with 191,840 votes, over 60,000 more votes than the second candidate. In the democratic period, Hsu won election to the legislature in 1998, 2001 and 2004.

Huang Tien-fu 黃天福 was the younger brother of Huang Hsin-chieh. He ran for the legislature from Taipei Municipality in the December 1980 election and won. However, he failed in his bid for re-election in 1983. (In that election, the *dangwai* did elect two key members from Taipei Municipality, Chiang Peng-chien and Kang Ning-hsiang.) Huang Tien-fu won another term as legislator in 1995.

Conclusion

At the time of the Kaohsiung Incident, Taiwan had been undergoing a phase of "liberalization" for some seven years. After the Kaohsiung Incident, the state-controlled media grossly exaggerated the level and significance of the violence that had occurred, accusing the demonstrators of violent behavior when in fact the security agencies perpetrated all of the violence that occurred. The arrests and imprisonment of the Kaohsiung Incident leaders ended the period of liberalization and began a period of strong oppression. But Taiwan's democratic activists would not be repressed. They continued to press hard. The numbers of *dangwai* magazines published in Taiwan in the early 1980s increased exponentially. And, by 1983, the issue of "Taiwan" also came to the fore in the legislative election campaign in addition to the issue of "democratization."[11]

As we noted earlier, the "violence" of the Kaohsiung Incident cannot be compared to the Kwangju Massacre of May 18–27, 1980, six months after the Kaohsiung Incident, in south-western South Korea, when the Korean military

---

11   J. Bruce Jacobs, "'Taiwanization' in Taiwan's Politics," in *Cultural, Ethnic, and Political Nationalism in Contemporary Taiwan: Bentuhua*, ed. John Makeham and A-Chin Hsiau (New York: Palgrave Macmillan, 2005), pp. 22–33.

slaughtered at least 191 Korean citizens and injured many more. Certainly, the *Formosa Magazine* demonstrations were peaceful. But, and this is important, Taiwan's security agencies were much less peaceful. They tortured at least some of the defendants. They beat people such as in the Kushan Incident the night before the Kaohsiung Incident. And, they probably killed Lin I-hsiung's family, the first and only time in Taiwan's postwar history that family members of political prisoners have been killed. So, in fact, there was violence surrounding the Kaohsiung Incident, but it was state violence, not violence from demonstrators.

Taiwan's transition to democracy has proven reasonably peaceful and smooth. The one difficulty has been the absence of an official Truth and Reconciliation Commission. In South Africa and many other countries, people who perpetrated violence on behalf of the state can be forgiven, but they must first ask for forgiveness. Taiwan has never undergone this process. Thus many people who committed violence for the state have not sought forgiveness and, in fact, many are still honored. As a result, many difficult historical issues like February 28 (1947) remain unresolved. In the words of the poet Li Min-yung 李敏勇, Taiwan must "allow the flowers of the wounds to blossom soon 讓傷口的花早日綻放."[12]

In Part 1 we have analyzed the Kaohsiung Incident and its contributions to Taiwan's democratization. In Part 2 we examine the murder of Lin I-hsiung's mother and twin daughters and the "roles" of the writer.

---

12   Jia Bo 家博 (J. Bruce Jacobs), "Rang shangkou de hua zaori zhanfang 讓傷口的花早日綻放 [Allow the Flowers of the Wounds to Blossom Soon]," *Zhongguo shibao* 中國時報 [*China Times*] February 25, 1997, p. 11.

PART 2

Memoirs of a Foreign Big Beard
大鬍子外籍男子回憶錄

∵

CHAPTER 6

Memoirs of a Foreign Big Beard

The story of my becoming interested in Taiwan actually has a false start. My paternal grandparents had many Asian objects in their house. Their origin came from a grand uncle, Henry H. Hart (1886–1968), whom I never met. Henry H. Hart married my paternal grandmother's older sister, Alice (1889–1936). Alice died before I was born and I never met her either, though I did know her two daughters and her two grandchildren, my second cousins. Henry H. Hart had interests in Asia and published several books including two on Marco Polo,[1] a work on the early Portuguese navigators to Asia,[2] and several works on Chinese poetry and literature, which involved his own translation.[3] According to my grandparents, Henry H. Hart was not a nice person and he did not treat my Grand Aunt Alice well. Like many in my family, Henry H. Hart lived in San Francisco and went into the import-export trade with Asia. Apparently, he was not a good businessman and my grandfather had to bail him out. Thus, my grandparents had many Asian articles in their house including Chinese vases and paintings, Korean chests and Japanese prints. Such art did not particularly strike me as a boy, though I did find the locks on the Korean chests intriguing and I did look at the Japanese prints. But, as I suggested, this history had nothing to do with my becoming a scholar of Asia.

That began when I was an undergraduate at Columbia College of Columbia University. Columbia had (and still has) a program called the Core Curriculum of reading great books in a wide variety of areas as well as learning about music

[1] Henry H. Hart, *Venetian adventurer: being an account of the life and times and of the book of Messer Marco Polo* (Stanford: Stanford University Press, 1947). Henry H. Hart, *Marco Polo: Venetian Adventurer* (Norman: University of Oklahoma Press, 1967).
[2] Henry H. Hart, *Sea Road to the Indies: An Account of the Voyages and Exploits of the Portuguese Navigators, Together with the Life and Times of Dom Vasco da Gama, Capitão—Mór, Viceroy of India and Count of Vidigueira* (London, Edinburgh, Glasgow: William Hodge and Company, Limited, 1952).
[3] Henry H. Hart, *The Hundred Names: A Short Introduction to the Study of Chinese Poetry with Illustrative Translations* (Berkeley: University of California Press, 1933, 1938). Shifu Wang and Henry H. Hart, *The West Chamber. A medieval drama. Translated ... with notes by Henry H. Hart, etc.* (Stanford: Stanford University Press, 1936), also published London: Oxford University Press, 1936. Henry H. Hart, *A garden of peonies: translations of Chinese poems into English verse* (Stanford: Stanford University Press, 1938, 1943, 1947), the 1938 and 1943 editions were also published London: Oxford University Press.

and art history, a foreign language, science and mathematics, and a physical education requirement which included completing a 75-yard swim before one could graduate. (I later taught many students to swim so that they could complete their 75-yard requirement.) I was interested in human freedom and took special interest in what were called "totalitarian" regimes at the time, like those of Hitler and Stalin. I had studied some Russian and planned to become a Soviet specialist. In that context, I thought it would be useful to take Oriental Civilizations for my second year Contemporary Civilizations subject. My attitude was that I should know something about Asia and then would be done with it. I certainly had some strange preconceptions. For example, I remember seeing a Westerner in the Law Library studying Chinese and remembering how weird I found that! Clearly the Asian artifacts which filled my grandparents' house did not give me any particular insights.

Little did I know that I would be hooked by the China section of Oriental Civilizations. Later in the year, I screwed up my courage and went to see my professor, the very eminent William Theodore de Bary, and told him that I was interested in China and asked what I should do. Professor de Bary said that I should learn Chinese. I remember asking, "How do I do that?" Professor de Bary replied that I could study in the summer at Columbia and offered to help me get a scholarship. So, that summer of 1963, after my sophomore year and before my junior year of Columbia College, I began studying Chinese in hot New York. It was hard work and I only got grades of C+. Later, as a postgraduate student when my Chinese was much more fluent, I learned that Professor de Bary had only gotten Cs in his first year Chinese. So, maybe C+ was not so bad! Fortunately, my Chinese grades went up after that.

When I graduated from Columbia College in 1965, I wanted to go to China. However, the Cultural Revolution was getting underway and foreigners were not welcome. In addition, I was then an American citizen and that made going to China even more impossible. So I went to Taiwan and studied at the Graduate Institute of History at National Taiwan University for a year. That year was critical in my learning Chinese. Basically, I was rude and refused to speak any English. But my spoken and written Chinese improved exponentially. I returned to Columbia as a postgraduate student.

I found the writings of the Cultural Revolution quite boring (I later found out that my friends in China also found such writing boring) and I did not want to spend all of my time in Hong Kong interviewing refugees from China. Rather, I wanted to interact with Chinese society. Thus, I determined to do a field study of local politics in rural Taiwan. I did this for close to eighteen months before returning to New York. I taught two years in upstate New York at Clarkson College of Technology, where I completed writing my PhD in 1975, and then taught a year at Hofstra University on Long Island just to the east of New York City before accepting a tenured position at La Trobe University in Melbourne, Australia. On the way to Australia in 1976, I revisited Taiwan again and returned there in 1977, 1978, 1979 and 1980. In between my 1977 and 1978 trips to Taiwan, I also made my first trip to the People's Republic of China.[4]

By my 1978 trip, I had built a good relationship with Ding Mou-shih 丁懋時, then Director-General of the Government Information Office (GIO) and a very senior KMT leader. The GIO helped me arrange many appointments with key people in Taiwan and when I returned from China in early 1978, Ding hosted a fancy lunch for me with several senior officials where I was asked to speak quite frankly about what I had observed in China.

When I arrived in May 1979, I expected to meet the new Director-General of GIO, who was only eighteen months older than me. However, James Soong 宋楚瑜 was too busy. In the meantime, Chen Chu 陳菊 of the *dangwai* opposition had learned I was in town and quickly organized meetings with such people as Shih Ming-teh 施明德, who was just out of prison, Yao Chia-wen 姚嘉文, Lin I-hsiung 林義雄, Chang Chun-hung 張俊宏, and Annette Lu 呂秀蓮 among others. I also had the opportunity to attend the "birthday party" of Taoyuan County Executive Hsu Hsin-liang 許信良 on May 26, 1979 in Chungli 中壢, the site of the famous Chungli Incident (see Chapter 1) only eighteen months previously. With ten to thirty thousand people participating, the "Birthday Party" was the largest non-government sponsored, non-electoral peaceful gathering of people in Taiwan up until that time. This 1979 visit greatly widened my understanding of Taiwan's opposition and established long-lasting friendships with many people who later exercised considerable political leadership in Taiwan.

When I arrived in Taiwan on January 21, 1980, many of my *dangwai* friends had already been arrested and incarcerated. I went to the GIO and again James Soong had no time to see me. But I did have the opportunity to express my personal concern and the concern of the wider international society about the prisoners and about the arrests. My requests to see the prisoners in jail, of course, remained unanswered, but the GIO did arrange for me to visit the Ten Great Constructions Projects 十大建設, completed during the 1970s, and during this trip I also visited Taitung and Hualien for the first time.

When I arrived back in Taipei, much of my time was spent discussing the arrests and imprisonment of the *dangwai* leaders and members with a wide variety of people including academics, political activists, senior leaders, and

---

4 For more details on my trips to Taiwan from 1965 to 1980, see J. Bruce Jacobs, "Researching Taiwan in the 1970s," *Issues & Studies* 40, no. 3/4 (September/December 2004), pp. 403–418.

various political organizations. As one result of these discussions, on the evening of February 25 I was brought into contact with an Amnesty International delegation visiting Taiwan at the time. In fact, our preliminary judgments of the Kaohsiung Incident were quite similar, that the conflicts and arrests were more a tragedy of errors rather than some Kuomintang plot to destroy the *dangwai*. The Amnesty delegation asked me if I would be willing to pair with a lawyer and observe the trial of the Kaohsiung defendants. Of course, I was willing (tickets to the trial were very difficult to obtain). The Amnesty people also asked me to let them know if anything unusual happened.

I also spent time with *dangwai* friends and with the families of the political prisoners. In the company of other *dangwai* friends, we would spend time with the families just being friendly and supportive. I was living at International House 國際學舍 on Hsin-yi Road 信義路 near Hsin-sheng South Road 新生南路, where I had lived when I first went to Taiwan in 1965. This was close to Lin I-hsiung's house and, in the company of friends, I often spent evenings there just talking and playing with Lin's three daughters, who at the time were nine and six years old. (My own daughter was seven at the time.) We also visited with Yao Chia-wen's wife, Chou Ching-yu 周清玉, and their only daughter, Yao Yu-ching 姚雨靜, who was about ten at the time. I remember speaking to Yu-ching in Taiwanese (Hokkien) and being told that she did not speak Taiwanese. (This later came up at the trial, see Chapter 3.) This was quite a shock because Yao Chia-wen was in prison for advocating Taiwanese Independence while his daughter could not speak Taiwanese. Of course, this was quite common in Taipei at the time as parents tried to give their children every advantage in the school-entry examinations.

During this period I was also trying to conduct research about Taiwan's politics and on the afternoon of Thursday, February 28, 1980, I had two key interviews scheduled with Lien Chen-tung 連震東 (1904–1986) and Tao Pai-chuan 陶百川 (1902–2006). Both Lien and Tao were very senior and I believed (and still do) that one must prepare for such interviews very carefully. Thus, I spent the whole morning preparing and for lunch I went out and bought a box lunch 便當, which I brought back to International House. At lunch time, I called Lin I-hsiung's house to talk with his wife, Fang Su-min 方素敏, as I had learned that she had been to visit Lin I-hsiung in prison and because there were strong indications that Lin had been tortured. Fang Su-min was not there, but their younger twin, Lin Ting-chun 林亭均, answered the phone and we chatted for a while. I was about to hang up when she said that her older twin sister, Lin Liang-chun 林亮均, also wanted to chat. I told both girls that I would come over later that night and play "horse" (where I gave them rides on my back) with them.

That afternoon, before the interviews, I went to the Student Bookstore 學生書局 and bought the *Six Legal Codes* 六法全書 so that I had the complete text of all of Taiwan's laws. I then did the two interviews and remember that both interviews went very well. Lien, whom I had interviewed previously, was an important "Half-Mainlander" Taiwanese, who had gone to China to work with the Kuomintang (KMT) and its government during Taiwan's Japanese colonial period and who returned to Taiwan after World War II with the Kuomintang.[5] After World War II, Lien was the only Taiwanese member of the KMT Central Reform Commission 中央改造委員會 (1950–1952) and he was the first Taiwanese ever appointed a Minister when appointed Minister of the Interior in 1960. Although Lien may have been responsible for amassing the great wealth of the Lien family, he met me dressed very informally in the modest family home. He treated me, then a junior scholar, with courtesy and respect. During the interview, we talked mainly about the Central Reform Commission.[6]

I had also previously met Tao Pai-chuan, one of Taiwan's great liberal Mainlander leaders. Tao was a member of the Control Branch and issued a very strong critique of the government's handling of the Lei Chen 雷震 case in 1960. Tao then left the KMT, but retained considerable prestige. President Chiang Ching-kuo frequently consulted with Tao and one such consultation ultimately led to my release in late May 1980. I remember that we mainly talked about legal aspects of the Kaohsiung Incident cases.

When I got back, I was quite tired and saw Professor Parks Coble of the University of Nebraska, who was also living at International House, and invited him to have some Johnnie Walker Black Label Scotch Whisky that I had brought into Taiwan duty-free. In those days Johnnie Walker Black Label was very expensive and a bit special for us junior scholars. After relaxing and chatting

---

5 On the Half-Mainlander Taiwanese, see J. Bruce Jacobs, "Taiwanese and the Chinese Nationalists, 1937–1945: The Origins of Taiwan's "Half-Mountain People" (Banshan ren)," *Modern China* 16, no. 1 (January 1990), pp. 84–118.

6 Lien Chen-tung's father was Lien Heng 連橫 (also known as Lien Yatang 連雅堂), the author of the famous *General History of Taiwan* 台灣通史, originally published in 1920 and 1921. For a good biography of Lien Heng, see Shu-hui Wu, "Lien Heng (1878–1936) and the *General History of Taiwan*," *Journal of Third World Studies* 21, no. 1 (Spring 2004), 17–56. Lien Chen-tung's son, Lien Chan 連戰 (1936-) had an excellent political career becoming the first "Taiwanese" ambassador in 1975, the first "Taiwanese" foreign minister in 1988, and the first "Taiwanese" premier in 1993. Lien Chan was Taiwanese through the patrilineal Chinese system, but he was born in Xi'an, China, his mother was Chinese, his wife was Chinese and he behaved as a Chinese. Ultimately, although the KMT candidate for president in 2000 and 2004, he lost both elections.

for a while, I mentioned to Parks that I had to call Fang Su-min and rang their house. A man answered the phone and I asked for Fang Su-min. The man said that she was not home. I asked when she would return and he answered, "I don't know. Something has happened in the house" 不知道, 家裡發生事情. In the context of what we now know, I should have been alarmed, but, when Parks asked if I wanted to go to the house, I felt that if Fang Su-min was not there, there was no reason to go. In addition, the Johnnie Walker was precious and I said that we should finish the Scotch first.

After a while, I started to get more anxious and a bit before 6 PM, Parks and I went to the Lin family home. The house was surrounded by many police and reporters. I asked what had happened, but no one would tell me. I went to the door and rang the bell to go in, but no one answered. Several reporters took pictures of me ringing the doorbell. Since it was winter in Taiwan, it was already dark and reflections of their flashes can be seen in the photographs.[7] Later, when I was accused of going to the house at noon, these pictures—all with reflections of flashes—were used to "prove" the point.

Finally, someone told me that Fang Su-min had gone to the Jen-ai Hospital 仁愛醫院, which was not too far from the Lin family home. I ran there and saw Kang Ning-hsiang 康寧祥 when I arrived. Kang, who was then a *dangwai* legislator and the publisher of opposition magazines, and I had been good friends since the early 1970s. It was Kang who told me that Lin I-hsiung's mother and twin daughters had been murdered and that his eldest daughter was just then being operated upon in an attempt to save her life. Fang Su-min was in the hospital under sedation.

Many opposition people came to the hospital to lend support to Fang Su-min and to Lin Huan-chun 林奐均 and to hope that Lin Huan-chun came through her life-saving operation successfully. Several people told me that it was the security agencies that murdered Lin's mother and twin daughters, but my response was that the security agencies could not be so stupid. There were also many police in the hospital and I told the police including Group Leader Chang 張組長 that I had talked to the twins on the telephone around noon and would be happy to help them with establishing the time they were still alive. We stayed at the hospital for several hours, trying to provide support for Fang Su-min and Lin Huan-chun, but we were also numb with shock and only left

---

7 See, for example, the cover of *Yazhou shiji* 亞洲世紀 [*Asian Century*], No. 138, March 21, 1980. The caption reads, "Big Beard rings the door bell" 大鬍子按門鈴. Another photo, also taken that night, appeared in *Taiwan Xinshengbao* 台灣新生報 [*Taiwan New Life News*], March 3, 1980, p. 3. The caption on this photo says "The Mysterious Big Beard—Mr Bruce Jacobs" 神秘大鬍子 — 加 [sic] 博先生. My Chinese name was rendered in a number of different ways.

the hospital in the early morning hours. Apparently, I was not too nice to the press, partly because I was very upset and partly because I did not want my name in the newspapers as I still hoped I could observe the trial on behalf of Amnesty International.[8]

Not knowing what had happened, many people were quite frightened and several of us decided to stay together in the nearby Taipei Regency Hotel 財神大酒店. I remembered that I needed to inform Amnesty International about the murders and sent a telex from the hotel:

> February 28 Lin Yi-hsiung mother and two children murdered. Third daughter saved after prolonged surgery. Wife under police guard, under sedation in hospital. Lin Yi-hsiung released on bail after direct intervention by President Chiang Ching-kuo. All families under police guard.
> I was probably last person to talk to the two murdered girds[sic]. Talked on telephone about noon. Naturally upset and to hospital. Will probably be in all newspapers tomorrow. Understand if this causes change in plans.
> Sadly,
> Bruce[9]

The last sentence, apparently underlined by the police before they gave the telex to the press, meant that I understood if publicity would make it difficult for me to attend the trial for Amnesty International, though *The China Post* and others suggested this might have had some other, more sinister meaning. That night, several of us stayed in the hotel room together, but none of us got much sleep.

The next day, Friday, February 29, I kept an appointment to interview Shen Chang-huan 沈昌煥 at the Presidential Office. Shen had served in many senior KMT and government positions including as a member of the Central Reform Commission, ambassador to many countries including Spain (1959–1960), the Holy See (1966–1969) and Thailand (1969–1972), Minister of Foreign Affairs (1960–1966, 1972- 1979) and Secretary-General of the National Security Council (1979–1984), the position he held in 1980. This was not my first meeting with Shen Chang-huan as he was the father of a graduate student classmate at Columbia, Abraham Ta-chuan Shen 沈大川, and Shen Chang-huan had taken me to lunch when I visited Bangkok in 1971.

---

8   *Zhongguo shibao* 中國時報 [*China Times*], March 23, 1980, p. 3.
9   Text in *Taiwan Xinshengbao* 台灣新生報 [*Taiwan New Life News*], March 5, 1980, p. 3 and in *The China Post*, March 6, 1980, p. 12.

I had planned to interview Shen Chang-huan about the Central Reform Commission, but in fact we only talked about the murders of the previous day. For the first time at an interview with a senior person, I was in tears and asked that the imprisoned people in the *dangwai* be forgiven and released. I don't know if Shen made any reports of my visit, but my visit apparently had no effects on future events.

That night, I joined several *dangwai* friends and we spent the night at Lin I-hsiung's house. We felt safe because the house was guarded by police and we provided support to each other and to Lin I-hsiung's two younger sisters and his younger agnatic cousin, who were staying at the house. Lin I-hsiung's mother, Lim You A-mei 林游阿妹, whom I called Auntie (A-m 阿姆 in Hokkien, wife of father's older brother, the equivalent of 伯母 in Mandarin), was very religious. She had lost her husband many years before and from December 1979, Lin I-hsiung, the mainstay in her life, was in prison. While she recited many Buddhist prayers, she could only read a little and to take her mind away from her troubles, she did things like wash clothes for neighbors. One of the neighbors, for whom Auntie had washed clothes, came over and insisted on paying her bill. Lin I-hsiung's sister answered the door and was distraught at this attempt to pay for her late mother's work. At least, we were able to console her a little.

The next morning, the *United Daily* was delivered to the Lin house. The page 3 headline shouted, "Secret Witness Gives Police Clue. Search Everywhere for Bearded Foreign Male" 秘密證人向警方提供線索, 全面查尋大鬍子外籍男子.[10] The article said that the bearded foreigner had gone to the Lin house about noon. The article did not name me, but my friends were worried. I was not worried, because I had not gone to the house at noon and, to lighten the mood, I said to the police in the house, "I'm here if you want me!" They replied that they did not want me.

There had been reports that under questioning Lin Huan-chun had referred to the murderer as an "uncle" 叔叔. Several sources suggested that this meant that Huan-chun had known the murderer previously, though an "uncle" could also be any man who was younger than her father. However, the liberal *Taiwan Times* based in Kaohsiung, reported on March 1 that Lin Huan-chun had told her father, who had been released from prison following the murders of his mother and twin daughters, that she did not know the murderer.[11]

---

10 *Lianhebao* 聯合報 [*United Daily*], March 1, 1980, p. 3. The Chinese term *da huzi* 大鬍子 literally means a full beard as opposed to a mustache. I have generally translated this as "Big Beard" since that was the informal translation used at the time.

11 *Taiwan shibao* 台灣時報 [*Taiwan Times*], March 1, 1980, p. 3.

That afternoon, I went to the hospital to visit Huan-chun. Of course, there was a large security detail protecting Huan-chun since she could identify the murderer, but I had absolutely no trouble being admitted. Huan-chun greeted me warmly as "Foreign Uncle" 外國叔叔. Considering that an operation had saved her life only two days earlier, she seemed good and happy. The doctors and nurses took me to one side and made clear that Huan-chun had said that she did not know the murderer. This visit to Huan-chun was important to me for a number of reasons. In the political context of the time, I thought how brave the doctors and nurses were. And, later, after my difficulties with the police, I thought back on how the police had not had the slightest suspicion of me during this visit, nor had they prevented me from coming very close to Huan-chun.

That night, I returned to International House. The next morning, as usual, I bought several newspapers. The *United Daily* seemed to suggest that I might be the "bearded foreigner". The main headline on page 3 (social news) screamed, "Police Monitor Big Beard for the Entire Day" 警方全天候監視大鬍子！The first few lines of the article alarmed me: "... the foreign "Big Beard" who went to the Lin family house might have a PhD from Columbia University in the United States. Now he is teaching in Taiwan."[12] Although I was not teaching at the time in Taiwan, I was probably the only bearded foreigner with a PhD from Columbia at that time in Taiwan since many fewer foreigners lived in Taiwan then, especially during winter, and beards were also not that common. I did have good relations with the *United Daily* and it was known that I read newspapers, so I thought this might be a message. The article said that the police still had not made contact with the foreign "Big Beard," but that they would speak to him after they "had grasped genuine, strong evidence" 掌握確實有力的證據.[13]

What should I do? It was Sunday morning and offices were closed. I decided to ring two fairly senior KMT friends with whom I was sufficiently close to have their home phone numbers. Chao Shou-po 趙守博 and John C Kuan, also known as Kuan Chung 關中, were both young Deputy Directors of key Kuomintang central party departments, though their backgrounds were quite different. Chao was a Taiwanese encouraged by former governor and then Vice-President Hsieh Tung-min, while Kuan was a Mainlander with a reputation for advocating political reform. Later, they acted very differently, but on

---

12   *Lianhebao* 聯合報 [*United Daily*], March 2, 1980, p. 3. The original text is: ... 到過林宅的外籍 大鬍子", 可能是美國哥倫比亞大學的博士, 現在台灣任教.
13   Ibid.

this occasion they both gave the same advice: if you want, contact the Detective Bureau of the Police Force 刑事警察局.

I then called the Detective Bureau and asked if they wanted to see me. I explained that I had expected them to call because I had told the police on February 28 at the hospital that I had talked to the twins on the telephone at noon on the day they were murdered. In addition, I thought that the *United Daily* of that day also implied that I was the Foreign Big Beard. They said that, if I wanted to come in, they would be pleased to see me. So, we arranged that I would go that afternoon.

"Walking into the Tiger's Lair" 走進虎的巢穴

The afternoon of Sunday, March 2, about 2 PM, I went to the Detective Bureau. We had an extensive discussion of all I knew and the police were reasonably friendly. When, for example, they asked if I had communicated with anyone overseas, I said that I had sent a telex to Amnesty International. They asked what I had said and I showed them my copy of the telex. I never felt they doubted anything I said. They did take some video, which they said was just to remember the occasion, but I later learned that they showed the videos to "witnesses" who were asked whether I was the person who supposedly went to Lin I-hsiung's house about noon on February 28.

I had two goals. My first goal was to do all I could help to catch the murderer. My second goal was to keep my name out of the media for two reasons. First, I did not want to become a news item because this would make it difficult for me to attend the trial for Amnesty International. Secondly, if the murderer thought I had seen him, then what was my life worth!

Around 5 or 6 PM, I asked the detectives if they had anything further. They said they did not, so I said I would leave. They replied that there were reporters outside. As I did not want to become a news item, I accepted the offer of the detectives for them to "protect" 保護 me. This required that I sign a request every twenty-four hours to be protected. We discussed where I would be protected and finally I proposed the Grand Hotel 圓山大飯店 since I had never stayed there before. At the suggestion of the police, I went out hidden under my raincoat, an image that was published in the press later.[14] Several of my Taiwan journalist friends told me afterwards that, in fact, the police had called them to the police station. I do not remember when we finally left the Detective Bureau, but newspapers reported that I had been with the police for thirteen

---

14   *Lianhebao* 聯合報 [*United Daily*], March 4, 1980, p. 3.

hours and departed in the early hours of the morning.¹⁵ I had come under the control of the Special Task Force 專案小組 in charge of solving the Lin family murder case. In the words of my Taiwan friends, I had walked into the tiger's lair 走進虎的巢穴.

The next morning, the press was filled with my name. *The United Daily* was quite kind. The main article stated very clearly, "The police most definitely do not consider Bruce Jacobs a suspect in murder case" 警方並沒有認為家博涉嫌這起命案."¹⁶ On the same page, a close *United Daily* journalist friend, Wu Cheng-shuo 吳正朔, wrote a nice piece praising my scholarship and my person as well as my affection for the Lin daughters. The newspaper also printed a subdued photo of me with Kang Ning-hsiang at the hospital on February 28. The *China Times* was also reasonably kind. It stated that I had asked the police for protection and showed a photo of me at the hospital visiting Lin Huan-chun, captioned "his appearance is grief-stricken" 他神情哀傷. In another article on the same page, the *China Times* reported that Lin Huan-chun had stated that she could remember and identify the murderer and that he was tall and skinny.¹⁷ That afternoon, the *Min Tsu Evening News* made many errors in their reports, but they had a photo of *dangwai* Provincial Assemblywoman Huang Yu-chiao 黃玉嬌 and me at the hospital on February 28.¹⁸ In a light-hearted secondary article, the *China News* stated, "barbershops reported that their customers in the past few days included quite a number of foreigners who wanted to have their beard shaved to avoid embarrassing glances."¹⁹

I do not remember too much of the next two days in the Grand Hotel. We stayed in the new, front part of the hotel. I was very tired because I had slept very little since the murder of Auntie and her two granddaughters. I was hoping that the police would take me to a joint press conference and announce that I had nothing to do with the case. Not much happened and about the only interesting thing to occur was that all of a sudden I was moved from my original room to another room. It turned out that one of my closest friends, Don Shapiro, a classmate at Columbia University, whom I had known since our first week as undergraduates in September 1961 and a superb journalist based in Taiwan, almost found me, thus occasioning the change of room. During this time, one newspaper reported that the "secret witness" had said the bearded foreigner who went to the Lin house at noon "did not really look the same" 實

---

15   Ibid and *Zhongguo shibao* 中國時報 [*China Times*], March 4, 1980, p. 3.
16   *Lianhebao* 聯合報 [*United Daily*], March 3, 1980, p. 3.
17   *Zhongguo shibao* 中國時報 [*China Times*], March 3, 1980, p. 3.
18   *Minzu wanbao* 民族晚報 [*Min Tsu Evening News*], March 3, 1980, p. 2.
19   *China News*, March 3, 1980, p. 4.

在不像 as me.[20] Yet, the next day, the same newspaper screamed that "witnesses in unison identified the same person" 證人齊聲指認同一人.[21]

Early in the evening of Tuesday, March 4, the police told me to get ready. As stated earlier, I was hoping we were going to a joint press conference, but they took me to a "safe house" (the term used by American Institute in Taiwan [AIT] personnel) located a bit to the east of the old Taipei Municipal Baseball Stadium 台北市立棒球場 at the intersection of Nanjing East Road, Section 4 南京東路四段 and Dunhua North Road 敦化北路 where the Taipei Arena 臺北小巨蛋 is today. In 1980, this was still a very sparsely populated area and the two-storey safe house had its own plot of land.

Most of the second storey was one large room with several desks and chairs and at least one couch. The questioning started reasonably friendly, but then things got a bit more reserved. The police explained that they had verified that I had gone to see Lien Chen-tung and Tao Pai-chuan on February 28, but they had not been able to find the person who had sold me the box lunch. Thus, they believed I had gone to the house at noon and seen the murderer. In the course of the discussion, I asked them if they had pursued particular lines of investigation and almost always they responded that they had not. I was a bit astonished that an amateur like me was raising possible avenues for examination which I would have thought obvious to a professional.

Around 10 PM, I had to go to the toilet and was surprised when I was followed downstairs and watched. I still had not slept since the murders of Auntie and the twins and I was very tired. I thought we were not making any progress and I told them that I was going home. They replied, "You can't go home."

I asked, "What do you mean? Why can't I go home?" I then definitely knew that things had become much more complicated. By 2 AM I was exhausted.[22]

They had begun rotation questioning where one or two people would ask questions and then after an hour another one or two would ask the same questions. I asked why they were doing this. They said that others needed to talk to me. I told them that I was exhausted and said, "Okay. Have whoever wants to talk to me come now and we can all talk. After an hour, I need to sleep."

---

20 *Taiwan ribao* 台灣日報 [*Taiwan Daily*], March 4, 1980, p. 3.
21 *Taiwan ribao* 台灣日報 [*Taiwan Daily*], March 5, 1980, p. 3.
22 All of my discussion with the police and other security agencies were conducted In Chinese. The Chinese texts of these discussions may be found in Jia Bo 家博 (J. Bruce Jacobs), "Jia Bo (Bruce Jacobs) xiansheng fangwen jilu 家博 (Bruce Jacobs) 先生訪問紀錄 [Record of Visit with Mr Bruce Jacobs]," in *Koushu lishi: meilidao shijian zhuanji* 口述歷史: 美麗島事件專輯 [*Oral History: Special Collection on the Formosa Incident*], ed. Chen Yishen 陳儀深 (Taipei 台北: Institute of Modern History, Academia Sinica, 2004), p. 305.

They said, "Okay, okay." However, after an hour they wanted to have another rotation.

I was very unhappy and said, "You promised me to let me sleep. Now you won't let me sleep."

One policeman said that I had to speak the truth before they would let me sleep.

I was both really tired and really angry. I swore at the policeman in Taiwanese, "Fuck your mother's broken cunt" 姦爾娘破膣屄.[23] Immediately, I realized that I had been very rude and I apologized, "Excuse me, I should not have used that kind of language." That was probably the closest I came to being physically beaten. With my apology, the police sensed that they had won a victory and asked me what I wanted to say. Fortunately, my exhausted brain still worked.

I said, "I never thought…"

They asked, "What did you never think?"

I said, "I never thought… I never thought that the Republic of China used torture."

They were quite upset and asked, "What torture?"

I replied, "Deprivation of sleep is a very famous method of torture." Then, they finally let me sleep a bit, though I still found it difficult to doze and just rested.

After an hour or so of rest, we then prepared a written record 筆錄 of the interrogation. These records were quite stilted and I was quite particular about getting the content correct. They made several amendments at my request. When it came time to sign the document, I signed it in Taiwanese as "Bruce Jacobs wants to sleep" 家博愛睏. This established quite clearly in the permanent record that I had been deprived of sleep.

The police then said that we were going to International House. When we got there, they asked to see my research and interview notes. I warned them that if the police started checking the research and interview notes of foreign scholars, this could create problems for Taiwan in the future. They still asked to see them and so I showed them the notes. Fortunately, I took all of my notes in English and my handwriting is particularly illegible. They asked what the notes

---

23   Living in the Taiwan countryside in the 1970s and imitating the language of the locals, I learned to swear rather automatically as virtually every third word was "Fuck your mother," said in two slightly different ways. Such language was common among peasants in many cultures, e.g. Russian peasants. I would note that such language is now very rare in the Taiwan countryside. "Fuck your mother's broken cunt," on the other hand, was extraordinarily rude and not a part of everyday language in the 1970s countryside.

said, but I said, "I am showing them to you, but I will not tell you what they say." They had a look, but could not understand them, and returned the notes to me.

We returned to the "safe house." It later became clear that several cultural misunderstandings made the police question my status as a scholar. During the first parts of the interview, I walked around and I would occasionally sit on a desk. In a bureaucratic environment this was very rude, though I was not aware of this custom. They were also shocked that I swore and again believed that this showed that I could not be a scholar. These cultural misunderstandings continued and I was later able to use them to my benefit.

Taiwan's law at that time had a requirement that police could only interrogate a suspect for twenty-four hours and then they had to notify the family of the suspect. Of course this law was not obeyed in the case of the Kaohsiung defendants, but I was a foreigner. When I went to the "safe house", the people at the American Institute in Taiwan (AIT) were worried because I had disappeared. They spent the whole night trying to find me and contacting various security agencies. When the twenty-four hours were over, they were waiting for me. What a relief!

We had a three-way discussion between the police, AIT and me. Because the media had repeatedly said that I had seen the murderer, I felt that I should continue with police protection. However, we all agreed that the responsibility for protection would be given to the Foreign Affairs Police 外事警察 and that the police from the Special Task Force would be withdrawn. This worked very well and I would like to thank publically the head of my protection group, Wang Chao 王超. When I returned to Taiwan twelve years later, Mr Wang, who had then retired, was one of the very few police that I went to see to express my gratitude for his help. We also agreed that I would return to the Grand Hotel and the police agreed with three further conditions: (1) that I have a telephone which I could use at any time, (2) that I have a television which I could watch at any time and (3) I would be allowed to purchase and read all the Taiwan newspapers that I desired. AIT gave me a telephone number and told me that if I did not ring every twenty-four hours, they would come looking for me.

A New Stage of "Protection"

I was taken back to the Grand Hotel. This time I was in a basement room without a window. My protection detail was quite large. I was told it was bigger than that of a visiting premier, though not quite as big as that for a visiting president. The main difficulty was that there were always police in my room. The only place I could be by myself was in the bathroom, which also had no window. For one month, I did not see any sunlight. After a week or so, I could not take staying in the room, so it was agreed that I could go out at night for an hour's walk. Each time, I had three policemen with me. One was armed with a pistol and the other two also had weapons. I really was being protected!

On March 5, the *United Daily* reported that I was not allowed to leave Taiwan.[24] The *China Times* said that the American Institute in Taiwan (AIT), the officially unofficial American diplomatic post in Taipei, had asked the police to explain my involvement in the case.[25]

AIT suggested that I get a lawyer and helped arrange for me to meet Henry H.M. Rai 賴浩敏 of the Formosa Transnational Law Office 萬國法律事務所. It turned out that Henry Rai was a very close friend of Lin I-hsiung and, before he accepted my request to represent me, he checked first with Lin I-hsiung to find out whether Lin had any objection. Lin told Rai to help me as much as possible, so Henry Rai became my lawyer.[26] I wish to thank publically Lin I-hsiung that he had time to think of me in his time of terrible distress. I later learned that I was the first person in Taiwan able to hire a defense lawyer before being indicted. I also learned that James Soong wrote to Henry Rai and asked him to take on the task of being my lawyer. In Taiwan, there was some concern that I might face criminal charges without legal assistance.

The police Special Task Force constantly leaked "news" to the media. As we have seen, the police called the press to inform them that I was at the Detective Bureau on March 2. A cartoon in the *Min Tsu Evening News*, a newspaper with close links to the police, raised the issue. In the cartoon, a group of men labeled the Special Task Force for the Lin Family Murders is sitting around a table. The leader has a newspaper in front on him with a big headline, "Big Beard." The caption says, "We must investigate who leaked this news!"[27] The torrent of "news" from the police was huge and much of it was false. For example, on the morning of March 6, the newspapers were filled with the story of my interrogation, attempts to understand what kind of person I was, and news that was mutually contradictory. Thus, the *Central Daily News* stated that I was "cooperating completely" 十分合作 with the police, while the *United Daily* the next

---

24 *Lianhebao* 聯合報 [*United Daily*], March 5, 1980, p. 3.
25 *Zhongguo shibao* 中國時報 [*China Times*], March 5, 1980, p. 3. At this time I was an American citizen. I became a permanent resident of Australia in September 1976 and naturalized as an Australian citizen in January 1986.
26 After a long and varied career, in 2010 Rai was appointed President of the Judicial Branch 司法院 and Chief Justice of the Council of Grand Justices, Taiwan's Constitutional Court.
27 *Minzu wanbao* 民族晚報 [*Min Tsu Evening News*], March 11, 1980, p. 2.

day reported the police as saying that I "all along have not been very willing to cooperate" 一直不太願意合作.²⁸ The *China Times* headlined that "Bruce Jacobs ought not to have 'problems'" 家博應該沒「問題」, but a *Central Daily News* header stated, "Investigating the whereabouts of Bruce Jacobs, police have discovered some doubts" 警方調查家博行蹤 / 發現有些疑點.²⁹ On March 8, the *China Times* reported that six police might receive demerits for allowing me to enter Lin Huan-chun's hospital room, though the article said I went twice rather than once!³⁰ Contrary to other reports, the prosecutor said that he had never met me and had not sought to speak to me.³¹ While reports on me continued in virtually each day's newspapers, they diminished and it became clear the press did not know my location. On March 10, the police raised the reward for helping to solve the Lin Family Murder Case from NT$2 million to NT$5 million.³²

On March 12, I met with General Wang Ching-hsi 汪敬煦, the commander of the Taiwan Garrison Command. General Wang told me that they knew that I was not the murderer or a member of a plot to commit the murders. However, Wang believed that I had gone to the Lin family home at noon and, for some reason, I was not willing to admit this. I stated that I had not gone to the house at noon and I said that, if I had gone, I would have already told them what I had seen as I wished to solve the murder case as much as they did. Unfortunately, in his later oral memoirs, General Wang was much less polite! A nicer passage read: "Bruce Jacobs admits he is a liberal, but actually he is a leftist."³³

On March 14 the police made me a three-part proposition. If I told them what they wanted to hear, they would first give me NT$10 million (then more than US$270,000), an amount equivalent to six times my annual salary and twice the openly announced reward. Secondly, they would "restore my academic reputation" and, finally, they would insure a safe and secret trip to CKS Airport and exit from Taiwan. I responded, "The truth is given free. You can

---

28 *Zhongyang ribao* 中央日報 [*Central Daily News*], March 6, 1980 p. 3; *Lianhebao* 聯合報 [*United Daily*], March 7, 1980, p. 3.

29 *Zhongguo shibao* 中國時報 [*China Times*], March 7, 1980, p. 3; *Zhongyang ribao* 中央日報 [*Central Daily News*], March 7, 1980 p. 3.

30 *Zhongguo shibao* 中國時報 [*China Times*], March 8, 1980, p. 3.

31 *Dahua wanbao* 大華晚報 [*Great China Evening News*], March 8, 1980, p. 3.

32 *Lianhebao* 聯合報 [*United Daily*], March 11, 1980, p. 3.

33 Wang Jingxu 汪敬煦, *Wang Jingxu xiansheng fangtan lu* 汪敬煦先生訪談錄 [*Records of Interviews with Mr Wang Ching-hsi*] (Taibei 台北: Guoshiguan 國史館 [Academia Historica], 1993), pp. 158–161, quote from p. 158.

beat out falsehood, but you can't buy it. You have investigated me for so long and so clearly, but you still don't know what kind of a person I am."[34]

After about ten days in my basement room, newspaper reports began to suggest that things were getting worse for me. The Prosecutor informed relevant agencies that I was not to leave Taiwan.[35] According to the *United Daily*, I had "become an important, related person" 列為重要關係人 in the Lin family murder case. Another article on the same page called me "mysterious" 微妙,[36] a word that had been frequently been used in the press earlier as well. The police started releasing leaks that witnesses had seen me go to the Lin house at noon on February 28.[37] The afternoon newspapers of March 15 all quoted Kung Ling-sheng 孔令晟, the Commissioner of the Police Administration in the Ministry of the Interior, in testimony to the legislature that, according to the Special Task Force, they had three witnesses who said that I went to the Lin house, rang the doorbell and entered the house at 12.30 PM on the day of the murders.[38] This news appeared in all of the other newspapers the following morning.

On March 15, I wrote to Hu Wu-hsi 胡務熙, Chief of the Taipei Municipal Police Bureau with copies to Shih Ming-chiang 石明江, Chief Prosecutor of the Taipei District Procuracy, Kung Ling-sheng 孔令晟, Commissioner of the Police Administration in the Ministry of the Interior, and Wang Ching-hsi 汪敬煦, Commander of the Taiwan Garrison Command. My letter began, "I have decided to take Cathay Pacific flight 521 leaving 12.25 on March 22 from Taiwan to Hong Kong in order to catch a flight to Australia and begin my teaching at La Trobe University. Kindly please assign personnel to protect me and enable me to leave safely according to this itinerary." I also requested, "If the government of your honorable country still has any need for assistance from me, kindly please raise this before my scheduled departure. I will naturally help to my utmost in any way which does not affect my scheduled departure." On March 20, they formally advised me that I could not leave Taiwan.

---

34 From my Letter of Protest 抗議書, March 22, 1980, section 4b, to Wang Ching-hsi 汪敬煦, Commander of the Taiwan Garrison Command, Shih Ming-chiang 石明江, Chief Prosecutor of the Taipei District Procuracy, and Kung Ling-sheng 孔令晟, Commissioner of the Police Administration in the Ministry of the Interior.

35 *Zhongyang ribao* 中央日報 [*Central Daily News*], March 12, 1980 p. 3.

36 *Lianhebao* 聯合報 [*United Daily*], March 13, 1980, p. 3.

37 Ibid.; *Zhongguo shibao* 中國時報 [*China Times*], March 13, 1980, p. 3; *Zhongyang ribao* 中央日報 [*Central Daily News*], March 13, 1980 p. 3.

38 *Zili wanbao* 自立晚報 [*Independence Evening News*], March 15, 1980, p. 2; *Dahua wanbao* 大華晚報 [*Great China Evening News*], March 15, 1980, p. 3; *Minzu wanbao* 民族晚報 [*Min Tsu Evening News*], March 15, 1980, p. 2.

On March 22, I sent a Letter of Protest 抗議書 to Wang Ching-hsi 汪敬煦, Commander of the Taiwan Garrison Command, Shih Ming-chiang 石明江, Chief Prosecutor of the Taipei District Procuracy, and Kung Ling-sheng 孔令晟, Commissioner of the Police Administration in the Ministry of the Interior with a copy to the American Institute in Taiwan. The Letter of Protest began:

> Because of deep affection for those murdered in the Lin Family murder case, I have sacrificed considerable time and money, [and] neglected my employment and family in order to help the authorities of the Republic of China to solve this crime. I have cooperated with the prosecutors and the police investigating task force in a sincere manner, but some authorities have misled me and used methods which may possibly go beyond the limits prescribed by law. Even worse, the work of the prosecutor and police have at times been sloppy. These actions have infringed on my personal freedom, a freedom enjoyed by all persons in Taiwan irregardless of whether they be Chinese or foreign.

In the letter, I made a number of key points. I noted that the court had produced a document on March 4 prohibiting me from leaving Taiwan, but that I did not see this document until 4.30 PM on March 20. Although the document was not secret, I was only allowed to see the document through the intervention of AIT and even then I was not allowed to make a copy. I noted that this document, which stated that I was "under grave suspicion" 涉有重嫌, was "empty words" 空言 since persons responsible for the investigation in the police and General Wang himself had all personally assured me that I was not under suspicion. On March 14, in response to my question, Police Team Leader Chang Yu-wen 張友文 told me that my status was "important related person" 重要關係人. I replied that the term "important related person" had no legal status, and he replied, "that is, an important witness" 就是重要證人. In my Letter of Protest, I noted that according to ROC law, authorities do not have the power to prevent a witness from leaving the country. I concluded this point:

> Since the persons responsible for investigating the case believe I am not under suspicion, the prosecutor must also have no basis for saying I am under suspicion. Because of this, I believe there is no basis for saying I am under suspicion. The objective must be to prevent me from exercising my legal rights and privileges. I request that this illegal and unsuitable order be immediately rescinded.

The Letter of Protest also gave many examples of sloppy work on the part of the police. For example, on March 12 General Wang stated that I had received a phone call from "Dr Tien 田醫師."[39] (As I noted, I was then outside buying a box lunch.) I had seen no evidence of such a call and Dr Tien had told friends that he had made no such call. I had suggested to the police that the call might be from "Mr Tien", i.e Tien Yung-kang 田永康 of the Government Information Office, but this was never pursued.

In conclusion, I emphasized my friendly ties with Taiwan and my "hope to return frequently to Taiwan in the future." I ended with a threat. If my case is delayed further, "I will be forced to reveal all of these truths to the foreign and Chinese press and to concerned persons around the world in an effort to obtain justice."

Sometime during this period, the *United Daily* printed an article about me that I found quite distasteful.[40] Previously, I had had good relations with the *United Daily* and had bought many items from them. In addition, the Director of their Service Department, Chang Pao-chin 張寶琴, and I had established a social relationship which even included a lunch with our respective children. After the article was published, I tried to ring Chang Pao-chin, but she was overseas, so I rang her husband, Wang Pi-cheng 王必成, then publisher of the newspaper and son of the founder of the *United Daily*, Wang Ti-wu 王惕吾.

When I rang Wang Pi-cheng, I said, "We haven't met, but I know your wife."

He asked who I was and when I told him, he replied, "Oh!" and asked why I had called.

I replied, "We ought to be friends, but today your newspaper has been very impolite."

He told me that he had not read the newspaper and asked me to wait so that he could look at it. He then asked, "What's the problem?"

I responded, "First, your report is not true. And, secondly, it implies that I have a relationship to the murder case."

He answered, "You are a person in the news. Anything that is related to you can be reported."

---

39 Dr Tien, Tien Chao-ming 田朝明 (1918–2010), also known as Papa Tien 田爸爸, was a well-known member of the opposition. His wife, Tien Meng-shu 田孟淑 (1934-), has long been well-known among the opposition as Mama Tien 田媽媽. A lovely 2011 film of their life, available on DVD, is called 牽阮的手, translated as "Hand in Hand." Tien Chiu-chin 田秋菫, the daughter of the Tiens, found the severely injured Lin Huan-chun as well as her murdered grandmother and younger sisters. Tien Chiu-chin has served as a DPP legislator since 2004.

40 I have not been able to find the specific article.

I replied, "I know your wife. If the news media said that Bruce Jacobs, this person in the news, has a relationship 關係 with the wife of Wang Pi-cheng, would you be happy?"

He answered, "It is not that kind of relationship."

I agreed, "Of course, it is not that kind of relationship, but if other newspapers in Taiwan wrote that Bruce Jacobs and Chang Pao-chin, the wife of Wang Pi-cheng, have a relationship, would you be happy?"

Wang replied, "We'll study it" 我們研究, 研究.[41]

After that, the *United Daily* was very polite to me. I knew that my telephone call had proven successful when I learned that Wang and his wife were telling people the same story in a defensive way in an effort to prevent future problems. This was another case of a weak person winning out over the powerful. A nice additional aspect was that members of my police protection group were very supportive of my phone call and kept urging me on!

The military court trial of the eight Kaohsiung defendants began on March 18. Every evening after the trial, I would talk on the telephone to foreign and domestic reporters who had attended the day's proceedings. Of course, during these conversations, I would learn about the sensitive things which had occurred that day and, as explained in Chapter 3, the next day's issue of the *China Times* would have the material in the transcript. In my basement room, I—like many in Taiwan at the time—paid close attention to the trial. Fortunately, news of the foreign "Big Beard" declined at this time.

I acceded to the request of Wu Kuo-tung 吳國棟, a reporter for the *China Times*, for my first interview since I had come under police protection. The police cooperated with this interview, which was published on Sunday, March 23, a day with no news on the trial.[42] After answering a wide variety of questions about what I had done over the past few weeks, I concluded: "I hope the police can give me a specific date when I can go [home]. Although I have freedom, as the prosecutor said, I have freedom only within the boundaries of Taiwan. This is not what I want. I have all along cooperated. Now, I hope the police will cooperate with me. I need to return to Australia to teach and to take care of my daughter. I have already written a letter of protest to the Police Administration."

The final question asked, "Do you believe this kind of investigation is necessary?"

---

41   For the original Chinese of this conversation, see Jia Bo 家博 (J. Bruce Jacobs), "Jia Bo (Bruce Jacobs) xiansheng fangwen jilu," p. 309.

42   *Zhongguo shibao* 中國時報 [*China Times*], March 23, 1980, p. 3. This interview has helped me date some events described above.

I responded, "I believe it is necessary and I understand. I even thank the security personnel who have protected me these past twenty days. They have been extremely good to me, extremely good."

My Press Conference and Subpoena to Appear in the Prosecutor's Court

The Kaohsiung Incident Military Court Trial of the eight key defendants began on March 18 and continued until March 28. My lawyer, Henry Rai, said it would be desirable to keep my case separate from that of the Kaohsiung Incident case. Unfortunately, that proved impossible as the Prosecutor subpoenaed me on March 25, 1980 to appear in the Prosecutor's Court on Wednesday, March 26 at 2.30 PM.[43] The subpoena was labeled a "criminal subpoena" 刑事傳票 and I was registered as "the defendant" 被告 with the case described as "murder" 殺人.

This incident proved another case where cultural assumptions led to misunderstandings. The police and prosecutors thought that I would be quiet if they issued a subpoena. From their perspective, it was a disgrace to receive a piece of paper declaring that I was a "defendant" in a "murder" case. From my perspective, these accusations needed to be challenged. I was in a weak position as one person against a very powerful authoritarian state, which controlled the press and the courts, and I felt that being as open as possible would provide me with the best protection.

Thus, I called a press conference for 12.30 PM. Getting a venue for the press conference proved difficult, but we finally booked the Central Hotel 中央大飯店 and notified the press. We also prepared 75 photocopies of such key documents as my subpoena, my written record of interrogation for March 4–5 which I signed in Taiwanese "Bruce Jacobs wants to sleep," and my letter of protest against my inability to leave Taiwan and my need to return home to Australia.[44] The police in my protection detail were very helpful to me.

---

43   *Lianhebao* 聯合報 [*United Daily*], March 26, 1980, p. 2. The same page had a story from the AP, probably written by Edith (Edie) Lederer. *The China Post*, March 26, 1980, p. 12 also had a short story while the afternoon *China News*, March 26, 1980, p. 4 also noted that I had called a press conference at 12.30 PM on March 26. Two of the afternoon Chinese-language newspapers also reported the news of the subpoena and press conference, *Zili wanbao* 自立晚報 [*Independence Evening News*], March 26, 1980, p. 2 and *Minzu wanbao* 民族晚報 [*Min Tsu Evening News*], March 26, 1980, p. 2.

44   The text of at least two of these documents appears in *Taiwan shibao* 台灣時報 [*Taiwan Times*], March 27, 1980, p. 3.

I was quite surprised when 125 foreign and domestic journalists showed up for my press conference and my 75 photocopies of all the documents did not begin to meet the demand! In accord with advice from Henry Rai, I began my press conference explaining that I had been subpoenaed by the Prosecutor and did not know if I would be free to talk with them again. I made clear that I had absolutely no connection with the Lin family murder case. I noted that if I was incarcerated and later said something else, they could work out what had happened. Although stated very politely and obliquely, the journalists knew that I was referring to testimony in the Kaohsiung military trial that "confessions" had not been freely given.

I then opened the press conference to questions. No matter how rudely a question was asked and no matter how many times it was repeated, I answered each and every question politely and calmly.[45] Finally, after about one and a half hours, the police protecting me told me that we had to go to the Prosecutor. I thanked the journalists and concluded in "a sort of farewell tone" 惜別的口氣:

> I don't know after responding to the subpoena whether or not I'll be able to see everyone again. So, I must emphasize that, if in the future there is any confession, I most certainly did not write it. It most certainly would have been forced out. And, now my body is in excellent health. If in the future my health is not good, you can compare [the different states of health] and understand.[46]

When we arrived at the Prosecutor's Court, a huge number of reporters had already arrived including television reporters with cameras. Seeing so many reporters waiting to see whether I would emerge from the Prosecutors or be incarcerated, I suddenly felt assured. With so many reporters waiting to learn my fate, I felt that I was going to be okay.

Up to this time, my interactions with the police and prosecutors had all been in Mandarin and in Taiwanese (Hokkien). When we got into the Prosecutor's court, I demanded an English interpreter. I did this for two reasons. First, AIT had sent in a person to listen and I wanted to facilitate his ability to take notes. Secondly, I was sick and tired of being asked the same questions over and over again and I wanted to protest. The first interpreter they brought in was hopeless and finally they brought in someone who proved a bit better. Eventually, they did move to new questions and there appeared to be the open-

---

45 Some of the text of the press conference appears in *Taiwan shibao* 台灣時報 [*Taiwan Times*], March 27, 1980, p. 3.

46 *Zhongguo shibao* 中國時報 [*China Times*], March 27, 1980, p. 5.

ing up of new areas of inquiry. When this happened, I was happy to speak Chinese.

The Prosecutor's court session ended about 4.50 PM and I was free to go, though not leave Taiwan. I told the waiting journalists that I felt the Prosecutor had moved into new areas of inquiry and that I hoped they would follow certain suggestions which I had made for the investigation. I expressed my hope that the police would soon capture the murderer.

That evening, the three television stations all broadcast the news of my press conference and my visit to the prosecutor as the second news item after the Kaohsiung military trial. One of the stations actually broadcast footage of my stating that I had nothing to do with the murder case and that if I should say something different after incarceration, they could work out what had happened. So, even a weak individual could have some minor victories!

The next morning newspapers were reasonably objective in printing the content of my press conference and, as indicated above, one newspaper even printed some full texts of the documents that I had handed out. However, that afternoon the press primarily reported the police response. I later learned from journalist friends that the press conference had been too late for the deadlines of the afternoon press, so they were angry. Of course, it was the Prosecutor who had set the time of my subpoenaed appearance and this in turn set the time of my press conference. The one good news on March 27 was that Lin Huan-chun had recovered sufficiently and was able to leave the hospital.

Things quieted down after that. On April 5, in an effort to help me and demonstrate that I was a good scholar, the independent monthly *Great Epoch* 大時代 published a Chinese translation of my 1976 *China Quarterly* article on Taiwan's media as a research resource[47] and they also published an interview with me on Sino-American relations and the future of Taiwan.[48] But, a couple of days later the cover of a newsweekly had a picture of me at my press conference just below a picture of Wu Chun-fa 吳春發, who had been executed as a result of the Yu Teng-fa case of January 1979 (see Chapter 1).[49] Of course, being paired with an executed prisoner did not make me feel well!

---

47 Jia Bo 家博 (J. Bruce Jacobs), "Taiwan de baozhi meijie: zhengzhi de goutong huan ji yanjiu de ziliao laiyuan 台灣的報紙媒介: 政治的溝通環及研究的資料來源 [Taiwan's Newspaper Media: Political Communications Link and Research Resource]," *Da shidai* 大時代 [*Great Epoch*], no. 10 (April 5, 1980). The original was Jacobs, "Taiwan's Press," pp. 778–788.

48 Geng Lisun 耿立孫, "Jia Bo lun Zhongmei guanxi he Taiwan qiantu 迦博論中美關係和台灣前途 [Bruce Jacobs Discusses Sino-American Relations and Taiwan's Future]," *Da shidai* 大時代 [*Great Epoch*], no. 10 (April 5, 1980), pp. 23–24.

49 See front cover, *Yazhou shiji* 亞洲世紀 [*Asian Century*], No. 141, April 11, 1980. Wu Chun-fa, also known as Wu Tai-an 吳泰安 was arrested in October 1978 and executed on May 28, 1979. For details, see Jacobs, "Taiwan 1979," p. 90.

About this same time, the police began to release more unfavorable news about me. On April 8 the *United Daily* had an article which told a number of lies about my personal life. The article also stated that the words of the two witnesses testifying that I had gone to the Lin family house at noon on February 28 were confirmed, even though the two witnesses disagreed on the time and whether or not I had gone into the house! But the article also raised questions. The subpoena had formally said I was a "defendant," but I was not incarcerated. I could not leave Taiwan and I was eating and living at public expense. An interview with a member of the Special Task Force at the end of the article did not enlighten. According to the police, I was hiding something, but they felt the possibility of my helping them further was slight. The article concluded that the Prosecutor would "delay" 拖 and that I would have to spend more time in Taiwan.[50]

The next day an article in the *Min Tsu Evening News* revealed for the first time that I was staying at the Grand Hotel. The headline said that I was "eating and drinking a lot, refusing to cooperate and looking for an excuse to go quietly" 大吃大喝, 巨合作, 借故開溜. Although the police were paying for my food and room, the article said that I was refusing to cooperate honestly with the police.[51] A third article the following day, based on a "leak from the Special Task Force" stated that I had collected lots of materials which had no relationship to my academic research. This, the article stated, caused both the police and the prosecutor "to deepen further their doubts about Bruce Jacobs."[52]

My "Protection" Becomes More Relaxed

Sometime in early April, I could no longer handle having so many people in my room and not seeing the sun. So, after agreement, I was shifted to an upstairs room in the back of the old part of the Grand Hotel close to Yuan Mountain 圓 山. Here I had a room to myself and the police remained next door. Any dangers were reduced as I was at the end of the hall. The murder case was making little progress and I began to feel safer and to push the limits. I began to wander more and to run. I ran all over and around Yuan Mountain and I also ran with the Taipei chapter of Hash House Harriers, a place I made many new friends. The original policeman sent to run with me on the Hashes could not keep up, so another policeman, who had no problems keeping up, came running

---

50 Article by Tang Ching-lan 唐經瀾, *Lianhebao* 聯合報 [*United Daily*], April 8, 1980, p. 3.
51 *Minzu wanbao* 民族晚報 [*Min Tsu Evening News*], April 9, 1980, p. 2.
52 *Taiwan ribao* 台灣日報 [*Taiwan Daily*], April 10, 1980, p. 3.

with me. This policeman was named Chiang Yung-chen and I nicknamed him "Shadow."

When running by myself or going out to buy something, the police just asked that I not follow the same routine every day, but change times and routes. I also read a lot including such books as the Sui and Tang Dynasties volume of the *Cambridge History of China*, a volume that had been instantly pirated in Taiwan.[53] I remember thinking how the Sui and Tang dynasties resembled both the People's Republic of China and the Taiwan of that time in emphasizing the admission of guilt through confessions in criminal cases.

I also began to try to pressure the security authorities into considering their costs in maintaining me in Taiwan. They were spending a lot of taxpayers' funds to support me and I wanted the security forces to have to demonstrate that the expended funds were worthwhile to their superiors. On the other hand, I felt guilty spending too much of the Taiwan taxpayers' hard-earned income—I had many friends in the Taiwan countryside where I had conducted considerable field research, so I didn't waste food or drink, though I did eat virtually every type of dish that the Grand Hotel offered and, after a while, it did become boring. I should also note that I personally had several expenses which mounted quickly. I had to pay for my own laundry (as I just did not feel like washing my own clothes by hand) and I had to pay for my own telephone calls back home to Australia. In addition, my lawyer also cost a considerable amount. Altogether, my out of pocket expenses for three months totaled some US$6,500–7,500, a considerable sum in 1980.

On April 9 I wrote an "Request" 聲請 to the Prosecutor. I noted that two weeks had passed since I was questioned by the Prosecutor on March 26, but that on the basis of newspaper reports, the case appeared to have made no progress. I again raised issues concerning the truth of the testimony of the so-called "secret witness." In the letter I wrote, "This defendant himself knows he is without guilt and is not afraid of any scientific investigation method which can determine the truth; I only fear torture, interrogation without sleep, or other inappropriate methods to force statements which are not true; I fear even more the guessing and speculations which have limited and obstructed this defendant's freedom." I stated, "this defendant is willing to guarantee returning [to Taiwan]."

On April 11, Hung Chih-liang went on trial. *The Australian*, a key national daily in Australia, had provided me with journalist credentials as early as

---

53   Denis Twitchett, ed. *The Cambridge History of China, Volume 3: Sui and T'ang China, 589–906, Part I* (Cambridge, London, New York and Melbourne: Cambridge University Press, 1979).

mid-March. I rang the Taiwan Garrison Command and was encouraged to come and get a ticket to attend the trial. When I arrived, however, I was refused entry. The different afternoon newspapers responded differently. The *Independence Evening News* had a short item with a picture of me with my hand up towards the camera.[54] The *Great China Evening News* had a fairly prominent story with a large photo of me together with the chief of my protection detail (though this was not indicated in the story). The story's emphasis was that I was denied entry because I had not applied earlier.[55] The *Min Tsu Evening News* headlined that I was "intrusively creating a disturbance" 鬧鬧 with a photo of me leaning with my right arm raised against a wall and my left arm on my hip captioned "Look at his manner" 看他這樣子.[56] If I didn't know better, I would say that the person in the photo was arrogant! Most newspapers the next morning also carried the item, usually with a photo.

This press coverage on April 11 and 12 caused me to write to James Soong, Director-General of the Government Information Office on April 12. I wrote that "distorted and blatantly false stories about me... have damaged my personal and scholarly reputation here in Taiwan [and] have caused me great distress." I reiterated what had happened noting that I had made every effort to apply properly to the authorities, had gone to the Military Court at the request of a Taiwan Garrison Command official, was denied entry because I represented the foreign press and not because I had not applied, and that I did not create a disturbance. For verification of these statements, I asked James Soong to check with Mr Wang Chao, who was head of my police protection unit. The two-page letter concluded:

> Finally, it is my understanding that, according to Republic of China law, the press must publish corrections. I hope you will act in your capacity as Director-General of the Government Information Office and demand the same accuracy in the local press as you demand of the foreign press. As I am sure you can understand, the distorted and inaccurate press coverage of me, together with my inability to be reunited with my daughter or to conduct my teaching at La Trobe University, has caused me great personal distress and anguish. I hope you will see that the local press acts according to law at the earliest possible moment and that future press coverage of me "reports and not distorts."

---

54   *Zili wanbao* 自立晚報 [*Independence Evening News*], April 11, 1980, p. 2.
55   *Dahua wanbao* 大華晚報 [*Great China Evening News*], April 11, 1980, p. 3.
56   *Minzu wanbao* 民族晚報 [*Min Tsu Evening News*], April 11, 1980, p. 2.

I wrote, "I look forward to your early reply", but I received no response.

On April 14 I wrote a letter to the Chief Prosecutor, Shih Ming-chiang 石明江, thanking him for his response of April 12, but noting that his response had not answered any of the important points raised in my letter. I noted that, speaking frankly, it appeared that his office was conducting "investigations only in form" 形式調查 [57] and had not obtained any genuine results. I said that I had not yet met the Chief Prosecutor personally and expressed the hope that I could meet him within one or two days as the Lin Family Murder case was Taiwan's most important criminal case at the time. Chief Prosecutor Shih did not respond.

I had applied several times to leave Taiwan and each time the application was rejected. One newspaper headlined, "Handling [His] Application to Leave [Taiwan] is Difficult, Bruce Jacobs is like a Rubber Ball, Prosecutor and Police Kick Him Back and Forth."[58]

The Chief of the Detective Bureau, Tsao Chi 曹極, became famous because he told a committee of the Taiwan Provincial Assembly that he was certain the police would solve the Lin family murder case. Tsao emphasized this by stating that the chances of solving the case were 9,999 out of 10,000. The Commissioner of the Police Administration in the Ministry of the Interior, Kung Ling-sheng 孔令晟, was a little more pessimistic. Kung told the Taiwan Provincial Assembly that the police had put all their hopes on solving the case upon the foreigner, Bruce Jacobs, but now all they can say is the Bruce Jacobs is under suspicion, but they cannot "confirm" 肯定 that he participated in this case. Kung said that many cases cannot be solved in the short-term and need to be "pursued" 拖 for two or three years. Kung also stated that they absolutely would not allow any foreign influence on the case.[59]

I later had the opportunity to meet with Tsao Chi in his office. Among a variety of other topics, he asked why I was in Taiwan. I replied that I was conducting research. He launched into a criticism of John King Fairbank. I said that Fairbank was from Harvard and that I was from Columbia and asked whether he knew that Harvard and Columbia universities were the leaders of two different academic factions 學派 in Chinese studies? He was quite surprised and did not raise the issue of Fairbank again. The next year, Tsao Chi

---

57 I did not realize it at the time, but the term 形式調查 is a homophone of "criminal investigation" 刑事調查. My lawyer, Henry Rai, was excellent.

58 I am pretty certain the article is from *Dahua wanbao* 大華晚報 [*Great China Evening News*], April 11, 1980, p. 3. However, my source is a photocopy given to me by AIT. The original Chinese is: 申請離境處理為難, 家博好像皮球, 檢警踢來踢去.

59 *Lianhebao* 聯合報 [*United Daily*], April 22, 1980, p. 3.

published his memoirs about investigating the Lin Family Murder Case, memoirs in which my name does not appear.[60] Tsao never lived down his boast that 9,999 chances out of 10,000 he would solve the case.

On April 23 the *Central Daily News* reported that two weeks earlier the Taiwan police had written to Interpol to find out if I had any previous record. The previous day the Detective Bureau had received a letter from Interpol stating that I had no "bad" 不良 or other records. The FBI also sent a letter stating the same thing.[61]

The incompetence of the police repeatedly became apparent. For example, a fairly substantial report revealed that Commissioner of the Police Administration in the Ministry of the Interior Kung Ling-sheng stated that I was the only "defendant" in the Lin Family Murder case and again said that the police had put all their hopes on solving the case upon me. He said that I still had not made clear two issues. First, did I go to the scene of the crime the evening of February 28 at 5 PM or 6.30 PM? Since the police were there in great numbers, they would have known! At least, this was an improvement from the repeated police claims that I had gone to the house at noon. Secondly, and even more farcical, Kung stated that I had gone to China for two days before arriving in Taiwan on January 21. He asked, why had I not revealed this?[62] The answer, of course, was that I had not gone. How they obtained such incorrect false information beggars the imagination. Similar stupidity repeatedly stymied the investigation.

While in Taipei under police protection, I had been missing my friends in the Chiayi countryside where I had conducted field research in 1971–1973 and every year from 1976 through 1980. Finally, on April 30, the police agreed to take me to Chiayi and we spent the day there. My friends were very curious about what was going on! They knew from our living together over several years that I loved children and it did not seem likely to them that I had killed Lin's children. They also knew that the reports in the newspapers were not reliable. When we arrived, some of my friends took care of the police while others talked to me to find out what was really happening. I apparently told my closest friend there, my "brother" A-hiong 阿雄, two things. First, get your children

---

60 Cao Ji 曹極, "Zhencha Lin Yixiong jiashu ming'an huiyilu 偵查林義雄家屬命案回憶錄 [Memoirs of Investigating the Lin I-hsiung Family Murder Case]," *Lianhe yuekan* 聯合月刊 [*United Monthly*], no. 1 (August 1981), pp. 108–127.

61 *Zhongyang ribao* 中央日報 [*Central Daily News*], April 23, 1980 p. 3. The *Taiwan Daily* made virtually the same report, *Taiwan ribao* 台灣日報 [*Taiwan Daily*], April 23, 1980, p. 3.

62 *Minzu wanbao* 民族晚報 [*Min Tsu Evening News*], April 24, 1980, p. 2.

educated as much as you can. Secondly, stay out of politics. Twelve years later A-hiong reminded me of this. He had educated his children and he had stayed out of politics during the authoritarian years, though he had become involved in a minor way with the Farmers' Association after democratization.

The newspapers were confused about this visit. The *China Times* had the basics of the story, that I had conducted field research in Chiayi and had friends there. The article stated that my purpose was to see friends and "recreation" 要來玩.[63] In their short piece, the *Taiwan Times* had some facts correct, but puzzled over the purpose of the trip, suggesting that it might just be only a courtesy 禮貌上 trip to visit friends.[64] The *Taiwan New Life News* simply said I visited friends where I had conducted field research.[65] The *Commons Daily*, in a longer article, claimed that my visit caused a "commotion" 騷動 in Chiayi. The story made clear that I had lived there a "not short" time, but incorrectly stated that I had married a local girl.[66] The *Taiwan Daily* stated that I had seen eight friends, all of whom were connected to the church.[67] Clearly, much of the press was incompetent too.

On May 3, the *United Daily* said that the murder case had not been solved for over two months and that my situation was "difficult to handle" 辣手 for the prosecutor and the police. The article said they could not keep me in Taiwan indefinitely, but they could also not crack the case. According to a high-ranking police officer, the "police know that Bruce Jacobs could not possibly be the murderer in the Lin family murder case" 警方了解, 家博不可能是林宅血案的兇手. The article continued that if the Special Task Force could not obtain some powerful evidence, they would have to let me leave Taiwan.[68]

Three days later, the same newspaper reported that the police felt "overburdened" 不勝負荷 with the long-term protection of me. In addition to my living costs, the police also had to support the costs of ten policemen, though these numbers had been reduced to three or four. According to one source, the Detective Bureau had spent about NT$300,000 (US$8,300). The report continued that a high-ranking police officer said, if in the near future there was still no concrete development in the Lin family murder case, the police and prosecutor would cautiously have to consider the question of whether I could leave.[69]

---

63 *Zhongguo shibao* 中國時報 [*China Times*], May 1, 1980, p. 3.
64 *Taiwan shibao* 台灣時報 [*Taiwan Times*], May 1, 1980, p. 3.
65 *Taiwan Xinshengbao* 台灣新生報 [*Taiwan New Life News*], May 1, 1980, p. 3.
66 *Minzhong ribao* 民眾日報 [*Commons Daily*], May 1, 1980, p. 3.
67 *Taiwan ribao* 台灣日報 [*Taiwan Daily*], May 1, 1980, p. 3.
68 *Lianhebao* 聯合報 [*United Daily*], May 3, 1980, p. 3.
69 *Lianhebao* 聯合報 [*United Daily*], May 6, 1980, p. 3.

On May 6 I wrote another formal letter of "Request" to the Prosecutor. Much of the content repeated earlier letters, but I again asked to leave Taiwan and stated that this would be auspicious 幸甚 for me as well as for Sino-American and Sino-Australian friendship.

On May 15, an article in the *Great China Evening News* examined legal aspects of my case. Basically, the article said that if I was simply a "related person" 關係人, then I could not be forbidden to leave Taiwan. Making me a "defendant" 被告 enabled the government to forbid my exit and there was no time limit on this restriction. According to the article, I could not claim compensation for loss of earnings or any other costs.[70]

The circumstances of my enforced stay in Taiwan enabled me to understand who my true friends were. People like Dr Chao Shou-po 趙守博, Professor Hwang Yueh-chin 黃越欽, a professor at National Chengchi University and a future member of the Council of Grand Justices, Taiwan's Constitutional Court, and Professor Hu Fo 胡佛 of National Taiwan University responded to phone calls and came to see me at some risks to themselves. I can only admire their courage. Others proved less laudable. Wei Yung 魏鏞, Director of the Cabinet's Research, Development and Evaluation Commission 研考會, a person I had known in the United States from the early 1970s, repeatedly refused to accept a phone call from me. John C. Kuan 關中 answered the phone at home, but when he heard who I was, just dropped the phone and I listened to what was happening in his house for the next twenty minutes.

In addition to those mentioned earlier, I would also like to thank a variety of people for their assistance. Many people in AIT were both helpful and friendly. I especially appreciated the help from Mark Pratt. Mark gave me a bottle of single-malt Scotch whisky and changed my drinking habits forever! Mark also knew Taiwan and its politics extremely well. One night we were talking and I asked him how many security agencies Taiwan had. Mark instantly replied, "Thirteen." I asked him to name them and he immediately reeled off eleven. I said, "Mark, that's only eleven. What about the other two?" Mark replied that there had to be at least two more to look after the other eleven! In addition, to Mark, I must thank Charles Cross, the Director of AIT, and Richard Williams, Michael Klosson and Evans Revere, who were often on the end of the telephone line making certain that I was okay.

I also benefitted from my Australian connections. I would especially like to thank my then Vice-Chancellor [President] of La Trobe University, Professor John Scott. John wrote to Australian government officials and he wrote to President Chiang Ching-kuo and the Taiwan foreign minister. John also made

---

70   *Dahua wanbao* 大華晚報 [*Great China Evening News*], May 15, 1980, p. 3.

clear within La Trobe University that my detention resulted from my work and he made certain that my pay and employment continued without any difficulties.

As a result of communications from Professor John Scott and others, Andrew Peacock, the then Australian Minister of Foreign Affairs, wrote in a letter dated May 16, 1980 to Sir Billy Snedden, then Speaker of the Australian House of Representatives:

> I am disturbed that Dr Jacobs, an Australian resident with tenure at Latrobe [sic] University, is being forced to stay in Taiwan without proper explanation given to him. Although Australia is not officially represented in Taiwan, the Department of Foreign Affairs has conveyed through appropriate channels to the Taipei authorities the Australian Government's concern about Dr Jacobs' welfare, as well as our hope that he will be given the full protection of the law and not detained in Taiwan longer than is necessary. A number of Australian senators and members [of the House of Representatives] have expressed similar concerns in a letter to the Foreign Minister in Taipei.
>
> The Department of Foreign Affairs is closely watching developments in this matter. An officer of the Department has spoken to Dr Jacobs by telephone, and an officer of the Department of Immigration and Ethnic Affairs based on Hong Kong recently visited Dr Jacobs. The Department of Foreign Affairs is in close contact with United States authorities in order to ensure that our efforts on Dr Jacobs behalf are further coordinated with those of the United States.
>
> I believe that the Taipei authorities are aware of the extent of our concern at Dr Jacobs treatment. We will continue to take steps as appropriate to enable his early departure from Taiwan.

My Australian visitors included two senators, John Knight from the Australian Capital Territory and Baden Teague from South Australia. Both John and Baden spent a lot of time with me and also told their Taiwan interlocutors that the Australian government was very concerned about me. After returning to Australia, I also spent time with them at Parliament House in Canberra. Sadly, John suddenly died the next year in March 1981. I also had a visit from the Vice-Chancellor [President] of Griffith University, Professor John Willett. Professor Willett sent good wishes from Australia and from my university. He also expressed concern to the Taiwan authorities about my not being able to leave Taiwan.

In addition, I had support from major media in the United States and in Australia. Richard Bernstein wrote an early, prominent article in *The Washington Star*.[71] Ten days later, *The Washington Star* had a shorter article.[72] My classmate and friend, Don Shapiro, wrote prominent un-bylined articles for *Time* magazine[73] and the *New York Times*.[74] Edie Lederer of the Associated Press, whom James Soong had attacked for her coverage of the Kaohsiung trial,[75] visited and wrote several articles. In Australia, Hamish McDonald of *The Age* came down from Tokyo to Taipei and wrote two key early articles[76] as well as a later follow-up from Tokyo.[77] David Guthrie-Jones in *The Sun* wrote one of the earliest articles[78] and Jim Clark in *The Age* mentioned me in his piece about the Kaohsiung Incident military trial.[79] Various Australian radio stations also interviewed me. All of this attention was very helpful in what was "the bizarre, Kafkaesque, and occasionally a bit worrisome" experience that I was undergoing.[80]

Another Subpoena to See the Prosecutor

The United States and Taiwan had scheduled a huge conference, the Fourth ROC-USA Joint Business Conference and Trade Forum, to be held at the Grand Hotel May 26–30. This conference expected more than 1,000 government officials, businessmen and industrialists to participate.[81] Forty-eight of the fifty Lieutenant Governors in the United States planned to attend. The Americans

---

71 In the A.M. Extra edition, the article appeared as Richard Bernstein, "Brutal Taiwan Killings Jeopardize American, Top Island Dissident," *The Washington Star* March 17, 1980, pp. A-1, A-6. In the Capital Special edition, the same article was entitled "Taiwan Killings Imperil Dissident, American" and appeared on p. A-6.
72 "Taiwan Now Seeks Death for Dissidents," *The Washington Star* March 27, 1980, p. A-7.
73 "A Deepening Mystery," *Time* March 31, 1980, p. 13.
74 "American, Held in Murder Case, Hopeful of Leaving Taiwan Soon," *The New York Times* May 7, 1980, p. A8.
75 *Lianhebao* 聯合報 [*United Daily*], March 21, 1980, p. 1; *China Post*, March 21, 1980, p. 12; *China News*, March 21, 1980, p. 4. Several reporters privately commented that Soong attacked Lederer because she was a woman.
76 Hamish McDonald, "Lecturer Can't Go Home: Police," *The Age*, March 21, 1980; Hamish McDonald, "Lecturer given 'defendant' summons," *The Age*, March 26, 1980.
77 Hamish McDonald, "Teacher has to stay in Taiwan," *The Age*, May 12, 1980.
78 David Guthrie-Jones, "Lecturer under guard," *The Sun*, March 19, 1980, p. 13.
79 Jim Clark, "Prison unites an opposition," *The Age*, March 22, 1980.
80 "American, Held in Murder Case, Hopeful of Leaving Taiwan Soon," p. A8.
81 *China Post* (International Air-Mail Edition), May 24, 1980, p. 1.

told the Taiwan government that they could not control me during the Forum and that they expected I would speak to many of the delegates. In fact, Charles "Chuck" Cross, the Director of AIT in Taipei, told me two months before the Forum that he saw the Forum as a key time for me. Mr Cross said that he thought they would either let me leave Taiwan or would imprison me before the Forum.

Mr Cross was spot-on. I received a subpoena to see the Prosecutor on Wednesday, May 21. I was, of course, nervous because I did not know what to expect. The prosecutor brought forth a witness, who he said, had claimed that I had gone to the Lin family home at noon. He said that they had another witness, but that witness was too afraid to be in the same room as me.

The witness who testified was a woman in her fifties. She obviously did not have a high "cultural" level because she could not speak any language other than Hakka even though she lived in Taipei (opposite the Lin family home). She testified that she had seen me go to the Lin family home at noon on February 28. Then, the prosecutor told me that I could cross-examine the witness.

Cross-examination is a complex skill and I had not received any training in the area. Yet, this series of questions would determine whether or not I would be a free man. So, I thought a bit and then asked the woman, "How many foreigners with beards have you seen?"

She answered, "One" and made clear that I was the one she had seen.

I then asked, "If you have only seen one, then how do you know it was me?"

She replied, "Because I have seen only one, therefore I know it was you."

I felt the frustration of the Prosecutor sitting next to me! He realized that as a foreigner, I would have to have an open trial in Taiwan and that he now had no case. He told me that I could leave Taiwan that evening.

I later learned that the decision to let me leave Taiwan had been made by President Chiang Ching-kuo himself. Apparently, Professor Hu Fo 胡佛 went to see Tao Pai-chuan 陶百川 and the two discussed my difficulties. Tao then went to see Chiang Ching-kuo. Without the bravery of Hu Fo and Tao Pai-chuan, I might instead have languished in a Taiwan prison.

I had to arrange a "guarantor" 保證人 of ROC citizenship to guarantee that I would return to Taiwan if required. I booked my flight to Hong Kong and went back to the Grand Hotel to pack. The police arranged for my suitcase to go on the plane.

When I arrived at the Hong Kong Airport, I saw a sociology colleague from La Trobe University, Dr Yoshio Sugimoto, also in the luggage area. We had a big hug. Then I went to the apartment of John and Hsi-ching Dolfin, old friends from my postgraduate work at Columbia, where I stayed the night. It was so good to be with friends outside of the grip of Taiwan's security agencies. Later, I opened my suitcase and saw that everything had been checked and tossed about. I broke down and cried.

Of course, I had long before sent out the sensitive materials.

Who Committed the Murders?

As stated earlier, on Februrary 28, just after the murders, several friends said that they thought the security agencies had killed Auntie Lim, Liang-chun and Ting-chun. On the night, I said that the security agencies could not be so stupid. At the time, I did have a few hypotheses.

First, I thought it possible that a deranged person had committed the murders. The press in Taiwan was filled with hate towards the defendants and the addresses of the defendants were given with the indictments, which were widely published in the press. The Lin family home was on the first floor and relatively easily entered. The family of Yao Chia-wen, for example, lived on the fifth floor and escape from such a location would have been more difficult. So, I thought a deranged person might have committed the murder.

Second, I thought it was possible that the Chinese Communists had sent over an assassin to stir up social unrest in Taiwan. Such a person could have come to Taiwan on a morning plane and left that afternoon.

In considering these possibilities, one has to remember that neither the deaths of Chen Wen-cheng 陳文成 on July 2, 1981 nor that of Henry Liu (Liu Yi-liang 劉宜良, Jiang Nan 江南) on October 14, 1984 had yet occurred. Because Henry Liu was killed in the United States and because the FBI had wire-taps, we know that Taiwan's security forces were involved. In addition, we have to remember that, to the best of my knowledge, Auntie Lim, Liang-chun and Ting-chun are the only family members of political prisoners ever to be killed in Taiwan.

The murder case still remains unsolved.

Why did I become involved? Mark Pratt of AIT told me there was also a Frenchman who had a beard and who was under consideration. But I walked into the tiger's lair and my prominence in the media helped deflect public attention away from possible internal suspects, including the security agencies, in the murders. As a regular visitor to Taiwan for over fifty years, I can attest that early 1980 was the most xenophobic period I have ever experienced there. The United States had recognized Beijing as of January 1, 1979. On the same date, the United States gave Taiwan one year's notice that the Mutual Security Treaty between the United States and Taiwan would be terminated.

Thus, on January 1, 1980, the United States had no formal obligation to protect Taiwan from invasion and this created great uncertainty on the island. The government promoted "Self-Strengthening Year" 自強年. It was during this insecurity and xenophobia that my "Foreign Big Beard" case came to the fore.

The next chapter considers my return to Taiwan after twelve years. In that chapter, we will consider a report to the Ma Ying-jeou government and reconsider the issue of who might have committed the murders.

CHAPTER 7

Rip Van Winkle Returns to Taiwan

Although I did not know it—and I did not know it until I returned to Taiwan after twelve years, the Taiwan government placed me on the "blacklist" meaning that I was not allowed to return to Taiwan after I left in 1980. Thus, unknowingly, I had joined a group of people whom the authoritarian government feared. In fact, although I had many friends in Taiwan, I had no plans to apply to return as I had no desire to add to my ten weeks of "police protection."

An indirect test of my status occurred in October 1984 when my daughter's mother wanted to take my daughter, then eleven, to Taiwan to visit with her maternal grandparents and other relatives. Naturally, I was concerned about my daughter's safety, especially in the context of the murders of Lin I-hsiung's twin daughters, and I checked carefully with both the United States and Australian governments to ascertain whether or not they would advise my daughter taking such a trip. Both governments believed my daughter would be safe and I gave permission for her trip.

My daughter's trip went smoothly except that her luggage went missing. As she had no clothes, her relatives bought her new clothes. After a week her luggage was "found" and the contents had been tossed about as the security agencies checked carefully to see whether or not I had sent anything "illegal" into Taiwan. Of course, I had not as I did not want to endanger my daughter's life, but this was a reminder of the continuing important roles played by Taiwan's security forces at the time.

As I have written elsewhere, Taiwan began to democratize with the accession of Vice-President Lee Teng-hui to the presidency following the death of President Chiang Ching-kuo in January 1988.[1] The Taiwan representative in Australia at the time was Mr Francias Lee 李宗儒. Francias and I became good friends as he was initially based in Melbourne and we met frequently. Sometime in 1991 Francias noted that Taiwan had changed considerably and suggested that I apply to go to Taiwan. I said that I would not apply, but gave him permission to write that he had talked to me and that I was interested in returning to Taiwan if I would feel safe and able to leave when planned. Francias wrote to Taiwan several times, but received no response concerning me.

I had moved from La Trobe University to Monash University at the beginning of 1991 and in 1992 was appointed a member of the Australia-China

---

1   Jacobs, *Democratizing Taiwan*.

Council. In Australian terms, this was quite a senior appointment requiring approval of the Australian government and I joined several senior persons including the president of a major bank as well as several senior members of the Australian Department of Foreign Affairs and Trade in this role. Francias again wrote to Taiwan and this time he stated that I was now too important in Australia to ignore. Eventually, I received a visa and planned a trip for one month arriving in Taiwan on June 16 and departing on July 17, 1992.

Rip Van Winkle Returns to Taiwan

Francias issued me a sixty-day, single-entry visa which had the hand-written note in Chinese, "Bruce Jacobs, Issued in accord with Ministry of Foreign Affairs cable No. 898 of February 26, 1992" 家博, 依據外交部 81.2.26 第 898 電辦理. The Australian government office in Taiwan arranged a hotel for me not too far from their office. As I wrote upon returning to Australia:

> On the plane to Taiwan, I read "Rip Van Winkle", Washington Irving's story about a man who awakes to a changed world after a twenty-year sleep. Although I had slumbered for less than one-third of the previous twelve years and had followed Taiwan from afar, I discovered parallels between Rip and myself. Most importantly, the American Revolution occurred during Rip's sleep. Had Taiwan's major political changes of the last twelve years been revolutionary? And, I feared, like Rip, it would be "some time before he could get into the regular track of gossip, or could be made to comprehend the strange events that had taken place during his torpor ..."[2]

Things seemed to be going well the first few days. I started to meet with old friends. Then, I heard a knock at my hotel room. It turned out to be the policeman who had run with me in 1980, Chiang Yung-chen, whom I had nicknamed "Shadow." He gave me a big hug, but I was ambivalent about seeing him because I was hoping to be away from the police during this trip. I later was taken to see a senior policeman, who had been involved in the Special Task Force. He told me that they were concerned about my safety.

After a few days, I took the train to Chiayi and went to the countryside. I did not know that virtually everyone in the countryside now had a telephone and

---

[2] Bruce Jacobs, "Rip Van Winkle Returns to Taiwan," *Far Eastern Economic Review* May 13, 1993, p. 36.

so I had not contacted anyone before I arrived. As I wrote at the time: "[W]hen I returned to my 'home' in the countryside, I literally lost my way. 'Western' buildings had replaced virtually every 'traditional' farm house and even the road had been broadened and moved! Furthermore, standards of living in Taiwan's countryside, which had increased considerably from 1971 to 1980, had again risen remarkably."[3] Fortunately, when I got out of my taxi, an older woman saw me and asked, "Are you Bruce Jacobs?" 你是不是家博？I answered "yes" and she took me to the new home of my "family." They were extremely happy to see me and soon villagers were coming to see and welcome me.

Unfortunately, my arrival had also brought a visit from over a hundred security personnel who literally invaded the village. Many villagers pointed at the newcomers. I knew things had changed fundamentally when people made jokes like, "We won't have to lock our house tonight because we have so many people watching it."

In case I had any problems, the senior policeman had given me his card and asked me to call him should I have any difficulties. I rang him in Taipei and said that the invasion of the village was not necessary. I told him that I felt safe in the village and that the invasion had led to his people becoming the butt of jokes. He immediately drove down and we had a discussion with the local police chief at the local police station. The senior policeman agreed to withdraw all of his people. They originally wanted me to tell them if I left the village but I said that I felt safe in the whole of my field site. However, I agreed that if I went outside the area of my field site I would let the local police know. The senior policeman also asked if they could drive me back to Taipei. Since I had not yet been on the Sun Yat-sen Freeway, which had been built during my twelve years on the blacklist, I agreed.

I then spent the next several days in the countryside visiting many old friends. The police operated as agreed and stayed out of my way.

When I went back to Taipei, I did go with the police. Unfortunately, the freeway was very crowded and progress was very slow. Although the car was unmarked, at one stage the police put out their siren and flashing light and we went along the emergency lane on the shoulder a bit faster than most traffic.

In Taipei, I told the police where I was staying, though they already knew. I was quite surprised to find out that they had already booked the room next to mine. Needless to say, I found this quite depressing! The police continued to seek to maintain close contact with me. They frequently invited me out to dinner and we went to KTVs (where you can sing karaoke) as well. They explained to me the difference between KTVs with women as waitresses and KTVs with

---

3 Ibid.

women as hostesses. According to the police, if the woman kneels in front of you, you should not touch her, but if she sits next to you, then it is okay to be friendlier. We went to both types of KTVs, though I never took advantage of my new knowledge as I did not want the police to have any new data on me! (I was also married at this time.)

At the KTVs, the police especially played one song for me because, as they said, they knew it would tug at me emotionally. "The Skies of Taipei" 台北的天空 has the following chorus:

> The Skies of Taipei
> Have the smiles of my youth,
> And they have the places where we rested and enjoyed ourselves together.
> The Skies of Taipei
> Are often in our hearts,
> No matter how many the years of wind and rain, I just want to spend them with you.

> 台北的天空
> 有我年輕的笑容
> 還有我們休息和共享的角落
> 台北的天空
> 常在你我的心中
> 多少風雨的歲月我只願和你渡過

The final two sentences of the last verse say:

> I've been to many different locales, I've undergone many changes,
> But today, I've returned to my own place.

> 我走過異鄉我走過滄桑
> 如今我又再回到自己的地方

One time at a KTV with hostesses, I said I would like to take a photo to remember this "wonderful time." The police immediately said that I could not take a photo. I asked why not? They responded, "The girls would be embarrassed." Of course, it was the police who would have been embarrassed.

The police tried to stay with me constantly. One time I moved into a "love hotel" in an effort to get away. Within two days they had placed a policeman in the lobby letting me know that they knew where I was.

The police constantly asked me to keep both a "low profile" 低調 and to go home early. I noted that I was keeping a low profile, but that my trip would be a failure if I had to leave early. In fact, I gave only three interviews, all with trusted journalists and all of which were published on the morning of July 17, the day I left Taiwan. These interviews were the first time that Taiwan's public had the opportunity to learn about what had happened to me in 1980.

The first interview was with the *Independence Morning Post*.[4] With democratization the *Independence Morning Post* had joined its stable mate, the *Independence Evening Post*, which had continued from the authoritarian period. Both newspapers were quite popular during the early 1990s. Furthermore, the president of the *Independence Morning Post* was my old friend, Wu Cheng-shuo 吳正朔, who in 1980 had worked for the *United Daily*, but had also in October 1979 written a very important article on the Chungtai Hotel Incident (see Chapter 1) for the independent magazine, *Great Epoch*.[5]

The interview was in three parts. The main article was written by Hsu Lu 徐璐, who had been one of the first Taiwan reporters to go to China to report. Wu Cheng-shuo also wrote an article on "Seeing Bruce Jacobs Again" 又見家博. The third article, prominent on the page and entitled "Cursing Expletives,[6] Very Fluent! 罵三字經, 溜得很 !" made reference to my twenty-four hour police interrogation (Chapter 6).

At the request of a DPP friend, I gave the second interview to the *Taiwan Times*, a Kaohsiung-based newspaper which had increasingly demonstrated a Taiwan-centric viewpoint.[7] This interview received the main headline on page 1 and other content reprinted newspaper articles from 1980.

I gave the third interview to *The Journalist Magazine*, whose publisher, Antonio Chiang 江春男（司馬文武） had then been my friend for twenty years. The main interview by Chiu Ming-hui, like the other main interviews, covered what had happened to me in 1980.[8] Antonio wrote a very nice, more personal account of me, which stated that my involvement in the murder case

---

4　*Zili zaobao* 自立早報 [*Independence Morning Post*], July 17, 1992, p. 9.
5　Wu Zhengshuo 吳正朔, "Zhongtai binguan," pp. 7–19.
6　In modern Hokkien, the term "Three Character Classic" means "expletive" when used with the verb "Curse". An English equivalent would be a "four-letter word."
7　*Taiwan shibao* 台灣時報 [*Taiwan Times*], July 27, 1992, pp. 1, 3.
8　Qiu Minghui 邱銘輝, "Wo you yige yue de shijian meiyou kandao taiyang 我有一個月的時間沒有看到太陽 [I did not see the sun for a month]," *Xinxinwen* 新新聞 [*The Journalist*] July 19-July 25, 1992, pp. 10–15.

"from the beginning to the end was an extraordinarily preposterous blunder" 從頭到尾都是極荒謬的誤會.[9]

On the morning of the day I left Taiwan, I was able to accept an invitation to visit the Taipei Seminary of the Presbyterian Church and to talk to their people. During the question and answer period, someone said, "We read in today's paper that you can curse in Hokkien. Please show us!" I answered that I did not think it appropriate to curse in a seminary.

In reflecting upon this 1992 visit, I decided that Taiwan had undergone three major changes. "Taipei remained familiar, though it now had many European shops, Western restaurants and fast-food outlets, new skyscrapers, automatic teller machines at financial institutions and even automatic urinals, which give a small flush when they sense your presence and a big flush when you move away."[10] As noted earlier, the changes in the countryside were much greater.

As I wrote in my "Rip van Winkle" piece:

> The second great change has been the surge of "Taiwanese consciousness" sweeping the island. Until a few years ago the ruling Nationalist Party (Kuomintang) emphasised Taiwan's Chineseness and did not permit the accentuation of Taiwanese culture. Now, the publication of thousands of books concerned with Taiwan politics, history and culture has supplanted the dearth. Restaurants featuring Taiwanese cuisine, politically suspect not long ago, now flourish and have prominent places in major hotels. One hears much more Hokkien, the main Taiwanese dialect, in Taipei and on Taiwan's airwaves. Even mainlanders are learning Hokkien, which has become the language of electoral politics as well as business. Importantly, many mainlander youth, born and raised in Taiwan, possess this new sense "Taiwanese" identity.

Taiwanese now expressed overt pride in their culture. During my month in Taiwan, I was taken countless times to the Shin-yeh 欣葉 chain of restaurants specializing in Taiwanese cuisine. One highlight was a dinner with Chen Chu 陳菊, who took me the Penglai Village 蓬萊邨 Taiwanese restaurant in the Howard 福華 Hotel. Chen Chu told me that under Chiang Kai-shek and Chiang

---

9   Sima Wenwu 司馬文武, "Shi'er nian hou de Taibei tiankong: Jia Bo zheige ren 十二年後的台北天空: 家博這個人 [The Skies of Taipei after Twelve Years: Bruce Jacobs is This Kind of Person]," *Xinxinwen* 新新聞 [*The Journalist*] July 19-July 25, 1992, pp. 12–13 (quote from p. 12).

10 Jacobs, "Rip."

Ching-kuo, restaurants in major hotels had to have Chinese cuisine from Beijing, Shanghai, Sichuan, Hunan or Guangdong or else be foreign restaurants. Taiwanese cuisine was forbidden. During later trips other Taiwanese also took me to the Penglai Village as well as to the Shin Yeh chain and I in turn have introduced foreign friends to Taiwan cuisine at the Penglai Village and at various Shin Yeh branches.

Finally, on this 1992 trip,

> the degree of "democratisation" in Taiwan surprised and impressed me. The press now has "absolute" freedom (to use the word of an opposition publisher), though the broadcast media remain under Nationalist Party control. Even advocacy of Taiwanese Independence has become both legal and politically acceptable. Many old friends ranging from senior academics to ordinary farmers said they no longer fear the police. Clearly, the Nationalist Party, which one United States government study described as the world's richest political entity, will not be easily displaced, but important political conflict within the Nationalist Party itself has broadened the parameters of political debate. And the leaders of the opposition Democratic Progressive Party, all jailed or exiled during my 1980 trip, now have high status and respect.
>
> I was also greatly surprised by the lack of concern, even among opposition leaders, about the potential political roles of the military and security agencies, which played a crucial role in supporting Taiwan's strong authoritarian system from the late 1940s through the mid-1980s. These leaders argue that Taiwan's military is undergoing substantial re-orientation. The army, the greatest threat to civilian authorities, no longer requires the capacity to invade and occupy the mainland and is losing resources to the navy and air force, which have missions centred on the defence of Taiwan. The largely Taiwanese membership of the armed forces and the increasing Taiwanisation of the top military leadership also reduces the likelihood of military intervention in politics. Furthermore, the military has long had good systems of leadership rotation which prevent military commanders from gaining the personal loyalty of troops. Similarly, many political leaders lack concern about the security agencies and point, for example, to the recent abolition of the "Second Personnel Office" in government offices and educational institutions which enabled the Bureau of Investigation to keep files on everyone.
>
> Yet some people in Taiwan (and this writer) see the military and security agencies as a potential threat to Taiwan's process of democratisation. The military remains a relatively closed system separate from society as a

whole and has substantial armed force at its command. Furthermore, despite the constitutional provision that the military is a state body, not belonging to any political party, the Nationalist Party still maintains political officers at all levels of the military. The security agencies too continue to exist and have uncertain future roles. The government abolished the feared Taiwan Garrison Command on July 31, 1992, but the Minister of Defence only outlined the new arrangements for the Taiwan Garrison Command's military functions, leaving unexplained the future of its myriad security functions.

Assuming that Taiwan's military and security agencies remain under civilian control, the processes of increasing prosperity, democratisation and "Taiwanese consciousness" suggest that the *de facto* independence of Taiwan will continue indefinitely. Even the ruling Nationalist Party, officially committed to reunification of Taiwan with the Mainland, repeatedly stated "no one among the twenty million Chinese in Taiwan wants to unify with the Chinese Communists" during the December 1991 National Assembly election campaign. Thus, we can predict the Chinese Communist policy of incorporating Taiwan into the People's Republic of China through its "one nation, two systems" formula will continue to fail.

What will another Rip Van Winkle see a decade hence in Taiwan? A new generation of talented leaders, much more committed to democratisation and "Taiwan consciousness" as well as Taiwan's prosperity, will have completely replaced the older generation of Nationalist leaders which grew up on the mainland. Assuming current trends continue, Taiwan will have completed the transition to true democracy. Although no longer a military threat, Taiwan will pose a major ideological threat to the Chinese mainland because its existence will have decisively proven the dogma that "Chinese culture is incompatible with democracy" to be a canard.[11]

Later in 1992, I applied for a visa to observe the December 19, 1992 legislative elections. Despite support from Francias Lee in Australia and despite the fact that I had made three sets of plane reservations to go to Taiwan, I never received a visa and had to analyze the elections from Melbourne.

---

11   Ibid.

The Police Follow Me Constantly in 1993

In 1993 the Department of Political Science at National Taiwan University invited me to come to Taiwan for academic discussions. I received a single entry visa for "Two weeks only" with the further proviso that "No Extension will be Granted." I entered Taiwan on June 8 and left on June 22, 1993.

On arrival at the airport, a security person came up to the immigration desk and asked, "You don't have an American passport?"

I replied, "No, it is Australian."

He answered, "I thought it was American." Since I had arrived on my Australian passport in 1992, this was evidence of sloppy work.[12]

Another person stopped me and took a photocopy of my passport and details of my address in Taipei. Then, when I got a cab, another man asked, "Do you mind if I ride back with you?", adding, "You know who we are." I rejected his request and my taxi was followed. Then plainclothes police followed me into the apartment building and knocked at the apartment door, which was a private residence.

This trip proved different from 1992 in a number of ways. First of all, I was the house guest of the then head of the Australian mission to Taiwan, Mr Laurie Smith. Laurie and his wife lived in an apartment on Dunhua South Road. Secondly, the security forces no longer invited me out to dinner or to KTVs, but now they followed me everywhere I went. Initially three cars were assigned to follow me: a blue Ford with the license plate 162–4711, a silver Ford with the license plate AE-9723 and a brown YueLoong with the license plate AE-9685. These cars were situated so that they could follow me no matter where I went.

One morning I went to see several aboriginal friends including a legislator and a senior civil servant. I told my taxi driver that the car behind us was following us. He thought I was being silly, so I suggested that he do a full circle at the next traffic circle. He was surprised that the car continued to follow us and said, "You're right, that car is following us!" He then asked if I wanted to lose the tail. I said that the car was a police car, but that if he could drop the tail safely, that would be okay. In a short time, he had lost the car.

I asked, "How did you do that?"

He responded, "We frequently have male patrons whose wives follow. So we have lots of experience losing tails."

I responded, "I'm glad it was only the police and not my wife!"

---

12   I had naturalized as an Australian in January 1986.

After a lovely lunch with my aboriginal friends, the senior civil servant and I were walking back along a quiet street. I noticed one of the three cars was following us. I told my friend, "That car is following us".

He replied, "That is impossible!" I showed him my notes with the description of the car and the license plate number and he answered, "You're right, it is following us!"

After this, almost every time I got into a taxi, a policeman would bang on the windscreen with his mobile phone and tell the taxi driver that he should drive slowly as he was being followed.

After about a week, the tailing became quite oppressive. My postgraduate classmate at Columbia University, Parris Chang 張旭成, was then an Overseas Legislator and called a press conference on June 15, 1993 at the Legislature. In order to encourage reporters to attend, Parris had framed the press conference as about "another White Terror", but I did not buy into that description. Parris was very kind in portraying me as a scholar and also mentioning my role as a member of the Australia-China Council.

I made three points at the press conference. First, the attention from the security forces, which I was receiving, did not square with the obvious democratization that had taken place in Taiwan. Second, the attention from the security forces was leaving a "shadow" over me. I said, after thirteen years, the security forces should have investigated the case clearly and they should either indict me and have an open trial to judge their "evidence" or they should clear my name and give me freedom of movement in and out of Taiwan and within Taiwan to conduct academic research. Finally, both Australia and Taiwan consider their relationship important and both sides have worked to improve and strengthen the relationship. The restrictions on my entry and the attention I was receiving from the security forces did not assist the development of the relationship, especially considering my role as a scholar helping Australia better understand Taiwan as well as my membership of the Australia-China Council.

Most newspapers picked up the news and also printed the descriptions of the three cars with their license plate numbers. The response of the security forces was to maintain the original three cars and add two more, a blue-silver Toyota with license plate 135–5698 and a maroon Ford with license plate 135–6570. Now I had five cars tailing me.

In view of my status as a member of the Australia-China Council, the Australian office arranged a series of meetings for me including one with the foreign minister, Frederick Chien 錢復. Unfortunately, Chien began to get cold feet and before I was able to see Chien, I was downgraded to meet the head of the Department of East Asian and Pacific Affairs. When he got cold feet, they proposed an appointment with an even more inferior official. I had the Australian office cancel my appointment at the Ministry of Foreign Affairs.

During the two weeks, I did have one evening without my minders. I took the elevator to the basement and walked out through the garage door. Fortunately, my minders did not see me and I had a pleasant evening with an old friend.

The Australian office had also arranged an interview for me with the Secretary-General of the KMT, Hsu Shui-teh 許水德, an old friend dating back to 1971 when he was the Chief of the Kaohsiung Education Bureau and I was a young PhD student about to embark on my doctoral field research. This time, I did not mind having my minders follow me. I could hear them gasp in disbelief, "He's actually going in! He's actually going in!" 他真的要進去！他真的要進去！The minders could not follow into the KMT Central Party Headquarters.

Actually, Hsu was a bit late, so our meeting did not get underway immediately, but I was in the KMT Central Party Headquarters for more than an hour. When I came out, two attractive women breathlessly asked me, "Are you Bruce Jacobs?"

After ascertaining they were reporters, I answered, "Yes."

They then asked me, "Did you see the Secretary-General?" So I agreed to an interview with a reporter from the *Liberty Times* and a reporter from the Police Radio station, which then broadcast traffic reports. The next day, the *Liberty Times* had a fairly large headline across the middle of page 4 which simply stated, "Bruce Jacobs and Hsu Shui-teh Have Secret Talk" 家博與許水德密談.[13] Clearly, the newspaper felt that no further identification of either person was required.

The roads outside the former KMT Central Party Headquarters are extraordinarily complex and I could see that each of the five cars was in position so that I could be followed no matter where I went. I looked around and realized that I had not yet visited the Chiang Kai-shek Memorial Park, a huge construction that includes Taiwan's major concert hall and opera house. I also visited the Chiang Kai-shek memorial hall itself. While there, a man, who I recognized as the policeman who had run with me in 1980 and who had come to my hotel room in 1992, Chiang Yung-chen or "Shadow," appeared. Chiang began to swear quite nastily in English in quite an unfriendly and disconcerting way.

I still had my card that the senior policeman had given me in 1992 which said, "Report any suspicious person to the police." So, I saw a uniformed policeman and showed him the card and told him that "that person" is suspicious because he is swearing loudly in English at me. The policeman started talking

---

13   *Ziyou shibao* 自由時報 [*Liberty Times*], June 22, 1993, p. 4.

to the swearer and, as I escaped in a taxi, I saw Chiang bring out his identification card to show the police that he too was a policeman! Such triumphs were rare.

President Lee Teng-hui Helps Me in 1995

In 1995 I received an invitation to participate in a major conference commemorating the Centenary Anniversary of the Treaty of Shimonoseki. I again received a single entry visa valid for "Two weeks only" and with a handwritten statement on my passport giving both my name in Chinese and details of the specific cable authorizing the visa. I arrived on April 11 and departed on April 25, 1995. The conference was sponsored in part by the *Liberty Times*. After the conference, we all went to the Presidential Office and met President Lee Teng-hui 李登輝. Several of the conference participants, including me, had been on the "blacklist" and unable to enter Taiwan.

Before beginning, President Lee went around the room and met each person individually. When he met me, he said, "Bruce Jacobs, you really are famous!" 家博，你真有名！After meeting all of the conference participants, President Lee then read a formal statement on the Treaty of Shimonoseki, which concluded the Manchu-Japan War of 1894–1895 and which made Taiwan the first colony in the new Japanese Empire. President Lee then asked for questions. No one dared to ask a question and the chief editor of the *Liberty Times*, who was sitting next to me, said, "Bruce, raise your case with the President."

During my 1993 trip, I had met Jason Hu 胡志強, then Director-General of the Government Information Office. Jason later personally took my documents to the security agencies in an effort to secure me a visa. Unfortunately, even though a senior cabinet minister, Jason's efforts failed.

In my question to President Lee, I noted that a cabinet minister had been unable to help, so I asked if the president could assist. I told him that I was no longer on the "blacklist" 黑名單, but was on a "gray list" 灰名單, where I could sometimes get a visa, but that the result of my visa applications was always uncertain. He immediately raised this with the Presidential Office Secretary-General, Wu Poh-hsiung 吳伯雄, and through Wu's help the Taiwan government shifted from Taipei to Melbourne the right to decide whether or not I would receive a visa. This meant that I now could reliably obtain a visa and in late 1995 I was able to observe the legislative election and in 1996 to observe the presidential election.[14]

---

14   For some results of these visits, see Jacobs, *Democratizing Taiwan*, pp. 96–101, 108–126.

Despite now having the convenience of being able to come to Taiwan when I wished, I still had to wait for at least a half hour or an hour at the immigration desk. Once I asked what was wrong and the immigration person just turned his screen towards me and I saw it flashing quite forcefully. Usually, the immigration people asked where I was staying and after verifying this allowed me to enter. Once, when I was staying at a smallish hotel in Taipei, I found a Chinese-language note in my pigeon hole addressed to the Security Officer of the hotel asking him to ascertain when I was leaving. I don't know if the note was put in my box accidentally or on purpose, but it did verify that hotels still had "security officers." I tried to contact the Security Officer, but he was not in. I left as planned.

These arrangements infuriated Lu Hsiu-lien 呂秀蓮, who at the time was County Executive of Taoyuan County and the host of a conference on cross-Straits relations. Lu had organized that I be given VIP treatment and met at the plane door. When she learned that we had been delayed at the airport, which was in Taoyuan, she protested vigorously to the central government. This improved my treatment somewhat, but it was only with the election of Chen Shui-bian 陳水扁 as president in 2000 that I no longer had to wait at the airport before entering Taiwan.

The Report Commissioned by the Government of President Ma Ying-jeou

On March 13, 2009 the Taiwan High Prosecutors Office 臺灣高等法院檢察署 brought together the Forensics Research Institute of the Ministry of Justice 法務部法醫研究所, the Detective Bureau of the Police Administration in the Ministry of the Interior 內政部警政署刑事警察局, the Police Bureau of the Taipei Municipal Government 台北市政府警察局 and the Prosecutors Office of Taipei District Court 台灣台北地方法院檢察署 to form a working group to re-investigate the murder cases of Lin I-hsiung's family and Chen Wen-cheng.[15] Four and a half months later, on July 28, this working group released a 45 page analysis of the two cases entitled a *Report on the Re-Investigation of the Lin*

---

15   Taiwan gaodeng fayuan jianchashu 臺灣高等法院檢察署 [Taiwan High Prosecutors Office], "Taiwan gaodeng fayuan jianchashu xinwengao 臺灣高等法院檢察署新聞稿 [News Release of the Taiwan High Prosecutors Office]," <http://www.tph.moj.gov.tw/ct.asp?xItem=164912&ctNode=5093&mp=003>.

Family Murder Case and the Chen Wen-cheng Murder Case.[16] This report mentions my name twenty-one times. Yet, though written almost thirty years after the Lin family murders, the Report adds little new material and achieves virtually nothing.[17]

The Report first mentions me on page 8 where it says that a witness saw me go to the Lin family house twice at noon and that the second time I rang the doorbell and was let into the house. The text does say that I denied going to the Lin family house and ringing the doorbell and that the police did not find any evidence.[18] However, the Report does not say that the testimony of the "witness" was tested at the Prosecutor's Office on May 21, 1980 and found wanting (see Chapter 6).

The Report next mentions my name in connection with a Control Branch 監察院 report on the case prepared by Control Branch members Chiang Peng-chien 江鵬堅 and Li Shen-i 李伸一 in September 1996. The Report says that I was subpoenaed when in fact I appeared voluntarily.[19] Later, Chiang Peng-chien told me that the Control Branch had not been successful in obtaining requested material and that the Control Branch report was a great disappointment to Chiang and his colleagues.

On page 11, the Report reveals that a listening device recorded all of the telephone calls going into and out from the Lin family house. The Report states that four phone calls were received at the house on February 28, 1980 at 11 AM, at 1.12 PM, at 1.40 PM and at 4.30 PM.[20] Why does the Report omit reference to my phone call to the Lin family home at noon, when I talked to the twins, and why does it not mention my phone call after I returned from visiting Lien

---

16   Taiwan gaodeng fayuan jianchashu 臺灣高等法院檢察署 [Taiwan High Prosecutors Office], "Lin zhai xue'an, Chen Wencheng ming'an chongqi diaocha zhencha baogao 林宅血案、陳文成命案重啟調查偵查報告 [Report on the Re-Investigation of the Lin Family Murder Case and the Chen Wen-cheng Murder Case]," <http://www.tph.moj.gov.tw/ct.asp?xItem=164912&ctNode=5093&mp=003>. Also available from <http://www.tph.moj.gov.tw/public/Attachment/9101910301925.pdf>.

17   For my early evaluation see Bruce Jacobs, "Murder probe reveals nothing new," *Taipei Times* September 13, 2009, p. 8. For a Chinese-language version, see Jia Bo 家博 (J. Bruce Jacobs), "Jianshi Lin zhai he Chen Wencheng mousha an baogao 檢視林宅和陳文成謀殺案報告 [Examining the Report on the Lin Family and Chen Wen-cheng Murder Cases]," *Pingguo ribao* 蘋果日報 [*Apple Daily*] September 15, 2009, available from <http://tw.nextmedia.com/applenews/article/art_id/31941560/IssueID/20090915>.

18   Taiwan gaodeng fayuan jianchashu 臺灣高等法院檢察署 [Taiwan High Prosecutors Office], "Report" pp. 8–9.

19   Ibid., p. 9.

20   Ibid., p. 11.

Chen-tung 連震東 and Tao Pai-chuan 陶百川 around 5 PM? I had mentioned these phone calls to the police and they should have been in both police records and in the records of person listening to the phone calls to Lin I-hsiung's house.

The Report says that in my accommodation at International House, the police found two spots of old blood in a cupboard. They apparently tried to find information about my blood type including asking my ex-wife's relatives, who lived in Taiwan, and checking all hospitals in Taiwan to ascertain whether I had any hospital records giving information on my blood type. All of these attempts to discover my blood type failed.[21] Of course, if I had been asked, I would have willingly told them that my blood type was B-positive and I would have happily provided a blood sample as well.

The Conclusion to the discussion of the Lin family murder case states that at the time the units investigating the case felt that "international plotters" 國際陰謀份子 wanted "to strike at the government" 打擊政府 and that the only important link to this theory was the suspect, Bruce Jacobs. The Conclusion again repeats the canard that witnesses said I went to the Lin family home twice at noon. However, the report does say that I denied "this" 之 and that the police were unable to discover any positive evidence. According to the Report, the authorities had no way to surmise that I was a suspect and so the argument that international plotters were striking at the government could not obtain any support.[22] While the Report's conclusion is gratifying on a personal level, the many holes in its logic must leave readers exasperated.

Why, almost thirty years later and after twenty years of democratization, did the units writing the Report remain so incompetent? Could they really find only four phone calls to the Lin house on February 28, 1980 or did they deliberately wipe my two telephone calls from the record? The Prosecutors Office of the Taipei District Court participated in writing the Report. Did they not have a record of my interview with the "witness" on May 21, 1980? Was the Report of July 28, 2009 trying to protect someone or some office? Why, after almost thirty years, were those writing the Report unable to come up with some fresh evidence or some fresh lines of analytical thinking? And, especially in view of the failure of the September 1996 Control Branch report, has someone or some organization deliberately inhibited understanding of who actually killed Auntie Lim, Liang-chun and Ting-chun on February 28, 1980?

---

21   Ibid., pp. 13–14.
22   Ibid., p. 17.

Reconsidering the Lin Family Murder Case after 35 Years

At the end of Chapter 6, I stated that I would reconsider the issue of who killed Auntie Lim, Liang-chun and Ting-chun in this final chapter. First of all, I must emphasize that I have no inside information. I did have substantial contact with the security agencies, but such contact was primarily adversarial and they in no way "consulted" with me about the case.

Chapter 6 makes clear that in 1980 I believed the chance of the security agencies being involved in the murders was low. However, I noted that the Chen Wen-cheng and Henry Liu murders had yet to take place. Furthermore, the murder of family members of a political prisoner was unprecedented and this too suggested that the involvement of security agencies was not likely.

Now, thirty-five years later, I do believe the security agencies were most likely involved in the murders. Of course, the Chen Wen-cheng and Henry Liu murder cases indicate that at least some security agencies were involved in murder of political opponents. This is especially clear in the case of Henry Liu where, because the murder was committed in the United States, the FBI wiretapped the criminal conspiracy and we have clear evidence that Taiwan's security agencies were involved.

Two scenarios involving the security agencies seem plausible. First, it is possible that someone higher up in a security agency said something like, "We must teach these bastards a lesson." In this scenario, a lower-level person took such a general statement as an "instruction" and committed the murders. As noted earlier, the Lin family house was convenient to the street and entry would have been relatively easy. In this scenario, higher-levels in the security agency were shocked that a general statement was perceived as an "instruction" and all evidence was removed from the records and the security personnel who performed the murders were most likely also permanently silenced.

The second scenario is more pernicious. In this scenario, a security agency quite deliberately planned and performed the murders. Again, in this scenario, we would expect that the evidence would have been removed from the records and quite possibly those who committed the murders were permanently silenced. The fact that General Wang Ching-hsi 汪敬煦 actually boasted about the murder of Henry Liu adds to the possibility that this scenario explains the Lin family murders.[23]

---

23 "During a late lunch punctuated with frequent toasts, an inebriated Wang [Ching-hsi] told his [American] guests that the murder, really, was no big deal. Why, he himself even knew of it in advance, he bragged." See Kaplan, *Fires*, p. 462.

Both of these scenarios would explain why so many attempts after democratization to solve the Lin Family murders have made no progress. With no records and no witnesses except at very senior levels, the likelihood of a confession was always slim. Furthermore, as time has passed, the probability is very great that the senior people have also passed away. Unfortunately, this suggests that we will never know who ordered the murders of Auntie Lim, Liang-chun and Ting-chun and we will never know who actually wielded the knife.

Bibliography

Taiwan Newspapers and Magazines (cited without reference to a specific article)

China News.
China Post.
China Post (International Airmail Edition).
Dahua wanbao 大華晚報 [*Great China Evening News.*]
Lianhebao 聯合報 [*United Daily*].
Lianhebao (Guowai hangkongban) 聯合報 (國外航空版) [*United Daily News (Overseas Edition)*].
Meilidao 美麗島 [*Formosa*].
Minzhong ribao 民眾日報 [*Commons Daily*].
Minzu wanbao 民族晚報 [*Minzu Evening News*]
Taiwan ribao 臺灣日報 [*Taiwan Daily*].
Taiwan shibao 臺灣時報 [*Taiwan Times*].
Taiwan Xinshengbao 台灣新生報 [*Taiwan New Life News*].
Yazhou shiji 亞洲世紀 [*Asian Century*]
Zhongguo shibao 中國時報 [*China Times*].
Zhongyang ribao 中央日報 [*Central Daily News*].
Zhongyang ribao guoji ban 中央日報國際版 [*Central Daily News International Edition*]
Zili wanbao 自立晚報 [*Independence Evening Post*].
Ziyou shibao 自由時報 [*Liberty Times*].

Cited Sources

"American, Held in Murder Case, Hopeful of Leaving Taiwan Soon." *The New York Times*, May 7, 1980, A8.

Arrigo, Linda Gail. "Three Years and a Lifetime: Swept up in Taiwan's Democratic Movement, 1977–79." In *A Borrowed Voice: Taiwan Human Rights through International Networks, 1960–1980*, edited by Linda Gail Arrigo and Lynn Miles. 274–374 (even numbers). Taipei: Social Empowerment Alliance, 2008.

"Baotu Zai Gaoxiong Qunji Zishi ... 暴徒在高雄麇集滋事 ... [Violence in Kaohsiung Gathers to Disturb the Peace ...]." *Lianhebao (Guowai hangkongban)* 聯合報 (國外航空版) [*United Daily News (Overseas Edition)*], December 11, 1979, 2.

Ben she 本社 [Formosa Magazine]. "Dangwai Zhenglun: Minzhu Wansui 黨外政論：民主萬歲 [Dangwai Commentary: Long Live Elections]." *Meilidao* 美麗島 [*Formosa*], no. 1 (August 16, 1979): 4–9.

———. "Dangwai Zhenglun: Shaoshu Pai Yu Baoli, Ping Zhongtai Binguan Qian De Naoju 黨外政論：少數派與暴力，評中泰賓館前的鬧劇 [Dangwai Commentary: The Minority Faction and Violence, a Critique of the Farce in Front of the Chungtai Hotel]." *Meilidao* 美麗島 [*Formosa*], no. 2 (September 25, 1979): 4–5.

———. "Xuanju Bamianfa Cao'an Zuotanhui Jilu 選舉罷免法草案座談會紀錄 [Record of Forum on Draft Election and Recall Law]." *Meilidao* 美麗島 [*Formosa*], no. 2 (September 25, 1979): 34–41.

Bernstein, Richard. "Brutal Taiwan Killings Jeopardize American, Top Island Dissident." *The Washington Star*, March 17, 1980, A-1, A-6.

Bush, Richard C. *At Cross Purposes: U.S.-Taiwan Relations since 1942*. Armonk, NY and London, England: M.E. Sharpe, 2004.

Cao Ji 曹極. "Zhencha Lin Yixiong Jiashu Ming'an Huiyilu 偵查林義雄家屬命案回憶錄 [Memoirs of Investigating the Lin I-Hsiung Family Murder Case]." *Lianhe yuekan* 聯合月刊 [*United Monthly*], no. 1 (August 1981): 108–127.

Chen Qiude 陳秋德. "Feichang Jumianxia, Shengyiyuan Suowei Heshi? 非常局面下，省議員所謂何事？[under Unusual Circumstances, What Are Provincial Assembly Members to Do?]." *Meilidao* 美麗島 [*Formosa*], no. 2 (September 25, 1979): 20–23.

Chen Yishen 陳儀深, ed. *Koushu Lishi, Di 12 Qi: Meilidao Shijian Zhuanji* 口述歷史，第 12 期: 美麗島事件專輯 [*Oral History, No. 12: Special Collection on the Formosa Incident*]. Taibei: Zhongyang yanjiuyuan jindaishi yanjiusuo 中央研究院近代史研究所 [Institute of Modern History, Academia Sinica], 2004.

———. "Taidu Panluan Huo Minzhu Yundong? Meilidao Shijian Xingzhi Jiexi 台獨叛亂或民主運動？美麗島事件性質解析 [a Taiwanese Independence Rebellion or a Democratic Movement? An Analysis of the Nature of the Formosa Incident]". In *Meilidao Shijian 30 Zhounian Yanjiu Lunwenji* 美麗島事件 30 周年研究論文集 [*Compendium of Research Articles on the 30th Anniversary of the Formosa Incident*], edited by Zhang Yanxian 張炎憲 and Chen Chaohai 陳朝海. 91–107. Taibei 臺北: Wu Sanlian Taiwan shiliao jijinhui 吳三連臺灣史料基金會, 2010.

Clark, Jim. "Prison Unites an Opposition." *The Age*, March 22, 1980.

"A Deepening Mystery." *Time*, March 31, 1980, 13.

Fan Zhengyou 范政祐. "Qi Erba Taizhong Naoju Zhi Wo Guan: Gei Taizhong Shimin De Gongkai Xin 七二八台中鬧劇之我觀：給台中市民的公開信 [My Views on the Taizhong Farce of July 28: An Open Letter to Taizhong's Citizens]." *Meilidao* 美麗島 [*Formosa*], no. 1 (August 16, 1979): 74–76.

Fei Xiping 費希平, Huang Hsin-chieh 黃信介, and Kang Ning-xiang 康寧祥. "Jiu Women Suo Mianlin De San Xiang Zhengzhi Wenti Xiang Xingzhengyuan Sun Yuanzhang Tichu Zhixun 就我們所面臨的三項政治問題向行政院孫院長提出

質詢 [Interpellating Premier Sun About Three Political Questions Which We Face]." *Meilidao* 美麗島 [*Formosa*], no. 2 (September 25, 1979): 7–8.

Geng Lisun 耿立孫. "Jia Bo Lun Zhongmei Guanxi He Taiwan Qiantu 迦博論中美關係和台灣前途 [Bruce Jacobs Discusses Sino-American Relations and Taiwan's Future]." *Da shidai* 大時代 [*Great Epoch*], no. 10 (April 5, 1980): 23–24.

Gleysteen, William H. *Massive Entanglement, Marginal Influence: Carter and Korea in Crisis*. Washington, DC: Brookings, 1999.

Guthrie-Jones, David. "Lecturer under Guard." *The Sun*, March 19, 1980, 13.

Haddon, Rosemary. "The Sky-Blue Backpack: My Experience with Taiwan's Human Rights." In *A Borrowed Voice: Taiwan Human Rights through International Networks, 1960–1980*, edited by Linda Gail Arrigo and Lynn Miles. 283–301 (odd numbers). Taipei: Social Empowerment Alliance, 2008.

Hart, Henry H. *A Garden of Peonies: Translations of Chinese Poems into English Verse*. Stanford: Stanford University Press, 1938, 1943, 1947.

———. *The Hundred Names: A Short Introduction to the Study of Chinese Poetry with Illustrative Translations*. Berkeley: University of California Press, 1933, 1938.

———. *Marco Polo: Venetian Adventurer*. Norman: University of Oklahoma Press, 1967.

———. *Sea Road to the Indies: An Account of the Voyages and Exploits of the Portuguese Navigators, Together with the Life and Times of Dom Vasco Da Gama, Capitão—Mór, Viceroy of India and Count of Vidigueira*. London, Edinburgh, Glasgow: William Hodge and Company, Limited, 1952.

———. *Venetian Adventurer: Being an Account of the Life and Times and of the Book of Messer Marco Polo*. Stanford: Stanford University Press, 1947.

He Wenzhen 何文振. "Qi Erba Taizhong Shijian Zhenxiang 七二八台中事件真相 [the Truth About the Taichung Incident of July 28]." *Meilidao* 美麗島 [*Formosa*], no. 1 (August 16, 1979): 73.

Huang Hsin-chieh 黃信介. "Fakan Ci: Gongtong Lai Tuidong Xinshengdai Zhengzhi Yundong! 發刊詞：共同來推動新生代政治運動！ [Words on Launching Magazine: All Work Together to Push a Political Movement of the New Generation!]". *Meilidao* 美麗島 [*Formosa*], no. 1 (August 16, 1979).

Huang Huang-hsiung 黃煌雄. "'Sheng Zhuxi' Neng Zuo Shenme? '省主席' 能做什麼？ [What Can the 'Provincial Chairman' Do?]." *Meilidao* 美麗島 [*Formosa*], no. 1 (August 16, 1979): 34–36.

Huang Nian 黃年, and Chen Xiuling 陳秀玲. "Qie Ting Huang Xinjie Zenme Shuo! 且聽黃信介怎麼說 [Let's Hear What Huang Hsin-Chieh Has to Say!]." *Lianhebao (Guowai hangkongban)* 聯合報（國外航空版）[*United Daily News (Overseas Edition)*] December 14, 1979, 2.

Huang Shun-hsing 黃順興. "Wei Nongmin Quanyi Xiang Xingzhengyuan Sun Yuanzhang Zhixun 為農民權益向行政院孫院長質詢 [Interpellation of Premier Sun on the

Rights and Interests of Farmers]." *Meilidao* 美麗島 [*Formosa*], no. 3 (October 25, 1979): 35–42.

———. "Xiang Xingzhengyuan Zhixun San Ze 向行政院質詢三則 [Three Interpellations of the Cabinet]." *Meilidao* 美麗島 [*Formosa*], no. 1 (August 16, 1979): 10–11.

"Huang Xinjie Zuo Shuoming Gaoxiong Shijian Jingguo ... 黃信介昨說明高雄事件經過 ... [Yesterday, Huang Hsin-Chieh Explained What Happened in the Kaohsiung Incident ...]." *Lianhebao (Guowai hangkongban)* 聯合報（國外航空版）[*United Daily News (Overseas Edition)*], December 13, 1979, 2.

International Committee for the Defense of Human Rights in Taiwan (ICDHRT). "An Account of Chen Chu's June 23rd Arrest, Detention and Release." In *A Borrowed Voice: Taiwan Human Rights through International Networks, 1960–1980*, edited by Linda Gail Arrigo and Lynn Miles. 317, 319. Taipei: Social Empowerment Alliance, 2008.

Jacobs, Bruce. "Murder Probe Reveals Nothing New." *Taipei Times*, September 13, 2009, 8.

———. "Rip Van Winkle Returns to Taiwan." *Far Eastern Economic Review*, May 13, 1993, 36.

Jacobs, J. Bruce. "Chiang Ching-Kuo Was No Democrat: The Difference between Liberalization and Democratization." In *Zhonghua Minguo Liuwang Taiwan 60 Nian Ji Zhanhou Taiwan Guoji Chujing* 中華民國流亡台灣 60 年暨戰後台灣國際處境 [*the Republic of China's Sixty Years of Exile in Taiwan and Taiwan's Difficult Postwar International Situation*], edited by Taiwan jiaoshou xiehui 台灣教授協會 [Taiwan Association of University Professors]. 435–480. Taibei: Qianwei 前衛, 2010.

———. *Democratizing Taiwan*. Leiden and Boston: Brill, 2012.

———. *Local Politics in Rural Taiwan under Dictatorship and Democracy*. Norwalk, CT: EastBridge, 2008.

———. "Political Opposition and Taiwan's Political Future." *The Australian Journal of Chinese Affairs*, no. 6 (July 1981 July 1981): 21–44.

———. "Recent Leadership and Political Trends in Taiwan." *The China Quarterly*, no. 45 (January-March 1971 January-March 1971): 129–154.

———. "Researching Taiwan in the 1970s." *Issues & Studies* 40, no. 3/4 (September/December 2004): 403–418.

———. "Taiwan's Press: Political Communications Link and Research Resource." *China Quarterly*, no. 68 (December 1976): 778–788.

———. "Taiwan 1972: Political Season." *Asian Survey* XIII, no. 1 (January 1973 January 1973): 102–112.

———. "Taiwan 1978: Economic Successes, International Uncertainties." *Asian Survey* XIX, no. 1 (January 1979 January 1979): 20–29.

———. "Taiwan 1979: 'Normalcy' after 'Normalization'." *Asian Survey* XX, no. 1 (January 1980 January 1980): 84–93.

———. "Taiwan and South Korea: Comparing East Asia's Two 'Third-Wave' Democracies." *Issues & Studies* 43, no. 4 (December 2007): 227–260.

———. "Taiwanese and the Chinese Nationalists, 1937–1945: The Origins of Taiwan's "Half-Mountain People" (Banshan Ren)." *Modern China* 16, no. 1 (January 1990 January 1990): 84–118.

———. "'Taiwanization' in Taiwan's Politics." In *Cultural, Ethnic, and Political Nationalism in Contemporary Taiwan: Bentuhua*, edited by John Makeham and A-Chin Hsiau. 17–54. New York: Palgrave Macmillan, 2005.

———. "Two Key Events in the Democratisation of Taiwan and South Korea: The Kaohsiung Incident and the Kwangju Uprising." *International Review of Korea Studies* 8, no. 1 (2011): 29–56.

Jia Bo 家博 (J. Bruce Jacobs). "Jia Bo (Bruce Jacobs) Xiansheng Fangwen Jilu 家博 (Bruce Jacobs) 先生訪問紀錄 [Record of Visit with Mr Bruce Jacobs]." In *Koushu Lishi: Meilidao Shijian Zhuanji* 口述歷史: 美麗島事件專輯 [*Oral History: Special Collection on the Formosa Incident*], edited by Chen Yishen 陳儀深. 294–316. Taipei 台北: Institute of Modern History, Academia Sinica, 2004.

———. "Jianshi Lin Zhai He Chen Wencheng Mousha an Baogao 檢視林宅和陳文成謀殺案報告 [Examining the Report on the Lin Family and Chen Wen-Cheng Murder Cases]." *Pingguo ribao* 蘋果日報 [*Apple Daily*], September 15, 2009.

———. "Rang Shangkou De Hua Zaori Zhanfang 讓傷口的花早日綻放 [Allow the Flowers of the Wounds to Blossom Soon]." *Zhongguo shibao* 中國時報 [*China Times*], February 25, 1997, 11.

———. "Taiwan De Baozhi Meijie: Zhengzhi De Goutong Huan Ji Yanjiu De Ziliao Laiyuan 台灣的報紙媒介: 政治的溝通環及研究的資料來源 [Taiwan's Newspaper Media: Political Communications Link and Research Resource]." *Da shidai* 大時代 [*Great Epoch*], no. 10 (April 5, 1980): 18–22.

The Kaohsiung Tapes. Seattle: International Committee for Human Rights in Taiwan, February 1981.

Kaplan, David E. *Fires of the Dragon: Politics, Murder, and the Kuomintang*. New York: Atheneum, 1992.

Kaplan, John. *The Court-Martial of the Kaohsiung Defendants*. Berkeley: Institute of East Asian Studies, University of California, Berkeley, 1981.

Kerr, George H. *Formosa Betrayed*. Boston: Houghton Mifflin, 1965.

Kihl, Young Whan. *Transforming Korean Politics: Democracy, Reform, and Culture*. Armonk, N.Y. and London: M.E. Sharpe, 2005.

Kim Yong-taek. *5.18 Kwangju Minjung Hangjaeng* [*the May 18 Kwangju Uprising*]. Seoul: Tonga Ilbosa, 1990.

"Kong Lingsheng Shuoming Baoli Shijian Jingguo ... 孔令晟說明暴力事件經過 ... [Kung Ling-Sheng Explains the Experience of the Violent Incident ...]." *Zhongyang* ribao (Guoji hangkongban) 中央日報（國際航空版）[*Central Daily News (International Edition)*], December 12, 1979, 2.

Lee, Katherine. "Taiwan's Dissidents." *Index on Censorship* 9, no. 6 (December 1980 December 1980): 54.

Lin Yixiong 林義雄, and Yao Jiawen 姚嘉文. *Huluo Pingyang? Xuanzhan Guansi Guo Yuxin* 虎落平陽？選戰官司郭雨新 [*Has the Tiger Descended to Pingyang? Election Battles, Court Battles and Kuo Yu-Hsin*]. Taibei: Gaoshan 高山, 1977.

Liu Fengsong 劉峯松. "Yiqian Babaiwan Ren De Taiwan Shi 一千八百萬人的台灣史 [the Taiwan History of Eighteen Million People]." *Meilidao* 美麗島 [*Formosa*], no. 3 (October 25, 1979): 69–76.

Lu Xiulian 呂秀蓮. *Chongshen Meilidao* 重審美麗島 [*Re-Examining the Formosa Incident*]. Taibei 台北: Qianwei 前衛, 1997.

Marks, Thomas A. *Counterrevolution in China: Wang Sheng and the Kuomintang.* London and Portland, Ore.: Frank Cass, 1998.

McDonald, Hamish. "Lecturer Can't Go Home: Police." *The Age*, March 21, 1980.

———. "Lecturer Given 'Defendant' Summons." *The Age*, March 26, 1980.

———. "Teacher Has to Stay in Taiwan." *The Age*, May 12, 1980.

"'Meilidao' Zazhi Zai Gaoshi Zishi ... '美麗島' 雜誌在高滋事 ... ['Formosa' Magazine Creates Disturbance in Kaohsiung City ...]." *Zhongyang ribao (Guoji hangkongban)* 中央日報（國際航空版)[*Central Daily News (International Edition)*], December 11, 1979, 2.

Presbyterian Church in Taiwan. "A Declaration of Human Rights." <http://www.taiwan-documents.org/pct04.htm>.

———. "A Declaration on Human Rights." In *The Future of Taiwan: A Difference of Opinion*, edited by Victor H Li. 186–187. White Plains, NY: M.E. Sharpe.

Qiu Chuiliang 邱垂亮. "Liangzhong Xinxiang 兩種心向 [Two Ways of Thinking]." *Taiwan zhenglun* 台灣政論 [*Taiwan Political Review*], no. 5 (December 1975): 31–34.

Qiu Minghui 邱銘輝. "Wo You Yige Yue De Shijian Meiyou Kandao Taiyang 我有一個月的時間沒有看到太陽 [I Did Not See the Sun for a Month]." *Xinxinwen* 新新聞 [*The Journalist*], July 19-July 25, 1992, 10–15.

Renquan Zhi Lu: Taiwan Minzhu Renquan Huigu 人權之路：臺灣民主人權回顧 [*the Road to Human Rights: Looking Back on Taiwan's Democracy and Human Rights*] Taibei: Yushan, 2002.

The Road to Freedom: Taiwan's Postwar Human Rights Movement Taipei: Dr Chen Wen-chen Memorial Foundation 2004.

"Shelun: Dong Kou, Ying Jia Kuanrong; Dong Shou, Jue Bu Ying Kuanrong! 社論：動口，應加寬容；動手，絕不應寬容！ [Editorial: If One Moves the Mouth, Then When Must Be Lenient; If One Moves the Hand, Then One Most Definitely Cannot

Be Lenient!]." *Lianhebao (Guowai hangkongban)* 聯合報（國外航空版）[*United Daily News (Overseas Edition)*], December 12, 1979, 1.

Shi Mingde 施明德. "Taiwan Minzhu Yundong Huashidai De Yitian: Dangwai Renshi Wei Yu Dengfa an Youxing Kangyi Jishi 台灣民主運動劃時代的一天：黨外人士為雨余登發案遊行抗議記實 [An Epoch-Making Day in the Taiwan Democratic Movement: A True Account of the *Dangwai* Personnages Marching to Resist the Yu Teng-Fa Case]." *Meilidao* 美麗島 [*Formosa*], no. 4 (November 25, 1979): 82–88.

Sima Wenwu 司馬文武. "Qi'er, Zhengzhi He Lishi 妻兒，政治和歷史 [Family, Politics and History]." *Zili wanbao* 自力晚報 [*Independence Evening Post*], February 29, 1980, 2.

———. "Shi'er Nian Hou De Taibei Tiankong: Jia Bo Zheige Ren 十二年後的台北天空：家博這個人 [the Skies of Taipei after Twelve Years: Bruce Jacobs Is This Kind of Person]." *Xinxinwen* 新新聞 [*The Journalist*], July 19-July 25, 1992, 12–13.

"Sun Yunxuan Yuanzhang Da Liwei Zhixun ... 孫運璿院長答立委質詢 ... [Premier Sun Yun-Suan Answers the Interpellation of a Legislator ...]." *Lianhebao (Guowai hangkongban)* 聯合報（國外航空版）[*United Daily News (Overseas Edition)*], October 3, 1979, 1.

Taiwan gaodeng fayuan jianchashu 臺灣高等法院檢察署 [Taiwan High Prosecutors Office]. "Lin Zhai Xue'an, Chen Wencheng Ming'an Chongqi Diaocha Zhencha Baogao 林宅血案、陳文成命案重啟調查偵查報告 [Report on the Re-Investigation of the Lin Family Murder Case and the Chen Wen-Cheng Murder Case]." <http://www.tph.moj.gov.tw/ct.asp?xItem=164912&ctNode=5093&mp=003.

———. "Taiwan Gaodeng Fayuan Jianchashu Xinwengao 臺灣高等法院檢察署新聞稿 [News Release of the Taiwan High Prosecutors Office]." <http://www.tph.moj.gov.tw/ct.asp?xItem=164912&ctNode=5093&mp=003>.

Taiwan Lishi Nianbiao (1966–1978) 台灣歷史年表 [*Chronology of Taiwan History*]. Vol. II, Taibei: Guojia zhengce yanjiusuo ziliao zhongxin, 1990.

Taiwan Lishi Nianbiao (1979–1988) 台灣歷史年表 [*Chronology of Taiwan History*]. Vol. III, Taibei: Guojia zhengce yanjiusuo ziliao zhongxin, 1990.

"Taiwan Now Seeks Death for Dissidents." *The Washington Star*, March 27, 1980, A-7.

Tao Bai-chuan (editor) 陶百川（編）. *Zuixin Liufa Quanshu* 最新六法全書 [*the Most Recent Complete Six Legal Codes*]. Taipei 台北: Sanmin shuju 三民書局, 1980.

Taylor, Jay. *The Generalissimo's Son: Chiang Ching-Kuo and the Revolutions in China and Taiwan*. Cambridge, MA and London: Harvard University Press, 2000.

Twitchett, Denis, ed. *The Cambridge History of China, Volume 3: Sui and T'ang China, 589–906, Part I*. Cambridge, London, New York and Melbourne: Cambridge University Press, 1979.

Wang Jingxu 汪敬煦. *Wang Jingxu Xiansheng Fangtan Lu* 汪敬煦先生訪談錄 [*Records of Interviews with Mr Wang Ching-Hsi*]. Taibei 台北: Guoshiguan 國使館 [Academia Historica], 1993.

Wang, Shifu, and Henry H. Hart. *The West Chamber. A Medieval Drama. Translated ... With Notes by Henry H. Hart, Etc.* Stanford: Stanford University Press, 1936.

Wen Chaogong 文抄公. "Ni Kan De Shi Shenme Bao? Ge Bao Dui Zhongtai Shijian De Baodao 你看的是什麼報？各報對中泰事件的報導 [What Newspaper Do You Read? The Reports of Different Newspapers on the Chungtai Incident]." *Meilidao* 美麗島 [*Formosa*], no. 2 (September 25, 1979 September 25, 1979): 83–87.

Wu, Shu-hui. "Lien Heng (1878–1936) and the *General History of Taiwan*." *Journal of Third World Studies* 21, no. 1 (Spring 2004): 17–56.

Wu Zhengshuo 吳正朔. "Zhongtai Binguan Shijian Shimo 中泰賓館事件始末 [the Chungtai Hotel Incident from the Beginning to the End]." *Da shidai* 大時代 [*Great Epoch*], no. 4 (October 5, 1979 October 5, 1979): 7–19.

Xingzhengyuan 行政院 [Cabinet]. "Fulu: Dui Huang Weiyuan Shunxing Zhixun Zhi Shumian Dafu 附錄：對黃委員順興質詢書面答覆 [Appendix: Written Answers to the Interpellations of Legislator Huang Shun-Hsing]." *Meilidao* 美麗島 [*Formosa*], no. 1 (August 16, 1979): 12–16.

Yang Ching-chu 楊青矗. *Meilidao Jinxing Qu* 美麗島進行曲 [*Songs on the Development of Formosa*]. 3 vols Taibei 台北: Dunli 敦理, 2009.

Ye Fengsheng 葉逢生. "'Shida Shengyiyuan' Xuanba Yupo '十大省議員' 選拔餘波 [Trouble after Selecting the Best 'Ten Great Provincial Assembly Members']". *Meilidao* 美麗島 [*Formosa*], no. 2 (September 25, 1979): 24–25.

"Zaiyedang Ji Wudang Wupai Renshi Duiyu Ben Jie Difang Xuanju Xiang Guomintang Ji Zhengfu Tichu De Shiwudian Yaoqiu 在野黨及無黨無派人士對於本屆地方選舉向國民黨及政府提出的十五點要求 [Fifteen Demands from Opposition Parties and from Non-Partisans Addressed to the Kuomintang and the Government Concerning the Current Local Elections]". *Ziyou Zhongguo* 自由中國 22, no. 7 (April 1, 1960): 30.

Zhang Fuzhong 張富忠, and Qiu Wanxing 邱萬興. *Lüse Niandai: Taiwan Minzhu Yundong 25 Nian, 1975–1987* 綠色年代：台灣民主運動 25 年, 1975–1987 [*the Green Era: Twenty-Five Years of Taiwan's Democratic Movement, 1975–1987*]. II vols. Vol. I, Taibei: Caituan faren lüxing wenjiao jijinhui 財團法人綠色旅行文教基金會, 2005.

Zhang Yanxian 張炎憲, and Chen Chaohai 陳朝海, eds. *Meilidao Shijian 30 Zhounian Yanjiu Lunwenji* 美麗島事件 30 周年研究論文集 [*Compendium of Research Articles on the 30th Anniversary of the Formosa Incident*]. Taibei 臺北: Wu Sanlian Taiwan shiliao jijinhui 吳三連臺灣史料基金會, 2010.

Zhang Yanxian 張炎憲, and Wen Qiufen 溫秋芬, eds. *Gaoxiong Shijian: 'Taiwan Zhi Yin' Luyin Jilu Xuanji* 高雄事件：'台灣之音'錄音紀錄選輯 [*Witnessing Kaohsiung Incident: Selected Tape Recordings of 'Voice of Taiwan'*]. Taibei 台北: Wu San-lien Taiwan shiliao jijinhui 吳三連台灣史料基金會 [Wu San-lien Taiwan History Materials Foundation], 2006.

Zhen Boya 甄伯牙. "Linshi Wuju, Bumou Wucheng 臨事無懼，不謀無成 [If One Does Not Plan, One Cannot Successfully Approach a Crisis without Fear]." *Da Shidai* 大時代 [*Great Epoch*], April 5, 1980, 13–17.

Zhou Qingyuan 周清源. "Shi Da Shengyiyuan 十大省議員 [Ten Great Provincial Assembly Members]." *Meilidao* 美麗島 [*Formosa*], no. 1 (August 16, 1979): 37–39.

Ziliaoshi 資料室 [Reference Office]. "Baifen Zhi Sa Xuanpiao De Shuzi Moshu 百分之卅選票的數字魔術 [the Wizardry of the Thirty Per Cent Vote Figure]." *Jifeng* 疾風 [*Gust*], April 4, 1980, 49.

Index

American Institute in Taiwan (AIT) 63, 124, 126–127, 130, 134, 142, 145–146
Amnesty International 26, 116, 119, 122
Arrigo, Linda 31
Australia-China Council 157
Australian, The 137

Beard 120–123, 127, 132, 145–147
Bernstein, Richard 144
Big Beard (see Beard)
Birthday Party for Hsu Hsin-liang 15, 115
Blacklist 107, 148, 150, 159
Brink of Violence 54, 63, 79–80
Bruce Jacobs wants to sleep 125, 133
Bureau of Investigation, Ministry of Justice 11, 29, 34, 45, 47, 50, 52, 55–56, 58, 61, 65–68, 70, 72, 74–75, 77–78, 91, 96, 100, 154

Cartoon 127
Central Daily News 27, 39, 127–128, 140
Central Hotel 133
Chang Cheng-hsiung 46
Chang Chih-hsiu 24–25, 27
Chang Chin-tse 35, 46, 48, 58, 61–62, 81–82
Chang Chun-hsiung 54, 65, 76, 78, 106
Chang Chun-hung 10, 14, 18, 26, 28–29, 34–35, 39, 58, 60, 66, 78, 80, 84, 105, 109, 115
Chang Fu-chung 29n30, 91, 97, 106
Chang Fu-hsiung 35, 46–48
Chang Pao-chin 131–132
Chang Pao-shu 11
Chang, Parris 157
Chang Te-ming 18
Chang Tsan-hung 35, 46, 48, 76
Chang Wen-ying 100
Chang Yu-wen 130
Chao Chen-erh 98–101
Chao Hsiu-wa 9
Chao Shou-po 121, 142
Chen Chin-te 9–10
Chen Ching-chih 94, 98
Chen Chu 6, 11–12, 29n30, 33–35, 39, 58, 61, 67, 69, 81, 89, 94, 105, 115, 153

Chen Chung-hsin 29n30, 91, 97
Chen Fu-lai 96–97
Chen Ku-ying 6, 13–14
Chen Po-wen 31n38, 64, 89, 97
Chen Shui-bian 45, 47, 66, 73, 105–107, 160
Chen Wan-chen 13, 17, 63
Chen Wen-cheng ix–x, 146, 160–161, 163
Chen Yi-shen 29
Cheng Ching-lung 74
Cheng Kuan-ming 93, 98
Cheng Sheng-chu 106
Chi Wan-sheng 29n30, 93–97
Chiang, Antonio 40–41, 152
Chiang Chin-ying 101
Chiang Ching-kuo 3, 32, 41, 44, 86, 103, 117, 119, 142, 145, 148
Chiang Kai-shek 3–5, 7, 41, 44, 153, 158
Chiang Peng-chien 46, 65, 69–70, 82, 106, 109
Chiang Yung-chen ("Shadow") 137, 149, 158
Chien, Frederick 157
China Democratic Party 7
China News 88, 123
China Post 88, 119
China Times 13, 43, 46, 64–65, 84–85, 103, 123, 127–128, 132, 141
Ching-mei prison 104
Chiou Chui-liang 6
Chiu Chui-chen 16, 54, 95, 97
Chiu I-jen 6
Chiu Hungdah 77
Chiu Lien-hui 9, 30n36, 31
Chiu Mao-nan 30n36, 90, 97
Chiu Ming-chiang 97
Chiu Ming-hui 152
Chiu Sheng-hsiung 24, 33, 37, 41, 56
Chou Ching-yu (Mrs Yao Chia-wen) 83, 108, 116
Chou Hung-hsien 6
Chou Ping-teh 24n5, 28–29, 88, 94, 97
Chou Tsang-yuan 9, 84
Chungli Incident 9–10, 15, 115
Chungtai Hotel Incident 15–18, 20, 152
Civil Trial (civilian court) 31, 34, 86–88, 93, 103, 105

INDEX   175

Clark, Jim   144
Clarkson College of Technology   114
Coble, Parks   117
Columbia University   113, 121, 123, 157
  Columbia College   113–114
Commons Daily   141
Concealing (Hiding) a Criminal   32, 86–87, 98, 103
Confession   44–45, 47–50, 55, 58–60, 65–66, 68, 70–72, 74–81, 83, 85–86, 88–89, 91–92, 94–97, 101, 103, 134, 137, 164
Control Branch (*yuan*)   4, 15, 106–107, 117, 161–162
Council of Grand Justices   4, 127n26, 142
Cross, Charles (Chuck)   142, 145
Cross-examination   52–53, 65, 91, 95, 98, 101, 145

Dangwai   7–8, 11–26, 31–32, 40, 46, 50, 54–56, 58, 63–64, 79, 90, 104, 109, 115–116, 118, 120, 123
  Dangwai Election Assistance Group   12–13, 54
  Dangwai National Affairs Meeting   14
deBary, William Theodore   114
Department of Intelligence, Military Police Command   30, 34
Department of Security, see Taiwan Garrison Command.
Ding Mou-shih   115
Dolfin, John and Hsi-ching   145
Dulles, John Foster   79

Fairbank, John King   139
Fan Sun-lu   6
Fan Cheng-yu   90, 97
Fang Su-min   40–41, 46, 62, 83, 108, 116, 118
Fatigue bombing, see Sleep deprivation
February 28, 1947 (2.28) Uprising   3, 9, 41, 110
Feldman, Harvey   12
Five-Man Committee   63, 65–66, 71, 73, 77, 79, 81–82
Formosa Magazine   15–21, 23–29, 35–37, 45–48, 50–51, 53, 56–59, 61, 63, 71–74, 76, 79, 89–91, 93–96, 110
Fu Wen-cheng   9
Fu Yao-kun   92, 97

General Political Warfare Department   29, 103
Gleysteen, William H.   28
Government Information Office   73, 115, 131, 138, 159
Grand Hotel   122–123, 126, 136–137, 144–145
Gray list   159
Great China Evening News   138, 142
Great Epoch   135, 142
Gust Magazine   8, 16–18
Guthrie-Jones, David   144

Hart, Henry H.   113
Harvard University   77, 139
Hash House Harriers   136
Ho Chun-mu   9
Hofstra University   115
Hsiao Yu-ching   17
Hsieh Chang-ting   45, 80, 105, 107
Hsieh San-sheng   18
Hsieh Hsiu-hsiung   18
Hsieh Tung-min   121
Hsu Chi-tan   93, 98
Hsu Ching-fu   99–101
Hsu Chung-chi   38
Hsu Hsin-liang   9, 14–15, 18, 35, 54, 58, 63–64, 115
Hsu Jung-shu   81, 109
Hsu Lu   152
Hsu Shih-hsien   6–7, 18, 38
Hsu Shui-teh   158
Hsu Tien-hsien   91
Hu Fo   142, 145
Hu, Jason   159
Hu Wu-hsi   129
Huang Chao-hui   99, 101
Huang Hsin-chieh   5, 8–9, 12–14, 17–18, 23–25, 27–30, 32, 34–35, 39, 44–45, 54–57, 61, 66–67, 70, 72, 74, 81, 83–84, 86, 90, 93, 104, 109
Huang Huang-hsiung   18
Huang Lao-sheng   73
Huang Shun-hsing   6, 14, 18, 20
Huang Tien-fu   18, 74, 109
Huang Yu-chiao   9, 123
Huang Yu-jen   9
Human Rights Day   21, 23, 36, 89, 94, 100

Hung Chih-liang   34, 46, 54, 72–74, 77, 84–85, 87, 137
Hung X-fa   94, 97
Hwang Yueh-chin   142

Independence Evening Post (*Independence Evening News*)   40, 138, 152
Independence Morning Post   152
Intelligence Bureau, Ministry of National Defense   104
International House   116–117, 121, 125, 162
Interpol   140

Jen-ai Hospital   41, 118–119, 121–123, 128, 135
Johnnie Walker Black Label   117–118
Journalist, The   152–153

Kang Ning-hsiang   5–6, 8, 14, 18, 26, 32, 54, 64, 70, 82, 109, 118, 123
Kang Shui-mu   9
Kao Chun-ming   87, 98–99, 101, 103
Kao Jui-cheng   69
Kao Kuei-yuan   11
Kao Yu-shu (Henry Kao)   7
Kaplan, John   43–44
Kim Dae-jung   28
Klosson, Michael   142
Knight, John   143
KTV   150–151, 156
Kuan Chung (John C Kuan)   16–17, 121, 142
Kung Ling-sheng   59, 129–130, 139–140
Kuo Chi-jen   66, 80
Kuo Yu-hsin   6–7, 11, 31, 61–62
Kuomintang (KMT)   3–5, 7–8, 10–11, 13, 15–18, 29, 54, 63–64, 79, 88, 105, 115–117, 119, 121, 153, 158
    4th Plenum, Eleventh Central Committee   29, 103
    Central Reform Commission   117, 120
    Central Party Headquarters   158
Kushan Incident   24, 32–33, 37, 41, 57, 59, 110
Kwangju Massacre   28, 109

La Trobe University   ix, 115, 129, 138, 142–143, 145, 148
Lao Cheng-wu   17
Lederer, Edie   144
Lee, Francias   148–149, 155
Lee Teng-hui   ix, 5, 148, 159
Legislature   4–5, 11, 13, 22, 29–30, 32, 38, 75, 105–109, 129, 157

Lei Chen   7, 83, 117
Letter of Protest   129n34, 130–134
Li Chang-tsung   94, 97
Li Min-yung   110
Li Ming-hsien   94, 98
Li Shen-i   161
Li Sheng-hsiung   48, 76, 78, 107
Li Tchong-Koei   79
Li Wan-chu   7
Liberty Times   158–159
Lien Chen-tung   116–117, 124
Lim You A-mei   v, x, 40–41, 83, 108, 110, 118–120, 123–124, 146, 162–164
Lin Cheng-chieh   6
Lin Family Murders   ix, 40, 119–120, 124, 127–129, 146–148, 161–164
Lin Hung-hsuan   31, 34–35, 37, 39, 46, 48, 68, 75–76, 78, 89, 99, 101
Lin Huan-chun   40–41, 70, 108, 116, 118–121, 123, 128, 135
Lin I-hsiung   x, 6, 9–10, 14, 18, 26, 28–29, 33–35, 39–41, 44–46, 54, 58, 62–65, 69–71, 81, 83–84, 105, 108, 110, 115–116, 118, 120, 122, 127, 148, 160, 162
Lin Li-ching   76
Lin Liang-chun   v, x, 40–41, 70, 83, 108, 110, 116, 118–120, 123, 146, 148, 162–164
Lin Lo-shan   9–10
Lin Shu-chih   98
Lin Ting-chun   v, x, 40–41, 70, 83, 108, 110, 116, 118–120, 123, 146, 148, 162–164
Lin Wen-chen   99–101
Liu, Henry (Liu Yi-liang, Jiang Nan)   ix–x, 104, 146, 163
Liu Tai-ho   94, 98
Long and short-range power seizure plan   35, 52, 60, 65, 80, 82, 86
Lu Chuan-sheng   49, 70, 77–78, 107
Lu Hsiu-lien (Annette)   13, 17–18, 26, 28–29, 34–35, 39, 46, 48–49, 66–67, 70, 76, 78, 105, 107, 115, 160

Ma Ying-jeou   106–107, 147, 160
McDonald, Hamish   144
Military Police   28, 53, 60, 71, 88–89, 91–96
    Department of Intelligence   30, 34
Military Trial   31–33, 38–39, 41–44, 69, 78, 82, 84–87, 98, 101, 104, 132–135, 138, 144
Min Tsu Evening News   123, 127, 136, 138

INDEX

Monash University ix, 148
Mutual Defense Treaty 31, 146

National Assembly 4, 13, 105, 108, 155
National Taiwan University ix, 13, 55, 77, 82, 114, 142, 156

Pan Lai-chang 94–97
Park Chung-hee 21
Peacock, Andrew 143
Peng Ming-min 35, 55, 63, 70, 82, 95, 107
Press conference 11–12, 27–28, 41, 123–124, 133–135, 157
Police, Department of 9–11, 15, 17–18, 24–25, 33, 37, 41, 44, 47, 52–53, 56–57, 59, 87–88, 91–94, 96–97, 109, 118–137, 139–141, 145, 149–152, 154, 156–162
    Detective Bureau 30, 34, 122, 127, 139–141, 160
    Foreign Affairs Police 126
    Special Task Force 123, 126–127, 129, 136, 141, 149
    Three-part proposition 128–129
Police Protection ix, 17, 121–123, 126–127, 129, 132–134, 136, 138, 140–141, 148
Pratt, Mark 142, 146
Presiding Judge 44–53, 55–56, 58–74, 81–84, 88–89
Presbyterian Church 7, 11, 47, 98–99, 153
Prosecutor 44–45, 49–52, 58, 60, 65–66, 68–72, 74–76, 78–79, 81–83, 87, 93–95, 97–98, 128–130, 132–137, 139, 141–142, 144–145, 160–162
Prosecutors Office, Taipei District Court 160, 162

Rai, Henry H.M. 127, 133–134, 137, 139n57
Revere, Evans 142
Rip van Winkle 149, 153, 155

Safe house 124, 126
Scott, John 142–143
Sedition (treason) 32, 34–35, 38, 50, 64, 68, 70, 78, 86, 88, 95, 99–101
Self-Strengthening Year 31, 147
Shapiro, Don 123, 144
Shen, Abraham Ta-chuan 119
Shen Chang-huan 11, 119–120
Shih Jui-yun 101

Shih Ming-chiang 129–130, 139
Shih Ming-teh 12–15, 17–18, 21, 25–31, 34–37, 39, 45–47, 50, 53, 56–57, 59, 63, 65, 67, 69, 78, 82–83, 85–87, 89, 96, 98–101, 103, 105, 115
Skies of Taipei, The 151
Sleep deprivation 11, 44, 49, 68, 85, 95, 103, 124–125, 133, 137
Smith, Laurie 156
Snedden, Billy 143
Soong, James (Soong Chu-yu) 115, 127, 138, 144
South Korea 28, 104, 109
Su Chen-hsiang 95, 97
Su Chih-fen 24
Su Ching-li 14, 18, 33
Su Hung Yueh-chiao 9
Su Nan-cheng 9
Su Tseng-chang 45, 66, 80, 107
Su Tung-chi 9, 24
Subpoena 134, 136, 144–145
Sugimoto, Yoshio 145
Sun Yun-suan 22, 38

Tai Chen-yao 92, 97
Taichung Incident 15–16, 19
Taipei Municipality Council 4–5, 8–9
Taipei Regency Hotel 119
Taiwan Garrison Command ix, 3, 11, 32–33, 38, 40–42, 73, 84, 88, 90–94, 96, 98, 128–130, 138, 155
    Department of Security 30, 34, 40, 63, 69–70, 81–82, 100–101
    Southern District 24, 27, 90–92, 94, 96
Taiwan Daily 11, 141
Taiwan High Prosecutors Office 160
Taiwan Independence 11–12, 17, 34–35, 46–52, 55, 61–62, 67, 69, 71–72, 74, 76–77, 79, 82–83, 107
Taiwan New Life News 141
Taiwan Political Review 5–6, 8
Taiwan Provincial Assembly x, 7–11, 19–20, 26, 29–31, 62, 84, 107, 123, 139
Taiwan Times 120, 141, 152
Tang Kuang-hua 64
Tao Pai-chuan 39, 46, 86, 117, 124, 145, 162
Teague, Baden 143
Tear gas 25–26, 53–54, 58–60, 80, 91, 95–96
Ten Great Projects 12, 115

Tien Chiu-chin   6, 131n39
Tien, Dr (Tien Chao-ming)   131
Tien Yung-kang   131
Torture   40, 44–45, 49, 65, 67, 69–72, 85, 89, 91, 94, 96, 103, 125, 137
Treason (see Sedition)
Tsai Chieh-hsiung   9
Tsai Ching-wen   94, 98
Tsai Chui-ho   30n36, 92, 97
Tsai Hsiu-hsiung   88
Tsai Yu-chuan   31, 92, 97, 99, 101
Tseng Wen-po   9
Tsao Chi   139–140

United Daily   11, 26–30, 120–123, 127, 129, 131–132, 136, 141, 152

Voice of Taiwan   52

Wang Ching-hsi   11, 128–130, 163
Wang Chao   126, 138
Wang Hsi-ling   104
Wang Kun-ho   9
Wang Man-ching   94, 98
Wang Pi-cheng   131–132
Wang Sheng   29, 103
Wang Ti-wu   131
Wang Tuoh   14, 18, 29n30, 60, 77, 89–90, 93, 97, 105
Wang Yung-shu   11

Wei Lun-chou   84
Wei Ting-chao   18, 29n30, 95, 97
Wei Yung   142
Willett, John   143
Williams, Richard   142
Wu Cheng-shuo   123, 152
Wu Chen-ming   91, 97
Wu Chu-jen   38
Wu Chun-fa (Wu Tai-an)   50, 135
Wu Kuo-tung   132
Wu Nai-jen   6
Wu Nai-te   6
Wu Poh-hsiung   159
Wu San-lien   7
Wu Wen   98–100
Wu Wen-hsien   91, 96–97

Yang Ching-chu   29n30, 88–89, 96–97, 105
Yang Yi-yi   35, 46
Yao Chia-wen   6, 13, 18, 25–29, 34–37, 39, 45, 55–59, 63, 65–68, 70, 78–80, 82–83, 93, 105, 108, 115–116, 146
Yao Kuo-chien   24, 32–33, 37, 41, 56
Yao Yu-ching   82, 116
Youth Party   31
Yu A-hsing   93, 97
Yu Ching   47, 71–72, 79–80, 83
Yu Chen Yueh-ying   9
Yu Teng-fa   7, 9, 14–15, 21, 64, 135

www.ingramcontent.com/pod-product-compliance
Lightning Source LLC
Chambersburg PA
CBHW021407290426
44108CB00010B/419